Creating Subaltern Counterpublics

JAPANESE SOCIETY SERIES
General Editor: Yoshio Sugimoto

Lives of Young Koreans in Japan
Yasunori Fukuoka

Globalization and Social Change in Contemporary Japan
J.S. Eades, Tom Gill and Harumi Befu

Coming Out in Japan: The Story of Satoru and Ryuta
Satoru Ito and Ryuta Yanase

Japan and Its Others:
Globalization, Difference and the Critique of Modernity
John Clammer

Hegemony of Homogeneity: An Anthropological Analysis of Nihonjinron
Harumi Befu

Foreign Migrants in Contemporary Japan
Hiroshi Komai

A Social History of Science and Technology in Contemporary Japan, Volume 1
Shigeru Nakayama

Farewell to Nippon: Japanese Lifestyle Migrants in Australia
Machiko Sato

The Peripheral Centre:
Essays on Japanese History and Civilization
Johann P. Arnason

A Genealogy of 'Japanese' Self-images
Eiji Oguma

Class Structure in Contemporary Japan
Kenji Hashimoto

An Ecological View of History
Tadao Umesao

Nationalism and Gender
Chizuko Ueno

Native Anthropology: The Japanese Challenge to Western Academic Hegemony
Takami Kuwayama

Youth Deviance in Japan: Class Reproduction of Non-Conformity
Robert Stuart Yoder

Japanese Companies: Theories and Realities
Masami Nomura and Yoshihiko Kamii

From Salvation to Spirituality: Popular Religious Movements in Modern Japan
Susumu Shimazono

The 'Big Bang' in Japanese Higher Education:
The 2004 Reforms and the Dynamics of Change
J.S. Eades, Roger Goodman and Yumiko Hada

Japanese Politics: An Introduction
Takashi Inoguchi

A Social History of Science and Technology in Contemporary Japan, Volume 2
Shigeru Nakayama

Gender and Japanese Management
Kimiko Kimoto

Philosophy of Agricultural Science: A Japanese Perspective
Osamu Soda

A Social History of Science and Technology in Contemporary Japan, Volume 3
Shigeru Nakayama and Kunio Goto

Japan's Underclass: Day Laborers and the Homeless
Hideo Aoki

A Social History of Science and Technology in Contemporary Japan, Volume 4
Shigeru Nakayama and Hitoshi Yoshioka

Scams and Sweeteners: A Sociology of Fraud
Masahiro Ogino

Toyota's Assembly Line: A View from the Factory Floor
Ryoji Ihara

Village Life in Modern Japan: An Environmental Perspective
Akira Furukawa

Social Welfare in Japan: Principles and Applications
Kojun Furukawa

Escape from Work: Freelancing Youth and the Challenge to Corporate Japan
Reiko Kosugi

Japan's Whaling: The Politics of Culture in Historical Perspective
Hiroyuki Watanabe

Gender Gymnastics: Performing and Consuming Japan's Takarazuka Revue
Leonie R. Stickland

Poverty and Social Welfare in Japan
Masami Iwata and Akihiko Nishizawa

The Modern Japanese Family: Its Rise and Fall
Chizuko Ueno

Widows of Japan: An Anthropological Perspective
Deborah McDowell Aoki

In Pursuit of the Seikatsusha:
A Genealogy of the Autonomous Citizen in Japan
Masako Amano

Demographic Change and Inequality in Japan
Sawako Shirahase

The Origins of Japanese Credentialism
Ikuo Amano

Pop Culture and the Everyday in Japan: Sociological Perspectives
Katsuya Minamida and Izumi Tsuji

Japanese Perceptions of Foreigners
Shunsuke Tanabe

Migrant Workers in Contemporary Japan:
An Institutional Perspective on Transnational Employment
Kiyoto Tanno

The Boundaries of 'the Japanese', Volume 1:
Okinawa 1868–1972 – Inclusion and Exclusion
Eiji Oguma

International Migrants in Japan: Contributions in an Era of Population Decline
Yoshitaka Ishikawa

Globalizing Japan: Striving to Engage the World
Ross Mouer

Beyond Fukushima: Toward a Post-Nuclear Society
Koichi Hasegawa

Japan's Ultra Right
Naoto Higuchi

Social Stratification and Inequality Series

Inequality amid Affluence: Social Stratification in Japan
Junsuke Hara and Kazuo Seiyama

Intentional Social Change: A Rational Choice Theory
Yoshimichi Sato

Constructing Civil Society in Japan: Voices of Environmental Movements
Koichi Hasegawa

Deciphering Stratification and Inequality: Japan and beyond
Yoshimichi Sato

Social Justice in Japan: Concepts, Theories and Paradigms
Ken-ichi Ohbuchi

Gender and Career in Japan
Atsuko Suzuki

Status and Stratification: Cultural Forms in East and Southeast Asia
Mutsuhiko Shima

Globalization, Minorities and Civil Society:
Perspectives from Asian and Western Cities
Koichi Hasegawa and Naoki Yoshihara

Fluidity of Place: Globalization and the Transformation of Urban Space
Naoki Yoshihara

Japan's New Inequality:
Intersection of Employment Reforms and Welfare Arrangements
Yoshimichi Sato and Jun Imai

Minorities and Diversity
Kunihiro Kimura

Inequality, Discrimination and Conflict in Japan:
Ways to Social Justice and Cooperation
Ken-ichi Ohbuchi and Junko Asai

Social Exclusion: Perspectives from France and Japan
Marc Humbert and Yoshimichi Sato

Global Migration and Ethnic Communities:
Studies of Asia and South America
Naoki Yoshihara

Stratification in Cultural Contexts: Cases from East and Southeast Asia
Toshiaki Kimura

Advanced Social Research Series

A Sociology of Happiness
Kenji Kosaka

Frontiers of Social Research: Japan and Beyond
Akira Furukawa

A Quest for Alternative Sociology
Kenji Kosaka and Masahiro Ogino

Modernity and Identity in Asia Series

Globalization, Culture and Inequality in Asia
Timothy S. Scrase, Todd Miles, Joseph Holden and Scott Baum

Looking for Money:
Capitalism and Modernity in an Orang Asli Village
Alberto Gomes

Governance and Democracy in Asia
Takashi Inoguchi and Matthew Carlson

Liberalism: Its Achievements and Failures
Kazuo Seiyama

Health Inequalities in Japan: An Empirical Study of Older People
Katsunori Kondo

Creating Subaltern Counterpublics

Korean Women in Japan and Their Struggle for Night School

By

Akwi Seo

Kyoto University Press
Kyoto

Trans Pacific Press
Melbourne

First published in Japanese by Ochanomizu Shobō in 2012 as *Zainichi Chōsenjin josei ni yoru 'kai no taikō-teki na kōkyōken' no keisei – Ōsaka no yakan chūgaku o kaku to shita undō*.

This English edition published in 2017 jointly by:

Kyoto University Press
69 Yoshida Konoe-cho
Sakyo-ku, Kyoto 606-8315, Japan
Telephone: +81-75-761-6182
Fax: +81-75-761-6190
Email: sales@kyoto-up.or.jp
Web: http://www.kyoto-up.or.jp

Trans Pacific Press
PO Box 164, Balwyn North
Victoria 3104, Australia
Telephone: +61-(0)3-9859-1112
Fax: +61-(0)3-8611-7989
Email: tpp.mail@gmail.com
Web: http://www.transpacificpress.com

© Kyoto University Press and Trans Pacific Press 2017.

Designed and set by Sarah Tuke, Melbourne, Australia.

Printed by Focus Print Group, Burwood, Victoria, Australia.

Distributors

Australia and New Zealand
James Bennett Pty Ltd
Locked Bag 537
Frenchs Forest NSW 2086
Australia
Telephone: +61-(0)2-8988-5000
Fax: +61-(0)2-8988-5031
Email: info@bennett.com.au
Web: www.bennett.com.au

USA and Canada
International Specialized Book Services (ISBS)
920 NE 58th Avenue, Suite 300
Portland, Oregon 97213-3786
USA
Telephone: 1-800-944-6190
Fax: 1-503-280-8832
Email: orders@isbs.com
Web: http://www.isbs.com

Asia and the Pacific (except Japan).
Kinokuniya Company Ltd.
Head office:
3-7-10 Shimomeguro
Meguro-ku
Tokyo 153-8504
Japan
Telephone: +81-(0)3-6910-0531
Fax: +81-(0)3-6420-1362
Email: bkimp@kinokuniya.co.jp
Web: www.kinokuniya.co.jp
Asia-Pacific office:
Kinokuniya Book Stores of Singapore Pte., Ltd.
391B Orchard Road #13-06/07/08
Ngee Ann City Tower B
Singapore 238874
Telephone: +65-6276-5558
Fax: +65-6276-5570
Email: SSO@kinokuniya.co.jp

All rights reserved. No reproduction of any part of this book may take place without the written permission of Trans Pacific Press.

ISSN   1443–9670 (Japanese Society Series)

ISBN   978–1–925608–91–5 (hardcover)

Cover photos
Front cover: A sit-in which demands that the branch Korean class be made an independent school, supported by Korean instructors. Picture taken in October 1993. ©Taiheiji Night Middle School.
Back cover: Night junior high school students in Higashi-Osaka in 1990. © Uri Seodang

Contents

Figures	viii
Tables	ix
Photos	x
Acknowledgements	xi

1	Introduction: Conceptualizing Korean women in Japan through a feminist lens	1
2	Between ethnic rights and women's rights movements	43
3	Counterpublics and the Taiheiji Independence Movement	78
4	Life course: Illiteracy and Night Junior High School	111
5	Formation of oppositional subjects	141
6	Intergenerational solidarity and the reconstruction of ethnicity	185
7	Korean women in Japan and subaltern counterpublics	203

Notes	215
Bibliography	235
Name Index	251
Subject Index	252

Figures

1.1a: Percentage of male workers aged over 15 by industry and nationality – 1985 — 22
1.1b: Percentage of male workers aged over 15 by industry and nationality – 2005 — 23
1.2a: Percentage of female workers aged over 15 by industry and nationality – 1985 — 24
1.2b: Percentage of female workers aged over 15 by industry and nationality – 2005 — 25
1.3: Changes in number of married Koreans in Japan (1955–2010) — 31
2.1: Analytical framework of movement organizations — 52
3.1: Osaka's Ikaino District and location of night junior high schools — 85
3.2: Shift in the number of students in public night junior high schools in Japan by background (1981–2011) — 93
3.3: Students of night junior high schools in Japan at the time of the start of the movement: Percentage by background (1993) — 95
3.4: Students of night junior high schools in Japan at the time of the start of the movement: Percentage by age group (1993) — 95
3.5: Students of night junior high schools in Japan at the time of the start of the movement: Percentage by gender (1993) — 96
3.6: Shift in the number of students in Chōei Night Junior High School — 99
3.7: Correlation chart of 'subaltern counterpublics' around Korean women in Japan — 106
6.1: Shift in total population, child population and elderly population with South Korean or Chosun nationality — 190

Tables

2.1: Major movement organizations composed of Korean women in Japan   46
3.1 Number of students of public night junior high schools in Japan by prefecture and background (1993)   94
4.1 Profile of research participants   114

Photos

3.1: Classroom in Uri Seodang 104
5.1: Name plate at the time of independence 166
5.2: Women from Uri Seodang participating in the international festival 178
5.3: Rally with former comfort women for the Japanese military in front of the Embassy of Japan in Seoul 183
6.1: Charye at the day care home 201

Acknowledgements

It was the fall of the year 2001 at the cultural festival of the Korean residents in Japan in Ikaino, Osaka, when I first learned of the existence of the first-generation *halmoni* who were studying at night junior high schools. Sixteen years have passed since then. Following the publication of the Japanese edition of this work, now I have the great pleasure of having it published in English. I would like to express my deep gratitude to everyone who has given me help and support in my research.

Firstly, I offer my heartfelt thanks to the Korean women residing in Japan who participated in the campaign for the independence of Taiheiji night junior high school and shared their life stories for this research. They gave me precious time for interviews in their very busy schedules between work, family, study and campaigning for the night school. I was fortunate enough to receive a great deal of cooperation, ranging from access to informants, information on the community of Korean residents in Osaka, to detailed advice on my way around Higashi-Osaka, from Chung Kwi-mi, who has dedicated her heart and soul to improving the well-being of the elderly Korean women in her local area. I am also grateful to Nishio Yoshiaki and Hayashi Jirō who have been dealing with the Korean women in Japan for over thirty years as teachers at the night junior high school. Reverend Gōda Satoru, who was the representative of Nikkan Shimin no Kai and instrumental in negotiating with authorities, granted me interviews, introduced me to a number of contacts, and provided me with campaign materials. Sadly, he passed away suddenly in 2008. I also received valuable suggestions from Takano Masao, who started the nation-wide citizens' movement to establish more night junior high schools in the late-1960s and inspired woman activists in the Taiheiji campaign, Bang Chun-ja, an ardent feminist activist based in the Ikaino Korean community, and from Man Hee, who led the literacy education campaign in South Korea.

The members of the organizations that have been committed to improving the status of the Korean women living in Japan for many years – the Korean Democratic Women's League in Japan (Nyeomaeng), the Korean Residents Union in Japan Women's Association (Buinhoe), the Korean Women's Society in Japan for Democracy (Yeoseonghoe), Mearihoe, the now-disbanded Military Comfort Women Issue Uri Yeoseong Network, and the Korean Christian Church in Japan Women's Association – and other women who have been actively involved in the Korean-women-in-Japan community kindly explained to me the specific problems those women faced and a variety of approaches they employed for improvement. The people of the Korean community of Osaka trusted me and provided help and support for my research even though I was a Tokyo-sider who had had nothing to do with their community. Thanks to their broadmindedness and warmth, Osaka has become my second home.

On the academic front, I am deeply grateful to Prof. Ito Ruri my Ph. D. supervisor. She imparted her knowledge of sociological theories such as ethnicity, nationalism, social movement and citizenship from a gender perspective and provided detailed guidance from the research phase to the writing phase. My first encounter with Prof. Ito was in the late 1980s when I was a student at Sophia University. Reading French migration studies in her seminar put me on the path to undertaking research on migrant women in Japan from the perspective of transnational sociology at the graduate school of Ochanomizu University ten years later. Conducting research while raising a young son was very difficult, even though I had expected it to be so, and it took a very long time to finish my dissertation. I owe the completion of my project to Prof. Ito, who watched over me and acted as a guiding light with compassion.

Joining a study group called International Migration and Gender (IMAGE) formed by Prof. Ito after I began my Ph. D. course at Ochanomizu provided an important impetus to deepen my interest in migrant women's organizations. The aim of IMAGE was to analyze and understand the processes of mutual aid, organization and community initiative formation by migrant women. My participation in this joint study group was very beneficial at the start of my research. I would like to thank my fellow members of IMAGE, Sadamatsu Aya, Ogaya Chiho, Sawada Kayo, Shin Ki-young, Ohashi Fumie, Yu Young-suk, Eunice Akemi Ishikawa, Fukuda Tomoko, Inaba Nanako and Oishi Nana.

Acknowledgements

For the thesis examination, I was given frank criticism and advice from Prof. Adachi Mariko, Prof. Tachi Kaoru, Prof. Ishizuka Michiko, and Prof. Jung Young-hae. Receiving valuable advice in a variety of specialties such as sociology, geology, gender studies, feminist economics and Koreans-in-Japan studies during the examination process helped me broaden my perspective and deepen my research. Rigorous advice and encouragement from Song Younok and Kim Puja not only as researchers but also as activists helped me feel my way forward. I appreciated stimulating discussions and mutual encouragement with my fellow seminar members, Uzawa Yumiko, Fujikake Yoko, Shinozaki Kyoko, and Hashimoto Miyuki.

This study owes a great deal also to many researchers I met during my time at the University of Toronto, Sophia University, and elsewhere. In particular, I attended the late Prof. Tsurumi Kazuko's seminar at Sophia University, which had a profound impact on my subsequent decision to pursue sociological research while I was working after graduation. My encounter with Prof. Vicente Bonet led me to choose human rights and discrimination as my lifework.

I also thank Vera Mackie, Fukuoka Yasunori, Kashiwazaki Chikako, and Han Tong-hyon who gave me valuable advice from the planning phase.

This work would not have been possible without financial supports from the Toyota Foundation, the Matsushita Memorial Foundation, the 21st Century COE Program of the Ochanomizu University "Frontiers of Gender Studies", the Grant-in-Aid for Scientific Research (KAKENHI) for Prof. Ito's project, and the Korean Scholarship Foundation. Following the publication of the Japanese edition, the publication of this English edition was made possible with a Grant-in-Aid for Publication of Scientific Research Results from the Japan Society for the Promotion of Science (15HP6009). I would like to take this opportunity to thank them all.

Thanks to the extremely meticulous attention given to my work by the publisher of the Japanese edition Ochanomizu Shobō and the editor Hashimoto Iku, I had the honor of receiving the Yamakawa Kikue Award (research in women's studies) and the Word and Gender Award in 2012 for the Japanese edition. The publication of this English edition was made possible by Kyoto University Press and Trans Pacific Press of Australia. It gives me a great joy to see my work published by these publishers who have a long history of introducing excellent Japanese sociological studies to the English-speaking world. I have not enough words to thank Suzuki Tetsuya, Yoshio Sugimoto, Karl Smith and Yuri Kamada for their patience in helping me as I struggled with editing in English, which is not my native language. I received the assistance of Hong Jung-eun and Kim Mijin for alphabetical notation of proper nouns in the Korean language.

Lastly, I would like to express my gratitude to my family whose support for this work has been invaluable. In particular, I would like to dedicate this book to my mother, who is a constant source of moral support, and my two deceased grandmothers. I also thank my husband and son for their emotional support.

My sincere hope is that this book offers a chance for the English-speaking readers to take an interest in the postcolonial diaspora of the Korean women living in Japan and contributes to the advancement of studies on the formation of organizations, social participation and activism for and by migrant women.

October 2016 in Fukuoka

1 Introduction: Conceptualizing Korean women in Japan through a feminist lens

This book is an exploration of the subject formation of Korean women in Japan[1] focusing on various social movements led by Korean women around the issue of public night junior high schools, which flourished in Higashi-Osaka from the 1990s onward. The term 'Koreans in Japan' generally refers to the people who migrated to Japan from the Korean Peninsula during the period of Japanese colonial rule (1910–1945) and their descendants. They have always occupied a somewhat unique position among the ethnic minority groups in Japan due to the historical and political implications of the colonial past. Statistically, 457,772 South Korean and 33,939 North Korean nationals were registered as foreign residents in 2015.[2] They were the largest non-Japanese ethnic group inside Japan until they were overtaken by the Chinese in 2008. A total of 360,096 South and North Korean nationals became Japanese citizens between 1952 and 2015.[3] The combined number of Koreans in Japan, including those with South Korean, North Korean and Japanese nationality (through naturalization), is 851,807. If we include, on top of this, children who were given Japanese citizenship at birth for having a Japanese parent (or Japanese parents of Korean origin) the number of Koreans in Japan reaches almost 1% of total population in Japan (Fukuoka 1993: 73).

In Japanese society where the Japanese ethnic group and Japanese citizens form the mainstream, Koreans who reside in Japan have long been regarded as inferior to the Japanese people and have been marginalized politically, socially, economically and culturally, on the basis that they originate from a former colony or, in many cases, simply because they are foreigners. At the same time, their 'homeland' on the Korean Peninsula split after the war. Diplomatic relations were established under the Treaty on Basic Relations between Japan and the Republic of Korea in 1965 but there has been

1

no official diplomatic relations with North Korea up to the present day. After the war, as the international political system developed with the nation-state as its constituent units, Koreans in Japan found themselves in between the three nation-states – South Korea, North Korea and Japan – and their lives have been largely dictated by the three states and their political relationships.

Against this political and social background, Koreans in Japan have been engaged in unique postcolonial liberation movements. The post-war Korean people's movements in Japan can be classified according to two general tendencies; those that are related to nation-building or reunification of the Korean Peninsula and those that are concerned with protecting and advancing their interests in Japan. The former may be called nationalist movements, and the latter ethnic movements. Within these two streams are a multitude of movements leading in different directions, while the two general tendencies often coexist within one organization.

Korean women in Japan have actively participated in and played key roles in promoting ethnic liberation movements. However, for a long time after World War II, collective action by Korean women remained confined to ethnic organizations in which decision making was an exclusively male prerogative, and women's groups themselves remained under the aegis of male-dominated parent organizations. A gendered division of labor was taken-for-granted in these ethnic organizations. Men made decisions about campaign objectives and tactics and other operations while women were limited to the implementation of given decisions. Furthermore, women's roles and positions were aligned with the family norms of 'mother' and 'wife', and thus they were restricted to activities that would not threaten the dominant norms of male superiority despite their considerable contribution to the ethnic movements.

Since the late 1980s, though, this situation has changed. Korean women in Japan began to engage in political activities with relatively more autonomy – in the sense that they were not dependent on the dominant ethnic organizations – and established a new position within the social movement sector seeking to improve the status of minorities. Having formed more autonomous movement organizations than in the past and developed an ability to enter into negotiations on their own initiative rather than as part of androcentric ethnic organizations, Korean women began to engage directly with the mainstream Japanese society. They were no longer involved in social action 'merely' as wives or mothers but began to fight for improvements of their own social positions and human rights.

The struggle for public night junior high schools in Osaka, which is the focus of this book, was started by first- and second-generation Korean women who were born and raised in prewar Japan. While the aim of this movement was to demand that education authorities safeguard places for learning, it also facilitated a new subject formation of Korean women in Japan at the local level. Let us look at the brief overview of the night junior high school movements.

Soon after opening its doors, Chōei Junior High School Night Class in Higashi-Osaka City had the largest student body of any night junior high school in Japan. The vast majority of its students were middle- and older-aged Korean women. The night school was situated in Japan's largest Korean settlement. Most first-generation Korean women had not had access to schooling opportunities when they were school age and were therefore illiterate. In the early 1990s, when the number of students in the night class exceeded the number of their daytime counterparts and the facility was not capable of adequately accommodating them, the board of education forced almost half of the students to relocate to an extension class set up in the neighboring Taiheiji Junior High School.

The new extension class was a hastily established stop-gap measure which failed to meet the necessary standards of facilities and numbers of teaching staff for night junior high schools. The Korean women, who constituted the great majority of the effected students, were frustrated by the substandard educational environment and concluded that, in conjunction with the forced relocation of the students, they had been subjected to this unjust treatment because they were Korean. Although this interpretation may be questionable, there is no doubt that Koreans in Japan have generally been treated as inferior to native Japanese citizens and have been subjected to discriminatory treatment by Japanese institutions. The Korean women at the night junior high school were responding to a long history of oppression before this event took place.

In 1993 the student council of the night school started demanding that the board of education elevate the extension class to an independent night junior high school and improve the education environment to meet the standards of regular night junior high schools. The struggle continued for eight years before the extension class was finally recognized as an official night junior high school in April 2001. The social movement organization which waged this battle, the Taiheiji Night Junior High School Independence Movement, continues to thrive today, even after having accomplished its original goal. Today it serves as a social platform that underpins a range of activities initiated by Korean women who live locally. The women who led the movement graduated during the process of their campaign; however, an oppositional social space which formed through the movement – one in which Korean women play the central roles – maintains a tangible presence, as Uri Seodang, a learning institution for Korean women, as well as Sarangbang, a day service center facility for elderly Korean women.

As we will see, Korean women have been involved in a great many social movements and organizations in postwar Japan. There are three main reasons for choosing to focus on the night junior high school movement in Higashi-Osaka. These can be summarized as follows:

1. The Taiheiji Night Junior High School Independence Movement generated an organization that is autonomous of the dominant Korean ethnic organizations, allowing women to conduct campaigns by and for themselves as the negotiating subjects.
2. It was conducted independently of gender roles such as 'mother', 'wife' and 'daughter'.
3. It aimed to promote the rights and improve the situation of the women themselves, from their perspectives, based on their own life experiences.

Over and above its more explicit achievements, the Taiheiji Independence Movement made visible the Korean women who had been rendered invisible within both mainstream Japanese society and their own ethnic community. It empowered them in the local society as a group with a unique historical and social background. In more theoretical terms, the protest against the city and prefectural Boards of Education and the local Japanese society helped Korean women to establish themselves as political actors, by demanding redistribution of resources and recognition of their identity.

At a broader level, this movement interacted with diverse social movements concerned with minority rights which were active in the Kansai region. These included nation-wide night junior high school expansion movements, Korean ethnic rights movements, literacy movements, buraku[4] liberation movements and human rights movements for foreign residents. The new subjectivity of Korean women can be seen as a product of the interactions of many different movements, yet it remains original and unique. Those women, who came to be called *halmoni* (grandmother) or *omoni* (mother) – as signs of respect – are the linchpins of a human network built around night junior high schools. The critical space that they created through their involvement in local politics has laid a foundation for a wide array of activities by Korean women's agency in the local community. In this book, I present this oppositional social space as a 'subaltern counterpublic' following Nancy Fraser (1992) and examine this space as the cornerstone for a new subjectivity of Korean women in Japan. The questions I will be addressing include: What were the conditions in the 1990s that brought the night junior high school movement into existence and that shaped its development? How did this movement relate to the social situation and life trajectories of Korean women in Japan? Who were the actors of the movement? What challenges were posed by the female subjects who were formed through the movement and what changes did the movement bring to their social position in family, local society, and ethnic community? The ultimate goal is to analyze the characteristics of autonomous social movements pioneered by Korean women in Japan and to position the women involved in the movement as agents of social change.[5]

Theoretical framework of the study

Spatial and temporal axes

It was no coincidence that the autonomous movement by Korean women in Japan developed in Higashi-Osaka in the 1990s. This movement in which the women manifested as social actors was born at the intersection of the different time spans and the multilayered social spaces in which Korean women have been living in Japan. This section will describe the spatial and temporal axes of this movement at the macro, meso and micro levels.

For the spatial axes, there are three conceptual 'places': a transnational life space spanning from Osaka to the Korean Peninsula, the social space created by the interactions of minority social movements in Kansai and the community of Koreans in Japan. There are also three temporal axes to be addressed: the transition from Japanese colonial domination to a postcolonial structure of subordination; the aging of first-generation and prewar-born second-generation Korean women in Japan; and the life course pattern specific to this cohort of Korean women in Japan.

Spatial axes

Most of the women who waged the night junior high school independence movement campaign were first-generation Koreans who had migrated to Japan prior to the war or second-generation Koreans who had been born and raised in pre-war Japan. When they were growing up, the Korean peninsula was part of the Japanese empire – a colony that was referred to as *gaichi*, an 'external territory', a vassal of *naichi*, the 'interior territories'. In August 1945, Korea was liberated following Japan's defeat in the war. It is estimated that almost one and a half million of the more than two million Koreans who were living in Japan returned to Korea at that time. However, approximately 600,000 Koreans remained in Japan due to the political instability on the Korean Peninsula. Due to its close connections with Jeju Island, Osaka received thousands of illegal Korean immigrants smuggled across the sea, including refugees from the Jeju Uprising, which began on 3 April 1948. A decade later, nearly 93,000 Koreans moved to North Korea under a repatriation project (1959–67, 1971–84). Hence many of the Koreans who reside in Osaka have relatives in the divided nation-states on the Korean Peninsula and have maintained communications, forming a life space that transcends national boundaries. In addition to the obvious language and cultural ties and kinship, Koreans in Japan have been politically influenced from across the sea – from the two nations of the Korean Peninsula as overseas nationals. The second spatial axis is the largest community of Koreans in Japan, which is concentrated in particular areas of Osaka. Chōei Night Junior High School and Taiheiji Night Junior High School are located on the periphery of the area with the largest ethnic Korean enclave in Japan, which extends from the eastern region of Osaka City to Higashi-Osaka City. Hence, elderly Korean women constituted a significant majority of the students of these two schools. As of the end of 2015, there were approximately 10,642 residents with either North or South Korean nationality in Higashi-Osaka City, accounting for 63% of the total foreign residents of the city.[6]

Introduction

From the beginning of the Taisho era (1912–1926) to the end of the Showa era (1926–1989), the Hanshin area underwent rapid industrialization, raising demand for low-wage laborers. Meanwhile in Korea, the land survey project coupled with the *Sanmai Zōshoku Keikaku* program (Rice Production Development Plan) caused many agricultural villages to fail and many impoverished farmers made their way to north-eastern China (bordering the Korean peninsula) or Japan. Owing to the opening of a shipping channel to Jeju Island in 1923, Osaka became home to over 400,000 Koreans by the 1940s. Prior to WWII, Koreans worked as laborers on construction projects or as low-level workers in small and medium-sized chemical, metal and textile factories. Although not as numerous as Korean men, there were also many single women migrant workers who were often employed in cotton-mills (Sugihara 1998). The most common pattern of immigration was for a man to enter Japan seeking employment, followed by his family. That is to say, a great majority of the women who migrated to Japan came as family members. This is possibly one of the factors that kept Korean women in Japan highly dependent on men, especially on the 'heads of household', even after the war, both in terms of legal status and economic matters.

The Korean neighborhood in Ikuno Ward is commonly known as *Ikaino*. On the eastern side of Tsuruhashi Station on the Osaka Loop Line is a high concentration of Korean restaurants, grocers, and retail stores that carry Korean sundry goods, bedding items, clothes, furniture and books, as well as real estate agencies and financial businesses. Korean ethnic organizations and networks are highly developed in the area, including ethnic rights / interest organizations such as Chongryun, Mindan and Hantongryun; religious organizations; and provincial associations, which are social groups for people from the same Korean province. Ikaino is a space that exhibits strong ethnic characteristics where the Korean lifestyle is relatively secured. Commercial business and voluntary associations, as well as a wide range of culturally appropriate services, enables Koreans to maintain a Korean lifestyle. With this large population of Koreans, ethnic rights movements were active in Osaka, and many campaigns for ethnic rights, over education, eligibility for public sector jobs, employment discrimination and cultural activities took place in Osaka.

Thirdly, Osaka is at the very center of the Kansai region – and hence the Korean community there shares culture, economic and political interests with others who are also positioned on the margins of this stratified urban society. There are many communities in Osaka, developed around areas inhabited by people who have been alienated from the mainstream Japanese society, including people from discriminated *buraku* communities, as well as Okinawans and day laborers. The people who provided the backbone for the industrialization of modern Osaka as low-wage laborers created their own settlements in the inner city areas; however, they were excluded discursively from and made invisible within the mainstream urban scenery due to class, racial and regional orders. The areas where those people dwelled were often lacking in urban infrastructure, which fueled campaigns for improved living conditions, giving rise to counter-cultural identities (Mizuuchi 2005a, 2005b). Minority groups in Kansai were able to make political progress, to some extent, at least, because of the mutual support among different activist groups and a wealth of resources that have accumulated through interactions between groups, including theories, methodologies and networks of social movements. The night junior high school independence movement in Higashi-Osaka built upon the subaltern counterpublics that had previously been formed by other minority movements in Kansai.

Korean women in Japan live in social spaces that are defined by these transnational, ethnic and local dimensions. They move back and forth between the imagined spaces where different languages and cultures are propagated on a daily basis. They produce and are produced by these spaces as they switch back-and-forth between languages and cultural codes. They speak their 'mother tongue' – the language of their hometowns on the Korean Peninsula – with their 'fellow countrywomen' and the Kansai dialect when speaking with local Japanese people. Switching identities from 'Kansai locals' to 'Koreans in Japan', then sometimes to 'overseas citizens of North Korea' or 'South Korean citizens' or simply 'Korean compatriots in Japan' or 'neighbors from the same village', they are inextricably bound up in a nation-state system that assumes agreement between language, ethnicity and nationality, while at the same time living in social spaces that are not readily defined by any singular nation-state framework.

Temporal axes

Almost all of the Koreans who study at night junior high schools in Japan are middle-aged or older women. Why are they women and why do they only begin studying at night junior high schools after they have reached their 60s or older? The first temporal axis we should look to for answers to these questions is a life course pattern specific to Korean women in Japan.

A life course is defined as 'the trajectory that ties together the history of various roles an individual pursues through their lifetime' (Iwakami 2003: 34). Humans live in social relationships that may involve schools, jobs, families and local communities. Life course research is an approach that uses transitions in an individual's positions and roles as analytical dimensions. In general, family is the most important social relationship in the life course of a Korean woman in Japan. Despite the fact a woman's position in the family changes from daughter to wife, mother, daughter-in-law, and mother-in-law, her mission remains substantially the same throughout all stages – to care for other family members and satisfy their needs. First-generation and prewar-born second-generation Korean women in Japan have been responsible for family chores and waged jobs all of their lives. Since education was not compulsory in Korea during Japanese colonial rule, people from poor farming households rarely received modern educations. Women especially were unlikely to go to school when they were school age due to a widespread belief that women did not need any formal education. Once they were married, they took sole responsibility for all child-rearing, household and nursing duties as well as engaging in home manufacturing and piecework, or else they did wage work in factories to support their families. Only in middle-age and freed to some extent from domestic duties, were they able to realize long-held dreams of 'going to school'. The night junior high school independence movement in Higashi-Osaka was influenced significantly by this life course specific to Korean women in Japan.

Although there has been almost no awareness of the illiteracy of Korean women in Japan, or it has been taken-for-granted as a non-issue, the women themselves have nurtured hopes of learning to read and write for more than half a century. When they finally entered night junior high school, they encountered fellow countrywomen in the classroom with pencils in their hands, trying to learn to read and write for the first time in their lives. The shared realization that illiteracy is not an individual problem became the foundation for the formation of an oppositional subjectivity during the course of a social movement fought over the right to an education.

The second temporal axis that should be examined is the colonial domination that has continued to be imposed on Korean women in Japan into the postcolonial era. While literally meaning 'after the colonial period', the term 'postcolonial' here points to the understanding that a variety of discourses, sets of values, forms of awareness, policies, systems and practices which had been devised by the colonizer to subordinate the colonized, remain in place today and are going to be carried into the future in reconstructed forms (Motohashi 2005: iv–vii). The Korean women who led the night junior high school movement have first-hand experience of colonial rule in Korea and Japan from the 1920s and '30s. Those experiences are deeply inscribed, as we will discuss in more detail.

They continued to be subject to prejudice and discrimination as migrants from a former colony even after the end of the empire. The racism that conceives of Koreans as inherently inferior was characteristic of the Imperial Japanese colonization of East and Southeast Asia, and continued to be prevalent in Japanese society throughout the 20th century. In the 1990s, their long experience of colonial oppression turned into indignation when they were transferred from a standard night junior high school to an extension class with substandard facilities and staffing. This indignation at continuing racial discrimination became the driving force of their resistance against local authority.

The third temporal axis is generational change. The night junior high school independence movement was an extraordinary event for both the local Korean society and the mainstream Japanese society because the activists were primarily older first-generation women. The movement came to be known as the '*halmoni* movement' – *halmoni* means grandmother or old woman in the Korean language. It received significant support from local second- and third-generation women and thus became a catalyst for women's intergenerational solidarity, which is essentially different from women's intergenerational relationship in family (between daughter and mother, or bride and mother-in-law), which are based on patriarchal values.

In the course of the night junior high school independence movement, a self-directed learning institution and a livelihood support facility were founded for the aging first- and second-generation women. These facilities provide a place for younger women to offer assistance in the daily living of older Korean women, including liaising with administrative services and the local society. These places facilitated social-cultural mediation by younger-generation women as well as public recognition of their mutual assistance. The older women receive assistance from the younger, and in exchange play a role in transmitting the language and culture of Korea, as well as their historical experiences as Korean migrants in Japan, to the younger women. The night junior high school independence movement brought local Korean women together.

As we have seen, the particular life course, the continuation of colonial domination in the postcolonial era and intergenerational solidarity are three temporal axes which are critical for analyzing the night junior high school independence movement.

Subaltern counterpublics

This book aims to analyze the formation of subjectivity by Korean women in Japan by exploring the social space that developed out of the night junior high school independence movement in Higashi-Osaka drawing on the concept of 'subaltern counterpublics' outlined by Nancy Fraser (1992). The public sphere is a concept originally proposed by Jürgen Habermas (1989) which refers to a public arena that is generated as private persons engage freely and on equal terms as 'peers' in debates on matters of common concern. The public sphere is a site where discourses that in principle are critical of the state are produced and circulated. It aims to mediate between society and the state. Habermas derived the ideal type of the bourgeois public sphere from the historical contexts of modern British, French and German developments, drawing on the history of the development of mass media, including books, journals and papers; the establishment of libraries, and reading societies as social nodes of a literary culture. In addition to these language-based media, Habermas also emphasized the role of new associations – such as awareness-raising organizations and education clubs – as communication channels for citizens (Habermas 1989).

Fraser outlined a number of important objections to Habermas' idealization of this model of the public sphere. First, the historical formation of the public sphere is conditional upon the rise of bourgeois citizens. Hence, it necessarily and intrinsically creates groups of people who are marginalized, such as women, lower-class men, racialized ethnicities of all classes, and foreigners. Fraser questions Habermas's conception of the public sphere as open and accessible to all, pointing out that bourgeois conceptions of the public sphere require bracketing inequalities of status (Fraser 1992: 118). Feminists have clearly demonstrated that gender provides the core of the public/private dichotomy in Western modernity. Habermas responded that the exclusion of women has been constitutive for the political public sphere in that its structure and relation to the private sphere has been determined in a gender-specific fashion (Habermas 1992: 428).[7]

Habermas envisaged the public sphere as a single comprehensive entity contraposed to the state. One problem with this is the difficulty for members of marginalized minority groups to be heard within an all-encompassing mainstream public sphere. They must therefore create their own spaces for communication, where they can discuss their own interests and strategies without being overridden by the majority. Revisiting historical developments from this perspective, it becomes apparent that when the bourgeois public sphere emerged, many competing public spheres also existed, such as a nationalist public sphere, an elite women's public sphere and a laborers' public sphere.[8] Fraser thus notes the existence of multiple, alternative competing spaces for discussions developed by non-mainstream, minority groups and named these alternative spaces 'subaltern counterpublics' (Fraser 1992: 123). Subaltern counterpublics are discursive arenas that enable members of subservient social groups to produce counter discourses that challenge the negative identities or stigma that have been attributed to them by mainstream society. Subaltern counterpublics are characterized by multiplicity, equality of participation, openness and interactivity.[9] Moreover, Fraser believes that communication across lines of cultural difference is possible if the differences are not bracketed. Such intercultural communication could be promoted by porousness, outer-directedness and the open-endedness of publics (Fraser 1992: 127). In this move Fraser attempted to broaden the horizons of the public sphere in such a way as to recognize and include racial/ethnic minorities who had been historically excluded from the 'citizenry'. The subaltern counterpublics model treats alternative public spheres as an accomplished fact; however, it needs to be explained how individuals, such as migrant women, who are embedded within multi-layered structures of oppression based on differences in race/ethnicity, class, nationality and gender, who lack the very foundations for forming collective bodies, are able to create their own public spheres. In particular, lack of proficiency in the language of the host society, especially when coupled with low literacy skills, means lack of means of communication and makes participating in any public discussion a significant challenge. Investigating the conditions that underpinned the formation and development of the night junior high school independence movement by Korean women in Japan will contribute to an empirical examination of the process of the formation of subaltern counterpublics.

Nation and gender

Racial/ethnic minority groups are incorporated into a society's structures of oppression. As a result, the personal domain – such as family and ethnic community – takes on added importance for individuals, acting as a refuge from the discrimination in mainstream society, a human relationship where those subordinated can foster self-esteem (hooks 1984), or at least the degree of individual dependency on family is assumed to increase. Unfortunately, too often this contributes to the perpetuation of gender inequalities within ethnic communities and families, binding individuals – especially female individuals – more tightly within gender norms. As discussed in Chapter 2, in the Korean ethnic rights movements in Japan, women's roles in the family, such as 'mother' and 'wife', were usually given greater emphasis than their identity as 'women'.

Social theories of nation and ethnicity have suggested that the creation of a modern nation-state entails the construction of imagined communities that are based on 'homogeneities' such as common language, culture and religion. Migration studies from a gender perspective have looked at the structures of gender as well as the gendered division of labor within nations and ethnic groups, revealing that communities are ordered on a gender-basis

(Yuval-Davis and Anthias 1989; Yuval-Davis 1993; Stasiulis and Yuval-Davis 1995; Enloe 1989). Yuval-Davis and Anthias identified five gender-specific roles imposed upon women in their theory of correlation between nation and gender:
1. biological reproducers of ethnic collectivities
2. reproducers of the boundaries of ethnic/national groups
3. central participants in the ideological reproduction of the collectivity and as transmitters of its culture
4. signifiers of ethnic/national differences
5. participants in national, economic, political and military struggles (1989: 6–7).

The theory of correlation between nation and gender highlights differences within minority collectives that are obscured by the confrontation with the majority. It also argues that women are prescribed special roles that serve as psychological boundaries for the community (Yuval-Davis and Anthias 1989).

Enloe also focused on the roles assigned to women in carrying on the legacy of the community and nurturing the next generation (Enloe 1989: 54–64). Driven by a sense of threatened survival, oppressed ethnic minorities tend to regard reproduction to be of the utmost importance and encourage heterosexual marriage as well as the 'wise mother and good wife' norms. At the same time, nationalist movements mobilize women for achieving political goals. Women – who have typically been confined within the domestic domain – welcome this opportunity and voluntarily commit to the movements, as a way to expand their range of activities beyond the private / domestic sphere. Hence, participating in a nationalist movement can be a means of improving a woman's status, fulfilling her desires to be acknowledged as a 'national citizen'. There is thus a two-fold dimension to nationalist movements for women: on one hand, they impose traditional gender roles and the gendered division of labor, but on the other hand, they open up possibilities for women to be involved in public sphere politics, albeit under the control of men.

This tension becomes even more complicated in the context of competition between different social movements and mobilizations. For example, during the 1960s, the United States experienced widespread structural change driven by the civil rights movement, left-wing political movements and the women's liberation movement. In many respects, though, minority women 'fell through the gaps' of these diverse liberation movements.[10] Furthermore, competition was fierce in the social movement space in the 1960s and androcentric civil rights and left-wing movements sought the support of women. For women who were working alongside men toward the shared goal of achieving racial/ethnic-based or class-based human rights, it was difficult to raise issues of gender inequality within the minority group due to concerns that any gender-based schism would weaken the larger group movement. African-American women who joined white-dominated women's emancipation movements were often considered as traitors. This is one reason why Chicana and African-American women did not join white women's liberation movements but created their own movement: so that they could justify their activism to their communities (Roth 2004).

In Chapter 2, I will examine a wide spectrum of social movements that were led by Korean women in postwar Japan, in preparation for analyzing the night junior high school independence movement in Higashi-Osaka. I will pay particular attention to gender roles in nationalist movements and ethnic minority liberation movements and use that, in combination with autonomy from androcentric parent organizations, as the analytical framework for discussion.

Intersectionality of oppressions and subaltern women

The idea of 'intersectionality of oppressions' points to those situations in which multiple dimensions of oppressions such as those based on race/ethnicity, gender and class intersect. At these intersections, the different dimensions of oppression do not simply accumulate; rather, the oppression is amplified and distinct forms of oppression emerge. A prime example is the case of African-American women, who face a unique structure of oppression; a product of the interaction and amplification effects of racial oppression and gender oppression rather than a simple accumulation of the two (Crenshaw 1989, 1994; Chow 1996; hooks 1984).

The challenges faced by Korean women in Japan can be traced to a distinct form of oppression that occurs at the intersection between the racial order and the gender order. Their struggles therefore cannot be understood through the lens of a single category. Korean women in Japan have been silenced, marginalized and excluded in both the ethnic rights movements spear-headed by Korean men and in the Japanese women's liberation movement. As will be shown in Chapter 2, efforts to address the difficulties specific to Korean women in Japan only started to appear in the public sphere in the late 1980s, and these were primarily initiated by second- or later-generation Korean women.

The final point to be noted here is the framework used in this research to account for subjectivity. Social subjects do not become subjects on their own. As individuals discursively construct themselves as subjects, they are 'interpellated' or 'spoken to', and they become represented as identities. Althusser theorized modern subjects as those that submit to interpellation on their own initiative. According to Althusser, individuals become concrete subjects who assert an ideology by being interpellated by the power structure and identifying themselves with the interpellated other. Thus, subjects do not exist a priori but are constructed as subjects who are 'spoken to' as they become subjected to, and choose to submit to, a specific ideology or discourse (Althusser 1976).

If the construction of subjects is dictated by authority, then we must ask how those individuals who are not even subjected to the power structure can become independent concrete subjects. I will try to answer this question in light of Spivak's notion of 'subaltern women'. Subaltern has the meaning of 'lower status' and 'dependent'; it is defined here as 'subordinate class'. Spivak considered women whose identities had been denied by the patriarchal ideology even within the invisible populace class and referred to them as historically silenced 'subaltern women'. Subaltern women's voices cannot be heard; they cannot speak and therefore have no other choice than to be silent/silenced (Spivak 1988). The field of subaltern studies in India has uncovered various underclass social groups separated from the elite class, focusing on those who have no means to present/represent themselves. However, this field has completely overlooked female subjects. Despite being as committed as men to India's anti-imperialist resistance movement, women were merely used as discursive / symbolic objects with no substance in the movement. Spivak argued that women were essential to the structure in which subaltern populations find themselves and therefore the subjectivity of these women ought to be examined (Spivak 1985).

Koreans in Japan have long been actively engaged in struggles seeking post-war redistribution and recognition of their identity, but women have been excluded from the liberation discourses; rendered invisible because the Korean ethnic rights movements were patently androcentric. Hence, consistent with Spivak's notion of the subaltern woman, Korean women in Japan could not represent themselves and found themselves in a position in which it was difficult to speak up. They have been othered both because they come from a former colony and because they are women. As Butler argues, identity is constructed in a performative manner through a set of repeated acts. Butler rejected approaches that presume unvarying subject categories such as 'women'. Identity is constructed through the action of 'performing' and subjects do not exist before action (Butler 1990). The struggle over night junior high schools in Higashi-Osaka was the first event in which women, who had been invisible, emerged as subjects in the local public space. By repeatedly protesting against the administration and the local community, they made the emancipatory identity 'Koreans in Japan' their own while at the same time constructing female oppositional subjects.

Intersectionality of Korean women's oppression in Japan

Subjectivity of Korean women in Japan

Korean women in Japan cannot be generalized since they are a diverse group in terms of nationality (South Korean, North Korean, Japanese and other), educational background (ethnic school, Japanese school or overseas), as well as the ethnicity of parents and spouses (Koreans in Japan, Japanese or other ethnic backgrounds). For the purpose of this book, I categorized a broad spectrum of women who have their roots in the Korean Peninsula as 'Korean women in Japan', regardless of differences in nationality, the ethnic backgrounds of their parents and spouses or their explicit self-identification as a Korean in Japan. In respect of the night junior high school independence movement in Higashi-Osaka, the subject of this study, the activists generally stressed the identity 'Koreans in Japan' but the word 'women' was rarely brought to the fore. The fact that the word 'women' was left out despite almost everyone being a woman will be discussed in separate chapters (Chapter 3 and Chapter 5), it should be noted here that this book employs the term 'Korean women in Japan' as an analytical category.

The expression 'Korean women in Japan' has long existed as a common noun, but it was only from the 1980s that it began to be widely used as political identity to signify a unique existence, distinct from both Korean men in Japan and Japanese women, as those who are subjected to and struggle with the system of multiple oppressions based on race, gender, nationality and class. The turning point came when second-generation women began to object to the patriarchy[11] in the families and communities of Koreans in Japan. Second-generation women recognized that the Korean community managed to survive in the highly exclusive Japanese society because of their mothers' painstaking efforts to protect their family but at the same time they aspired to a different way of life from their mothers.[12] Second-generation women who received school education acknowledged the struggle and accomplishment of the first-generation women who were 'living in secluded pockets of society, socially and economically, without being allowed to even study due to old Korean customs and feudal ideology'.[13] However, at the same time, they also began to criticize the irrational gender order that subordinated women to men.

> Men had no other means to release stress from the outside world but to make much of their status as men inside the home and, especially with the longing for the stolen motherland, they are enshrining and passing on even the customs and conventions that have long been abandoned back in our home country. (Kim Young-Soon 1979: 131)

Second-generation women, who were educated and are competent in the Japanese language began to voice accusations against Korean men who were not only forcing women into unpaid labor in the home and family businesses but were also expressing their frustrating experience of inhumane treatment in Japanese society through violence against their wives and children.

Of course, their criticism was not only directed at Korean men and the Korean community in Japan. The struggles faced by Korean women in Japan are inseparable from the fact that Koreans are a minority in Japanese society. Korean men were positioned at the bottom of the Japanese capitalist system as cheap labor and their wives suffered from unstable family lives. Korean women in Japan have not been able to communicate freely with their own parents living in Korea (whether South or North) because of a tradition which makes women serve their husband's family, as well as their illiteracy, the postwar liberation of Korea from Japan and the subsequent division of the homeland. Korean tradition also treats self-sacrifice as a virtue, although accepting the role of 'wise mother and good wife' served to preserve the feudal system. Thus second generation women developed an awareness that women needed to reinvent themselves (Yoon Ga-ja 1987).

The development of a theory of women's liberation, or feminism, among second generation Korean women in Japan occurred in the context of their increasing education and the ability to express themselves in the Japanese language, but their encounter with Japanese feminism and life experiences in Western countries was also of immense importance in changing their relative assessment of themselves.[14] More recent generations were increasingly interacting with the world outside of their local ethnic community and began to explicitly reject the patriarchy that was subjugating women. In the 1990s, fueled by the disclosures of a comfort woman in South Korea who had come forward, the voices of Korean women in Japan calling for emancipation grew louder,[15] leading to the foundation of an organization called 'Jūgun Ianfu Mondai Uriyoson Nettowāku (Military Comfort Women Issue Uri Yeoseong Network)', which will be discussed in Chapter 2.

For Korean women in Japan, criticizing the patriarchy meant a struggle between two contradictory forces: the ethnic society that required them to be a 'wise mother and good wife' and women's liberation. While acquiring Korean identity is an important challenge for women of more recent generations, they must inevitably undertake the process of sharing 'Korean' culture with their 'fellow compatriots' in the course of the journey. During this process, women tend to internalize various contradictions inherent in Korean culture, including sexual discrimination. For men, insistence on 'Korean' culture and identity might bring a sense of pride; in contrast, women are forced to live in self-denial by the sexual discrimination of the same 'Korean' culture (Jung Yeong-hae 1994). For Korean women in Japan, liberation from the male-dominated 'family' was equally as important as liberation from racial oppression in Japanese society. For those who faced greater adversity, in particular, physical violence, it proved to be an even greater challenge than racial liberation.

This has been a brief introduction to the development of postcolonial feminist subjectivity by second generation Korean women in Japan. In the following section I will illustrate their social situation from the perspective of the host society, the ethnic society and the family, based on previous studies.

Host society

The Korean population in Japan has been significantly influenced by Japan's colonial domination and its aftermath. The population of Koreans in Japan was 790 before Japan 'annexed' Korea in 1910. It increased to about 30,000 over the next decade,[16] and continued to grow, reaching approximately 300,000 by 1930 and one million by 1940. Perhaps the single most important push factor contributing to this migration was the impoverishment of rural communities resulting from colonial policies such as the land survey project and the Rice Production Development Plan (*Sanmai Zōshoku Keikaku*) program. The growing demand for low-wage labor in Japan to satisfy the needs of rapid industrialization was an important pull factor. In the late 1930s, a large number of Koreans were forcibly deployed in the 'interior territories' (the Japanese Islands) as well as Japan's occupied territories under the National Mobilization Law and the National Requisition Ordinance. As a result, the population of Koreans in Japan skyrocketed to around two million by 1944. Following Korea's liberation in 1945, many Koreans returned home. The population of Koreans in Japan had shrunk to around 550,000 by the end of the Korean War (1950–1953) (Morita 1996: 33).

During the colonial period, Koreans were Japanese nationals. However, they were distinguished from their colonial oppressors, the 'proper Japanese',[17] through a separate family register. The Japanese colonial policy was thus contradictory; it included Koreans in the category 'Japanese nationals' yet at the same time gave them a different status through the application of different family registration systems (Oguma 1998: 161).

After the war, with the end of Japan's Empire, the legal status of Koreans in Japan gradually changed from 'second-class citizens' to outright 'aliens'. This was first officially decreed as an addendum to granting women's suffrage in December 1945, an addendum which suspended the voting rights of Koreans and Taiwanese who were not on a family register in Japan.[18] The Alien Registration Ordinance[19] of 1947 further specified 'Koreans and Taiwanese as 'aliens,' obliging them to register as aliens and to carry a certificate of alien registration. When the San Francisco Peace Treaty came into effect in April 1952, it was determined that Koreans and Taiwanese, including those who were living in the interior territories, would lose their Japanese nationality by the order of the Director-General of the Civil Affairs Bureau. Through this series of measures, people from Japan's former colonies were deprived of any formal membership in the state of Japan despite living in the Japanese nation-state. Their legal status in Japan came to be governed by the immigration control law in the same manner as other foreigners. Now they could potentially be deported and faced restrictions on entering and leaving the country. They were also subject to new obligations such as carrying a certificate of alien registration at all times and fingerprinting.[20] At the same time, as they were no longer Japanese citizens, they were excluded from the rights conferred by domestic law. It was argued that there was no basis for people from Japan's former colonies to claim the rights guaranteed for citizens despite having to meet the same legal and tax obligations as Japanese citizens. Having been forcefully incorporated into the Japanese nation-state through Japan's colonization of Korea and then later simply excluded from the same nation-state which regarded them as aliens, Koreans in Japan have always found themselves at the mercy of the 'borders called nationality' (Jung Yeong-hae 2003: 106).

Economically, Koreans in Japan have generally been positioned at the bottom of the labor market, living precarious lives. More often than not, they lived in poverty due to the racial discrimination in employment practices by private sector Japanese companies as well as the nationality clause for public employment.[21] They were therefore generally self-employed or worked as physical laborers or in small businesses, with a very few holding secure white-collar jobs in solid companies. The harsh social reality of the time encouraged over 90,000 Koreans, including their Japanese spouses in many cases, to leave Japan in search of a new life in North Korea through the repatriation project which began in 1959.

Poverty increased the burden on women who assumed domestic responsibility. Women helped to support their families by attending to housework, child-rearing, and nursing care as well as engaging in paid work. It is undeniable that women's efforts to maintain the household as 'refuge' against racial discrimination served also to prop-up the patriarchy. Incidents of husbands and fathers venting frustrations about unstable employment through violent outbursts

Figure 1.1a: Percentage of male workers aged over 15 by industry and nationality – 1985

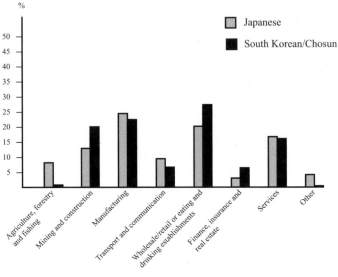

Source: Created by author from the *Final Report of the 1985 Population Census: Population Of Japan (Summary Report)* Table 10-13 and *1990 Population Census of Japan: Foreigners and Their Households* Table 8.

directed at wives and children are all-too-commonly found in the writings of Koreans in Japan. Yet Korean women, who were not only subject to racial discrimination but also sexist oppression, rarely had any choice other than to depend on the very family that abused them, as they were deprived of the necessary economic and social resources for living independently in Japanese society (Song Youn-ok 2005: 263–264). The expression '*areru aboji taeru omoni*' (violent father, resilient mother) – referring to the mother enduring the father's abuse in a desperate attempt to keep her family together – is too frequently repeated in the narratives of Korean women of more recent generations (Shin, Cho, Park and Jung 2000: 8).

Because of the limited opportunities to work in Japanese enterprises and the public sector, Koreans in Japan often engaged in small manufacturing at home. In family-run businesses, it is common for the entire family to work together. Women provide important labor. Let us review some statistics to illustrate these

Figure 1.1b: Percentage of male workers aged over 15 by industry and nationality – 2005

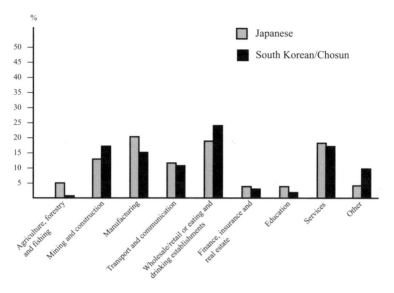

Source: Created by author from the *2005 Population Census of Japan Overview Series 6: Labor Force Status of Population Industry and Occupation of Employed Persons* (2008) Table 4 and 14.

points. First, according to the 2005 Population Census, the proportion of workers over 15 years of age who were self-employed was 11.0%.[22] However, for people with Korean nationality only, self-employed workers make up a much larger share at 18.5%.[23] Next, let us compare the employment rates for people with Japanese nationalities and people with South or North Korean nationality in various industries based on the 1985 population census – when the first-generation and prewar-born second-generation women in this study were studying in school – and the 2005 population census. The 1985 data for men shows a considerably higher proportion of Koreans than Japanese worked in construction, wholesale/retail and restaurants. This gap had narrowed only marginally by 2005 (Figures 1.1a and 1.1b). As for women, almost half – 44% – of Koreans worked in wholesale/retail or restaurants in 1985, a staggering 15% higher than the corresponding 28% of Japanese women (Figure 1.2a). There was very little change in the 2005

Figure 1.2a: Percentage of female workers aged over 15 by industry and nationality – 1985

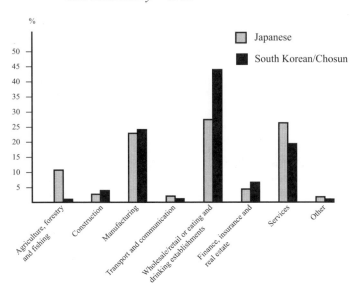

Source: Created by author from the *Final Report of the 1985 Population Census: Population of Japan (Summary Report)* Table 10-13 and *1990 Population Census of Japan: Foreigners and Their Households* Table 8.

statistics, at 42% and 29% respectively (Figure 1.2b). At the same time, the employment rate for Korean women in industries with relatively high rates of women, such as healthcare and social work, education and services, was lower than for Japanese women. These figures indicate a persistent tendency for Korean men to work in construction and Korean women to work in wholesale/retail or restaurants. In the latter case, they are most likely to be family employees.

Among other things this means that, as Chung Jang-yeon put it, Korean men in Japan cannot even experience the sorrow of being 'company men' (Chung Jang-yeon 1995: 65). 'While Japanese women have been oppressed by the "modern family ideology" which confines them to the role of wives who are expected to support their corporate warrior husbands, Korean women in Japan are responsible for all of the same domestic duties but must also work long hours in small home manufacturing businesses producing slip-on sandals

Figure 1.2b: Percentage of female workers aged over 15 by industry and nationality – 2005

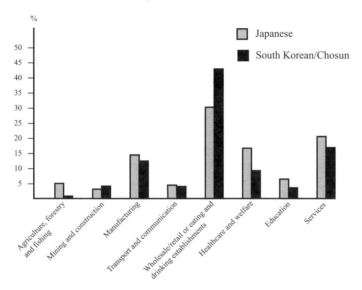

Source: Created by author from the *2005 Population Census of Japan Overview Series 6: Labor Force Status of Population Industry and Occupation of Employed Persons* (2008) Table 4 and 14.

and rubber products under demanding work conditions' (Kim Isaja 1994: 236–237). A second-generation woman who participated in my study said 'Koreans in Japan are mostly self-employed and women naturally have to help their husbands and on top of that, they have to take on household chores and childcare alone. So, gender equality can never be achieved'.[24] In short, Koreans in Japan have been excluded from the modern household model of the postwar Japanese corporate society, which assumes men are 'salarymen' and women are 'full-time housewives'. Second- and later-generation Korean women suffered much the same discrimination: they were unlikely to be hired by either private corporations or public institutions, and therefore had few alternatives to relying on the male-dominated family for work and life sustenance. It was quite unusual for them to advance to higher education, and thus their employment opportunities tended to be limited to either the bottom end of the hospitality industry or working in family manufacturing business

(Song Youn-ok 2002: 172), making it extremely difficult to achieve economic independence.

Since the 1970s, Koreans in Japan have organized a variety of campaigns to combat the discrimination that they endure, and especially to fight against their exclusion from the public domain. The anti-racial discrimination movements first gathered significant momentum in areas with large Korean populations such as Kanagawa, Osaka, Hyogo and Kyoto, under the lead of second-generation Koreans and in cooperation with Japanese human rights activists. One of the important early triggers was the Hitachi Employment Discrimination Incident, in which a second-generation Korean man was offered employment by the company, and then the offer was withdrawn on racial grounds. He sued, and achieved an overall victory, eventually joining the company.[25] Following this incident, Korean people's social movements in Japan began to point to not only the discriminatory practices of private companies but also to the injustice of the Nationality Clause for employment in public institutions and social security. Their struggles eventually lead to the repeal of the Nationality Clause from eligibility requirements for receiving the national pension, national health insurance and childcare benefit, accessing public housing and loans from the Housing Finance Corporation as well as employment as public school teachers, teaching staff in national universities, as local government employees and as apprentices at Supreme Court's legal Training and Research Institute. In the 1980s, there was a movement to refuse fingerprinting during alien registration, with critics seeing the requirement as a human rights violation. The requirement was abolished in 1999 after several revisions to the law (see note 20 above for more details).

A quite separate impetus for eliminating systematic discrimination and enhancing the legal status of non-Japanese residents was the United Nations led development of an international consensus on respecting human rights. The Japanese government amended a number of laws pertaining to the treatment of foreigners after signing the United Nations' covenants on human rights (1979) and the Convention relating to the Status of Refugees (1982). In the 1990s, acquiring local voting rights became one of the key issues for Koreans in Japan.

It is noteworthy that Korean postwar human rights activists in Japan have sought to obtain the same rights as Japanese while retaining their Korean nationality (either North or South), rather than campaigning to be granted Japanese nationality. Naturalization has generally been considered to be an act of betrayal by Koreans in Japan, a response to the history of forced incorporation of Koreans as Japanese Imperial subjects following Japan's annexation of Korea, as well as the Japanese administrations' long-standing emphasis on assimilation as 'Japanese'.[26]

These Korean social movements have contributed to elevating the status of Koreans and other foreign residents in the public domain and improving their living conditions. Tackling racial and ethnic discrimination in the public domain had tangible consequences, improving the situation of Koreans by expanding opportunities for employment and social security. The direct benefits for women, however, who continued to bear all domestic responsibilities, and who remained largely dependent upon male heads of household, were much more limited.

Ethnic society

The liberation of the Korean Peninsula from Japanese colonialism was followed by the North and South division at the 38th parallel. The two countries remain technically in a state of war today after the Korean War (1950–1953) ended in an armistice. North and South Korea have become two different societies believing in opposing ideologies, socialism and capitalism. The division into two opposed nations entailed a shared hope for unification among peoples on both sides of the 38th parallel, supported by a strong belief of national uniqueness. Moreover, decades of oppression by the Japanese inspired a belief in Korean superiority, fueling the struggle to overcome colonial legacy and regain national pride. Nationalistic discourses on both sides of the 38th parallel extol the homogeneity and unity of the Korean people. These discourses are oft-repeated and were translated into norms governing every aspect of citizens' lives. The Korean term *'uri'* (we) discursively creates the category 'we Koreans' by separating them from the 'outside' while at the same time, on the inside, seeks to essentialize the population by concealing differences. For example, in South Korean society, women's experiences were excluded from public memory and discourses because the gender gap was occluded by national discourses that suppress internal differences. Women had to remain silent within patriarchal social relations as they were symbolically interpellated in films and literature as passive, vulnerable, pure and self-sacrificing subjects (Kim Eun-shil 2000; Lim Jie-hyun 2000).

Koreans who live in Japan have been greatly affected by the political tensions in the Korean Peninsula. After the liberation of Korea from Japanese colonial domination, Koreans in Japan were separated into two ethnic organizations, the Korean Residents Union in Japan (Mindan) and the General Association of Korean Residents in Japan (Chongryun[27]), which support the nations of South and North Korea respectively. The tensions and differences wrought by the division in their homeland remain intact in the ethnic communities in Japan to the present day. The concept of the homogenous nation as well as the national unification discourse connected to patriarchy became entrenched within the ethnic organizations, which were significantly influenced by the governments of their respective countries. Meanwhile, the discrimination and alienation experienced by Koreans in Japanese society served to reinforce and accentuate the symbolic significance of the family, religion and ethnic community as a place of solace, which further reinforced patriarchy. Simply put, gender discrimination within the Korean community in Japan was further entrenched by the mechanisms that marginalized them socially and economically (Song Youn-ok 2005).

Koreans who lived in the country of their former colonizer tended to essentialize their culture and strengthen ethnic cohesiveness; in the process forming themselves as oppositional subjects. For example, *jesa*, a patrilineal succession ceremony, which serves to affirm the bonds among families and relatives, is a symbolic representation of their ethnic identity. Performed in each family, *jesa* has clearly defined gender roles where men, regardless of age, perform the ritual itself and women prepare the altar and food. Similarly, the genealogy book, a family tree that maps only patrilineage, has been viewed as reflecting the ethnic characteristics of Koreans in Japan, and in some cases is seen as evidence of their cultural superiority over the Japanese.[28]

Patriarchal practices are certainly not specific to the culture of Koreans in Japan. As discussed above, gender segregation often plays an essential role in the development of ethnicity. Although manhood and womanhood are not axiomatic, men and women in ethnic minority communities are expected to act appropriately as members of the communities; women in particular are forced into prescribed roles of biological reproduction and cultural transmission (Yuval-Davis 1994a: 413). Biological reproduction is seen as crucial for the continuation of the community; hence ethnic nationalism encourages childbirth and emphasizes the importance of marriage for that purpose (Parker et al. 1992: 6). The flip-side of this is that non-marriage, homosexuality and partnering with members of other ethnic groups is viewed negatively, seen as an act of terminating the bloodline of the group. This certainly holds true in the ethnic society of Koreans in Japan, where single women and women who married non-Koreans tend to be excluded for having deviated from the norms.[29]

Family

Criticisms of the gender order in Korean society often refer to the 'Confucian' influence. However, it is inappropriate to call Confucianism an ancient 'tradition' of Korea since it only became the social norm after the Confucian ideology was employed as the state governance philosophy in the Joseon dynasty (1392–1897). During the preceding Goryeo era (918–1392), the genealogy book and the patrilineal surname took root, but women were permitted to remarry and were entitled to an equitable distribution of property. Primogeniture was not established until the mid-17th century, and then was not enforced across all of Korea; for example, ultimogeniture has been observed in Hamgyeong Province and Jeju Province in modern times, and women's status varied (Song Youn-ok 2009).

During the Joseon dynasty, when the Confucian ideology became the governing principle of the country, people became increasingly stratified by status and women came to be strictly excluded from the public domain, resulting in the loss of their economic independence. The expansion of clan rule and the entrenchment of the patrilineal doctrine further increased women's dependence upon their androcentric family and they were expected to perform their duties as 'daughter-in-law', 'wife' and 'mother' in the family into which they married. Women could not be representatives of bureaucracy or patriarchal clans. They were confined to domestic activities, prohibited from participating in social activities without permission from their patriarch or husband and physically excluded from the public domain through restrictions on leaving the home

(Cho Hae-joang 2002; Moon Ok-pyo 1997; Jayawardena 1986). Korean expressions that reflect Confucian gender norms include: 'distinction between the sexes', 'women obey three masters (father, husband and son)', 'once married, no longer part of the family', 'the seven valid causes for divorce' and 'separation between the inside and the outside'.[30] Despite these strictures, women who gave birth to and raised an heir to the head of the family, that is a son, were granted some authority; and they were undoubtedly complicit in sustaining patriarchy in many ways, including dominating their children's families as the 'mother of the head of the family'. At the same time, the separation of the domain between the sexes created a world in which women had agency to initiate various activities, opening spaces in which they could engage freely in religious, cultural and other activities.

The 'Confucian' patriarchy has had a considerable impact on Koreans in Japan. It should be noted, though, that it changed in its transition to Japanese society. It became formally institutionalized with the introduction of the Family Registration Law during colonial rule. Industrialization and urbanization began and a Japanese-style education system was rolled out. During the colonial era women began to work in manufacturing as low-wage labor. There was a small increase in professional jobs for women, such as nurses and schoolteachers, but a substantial proportion of the female labor force was absorbed into Japanese industries that established in Korea, mainly textile, chemical and food manufacturing. The ethnic and gender orders were clearly evident in wage differences, with a Korean adult male and female being paid only one-half and one-quarter respectively, of the wages paid to a Japanese male (Lee Hyo-jae 1997: 350–351). The institution of the family was weakened and many farmers lost their land or were displaced. Many men left villages for Japan or northeastern China in search of work. The women who were left behind raised their children while pursuing paid work. With many of the men absent, households were managed by women (Cho Hae-joang 2002).

At the time, the majority of Koreans who migrated to Japan were from farming villages. Typically, the men would migrate to Japan to find work, mostly as factory laborers, and establish themselves to some degree. Once settled their families would follow. There was not much difference between Korean and Japanese families in terms of gender roles; in both cases women were solely responsible

Figure 1.3: Changes in number of married Koreans in Japan (1955–2010)

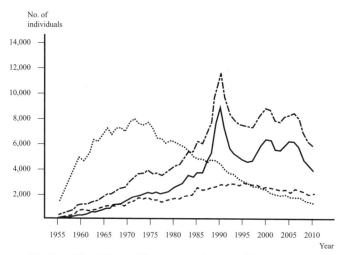

- - - - Number of South Korean/Chosun men who married Japanese women
——— Number of Korean/Chosun women who married Japanese men
—·—·— Total number of married individuals with South Korean/Chosun nationality whose spouse is a Japanese national (both men and women)
·········· Number of South Korean/Chosun individuals (both men and women) who married Korean/Chosun nationals

Source: Created by the author based on the *Vital Statistics* by the Ministry of Health, Labour and Welfare (1955–2010).

for household affairs. Nonetheless, it was no easy matter to be a migrant in Japanese society, where the culture and language were different and racial prejudice was prevalent. It is likely that this was the social condition that led to the description of first-generation Korean women in Japan as self-sacrificing 'great *omoni*'. First-generation migrant women were highly dependent on their families because of difficulties in communicating in Japanese and very limited employment opportunities.

Jung Yeong-hae discussed the closed nature of Korean families in Japan in her analysis of the representations of family in novels written by second-generation Koreans. Describing a family as comprising a tyrannical father who resorts to violence to make other family members obey him, a mother who submits to him, and children who despise such 'family', she argued that women and children were not protected by the father, as generally assumed, but were rather imprisoned in the family. She further explains that 'liberation from family' was an important impetus in Korean civil rights movements such as the anti-Alien Registration Act movement in the 1980s, in which several second-generation women participated as individuals rather than as members of ethnic collectivity (Jung Yeong-hae 1986).

Let us now try to infer changes in the family from the marital status of Koreans in Japan. Figure 1.3 shows the changes in the number of married persons among Koreans in Japan. Until the beginning of the 1980s, the number of couples in which both spouses were South Korean or Chosun nationals was larger than the number of South Korean/Chosun-Japanese couples but the phenomenon reversed in the early 1980s. The number of couples in which the husband is Japanese and the wife is a South Korean/Chosun national increased faster than the reverse combination. It should be noted that this statistic is intended to indicate a rough trend only, as the figures include marriages between newcomer Korean women and Japanese men. The upward trend of the number of marriage with Japanese is often viewed as a sign of the weakening ethnic consciousness of Koreans in Japan. In her study on spouse selection of Koreans in Japan of more recent generations, however, Hashimoto (2010) observed that many ethnic cultural practices are maintained even when Koreans are married to Japanese. She also interpreted the surge in the number of marriages between Koreans and Japanese resulting from the fact that inter-ethnic marriage has become a real 'option' today, in contrast to earlier periods in which interaction between Koreans and Japanese was limited. In contrast, Song Youn-ok suggests that the increased number of marriages between Japanese men and women with South Korean/Chosun nationality is 'likely to be related to the fact that more and more women sought freedom from gender bias to counter the culture of gender discrimination in the Korean community in Japan and aspired for a modern family with a Japanese spouse as a means of realizing their goals' (Song Youn-ok 2005: 267).

The situation of Korean women in Japan varies greatly depending on their nationality, generation, place of origin, place of residence, family relationships, education and occupation. Hence, the discussion in this chapter provides only a partial review of the family situation of Korean women in Japan. Nevertheless, it is reasonable to assume that patriarchy is as characteristic of Japanese society as it is in Korean ethnic communities, and that families have placed onerous restrictions on women's activities. Furthermore, the insecurity of the Korean population as a minority group in Japanese society was a special factor that reinforced patriarchy and negatively impacted upon Korean women.

Previous studies

Most of the significant previous studies on Koreans in Japan are historiographies that have sought to elucidate the development of ethnic organizations and leadership.[31] The historical studies have attempted to delineate their varied political involvement, inter and intra organizational relations and their transformation, focused on living conditions and legal status. More recent studies, like Tonomura (2004) for example, attempted to explore the consciousness of ordinary Koreans of Japan, which is not reducible to ethno-national movements, using resources such as statistics, novels and newspaper articles as references.

However, the earlier studies have been androcentric, in that the leadership positions of the ethnic organizations that have been studied have been occupied by men. In an effort to balance this, Kim and Kim (1993) presented a detailed examination of the issues and campaign activities specific to women, based on both primary written materials and interview data, focusing on the processes of establishing Korean women's organizations in Japan immediately after the war. Kim and Kim (1993) characterized the movements of Korean women in Japan as the pursuit of 'ethno-national identity', and the liberation of 'Koreans in Japan' and 'women'. Kajimura (1993) identifies two distinct perspectives characterizing Korean people's movements in Japan: one contributing to nation building on the Korean peninsula and the other aiming for the liberation of the Korean people in Japan from discrimination and the promotion of human rights to protect their basic livelihood. Kim and Kim's study raised a third perspective: the women's liberation movements.[32]

Since the 1990s there have been a number of sociological studies examining the identity of Koreans in Japan, particularly of more recent generations.[33] Most of the sociological research has focused on the identity politics in Korean ethnic movements contesting the Japanese government's policies on foreigners, primarily from an interactionist perspective. Kashiwazaki (2000) investigated the naturalization system and exclusionist policies on foreigners which entailed forced assimilation. This study illustrated the processes by which Korean ethnic movements came to share the Japanese government's logic equating nationality with ethnic identity even while protesting against Japan's 'assimilate or be removed' policy. Yamawaki (2001) demonstrated that a sense of belonging to Japanese society, rather than either of the two states on the Korean Peninsula, was the driving force of Korean social movements in the 1970s, when the permanent settlement of Koreans in Japan became more common and discussions about the validity of diverse identities began. These studies contextualized the Japanese government and social activism of Koreans in Japan, both of which were bound to a nation-state model in which race equates to nationality.

It is worth noting that research approaches that focus on the confrontation between a host nation and ethnic minority groups have overlooked intra-group conflicts and the implications of collective actions by women. A small number of studies, including Jung Yeong-hae (1986) and Ryang (1998), have attempted to rectify this shortcoming, discussing the particular problem of self-identification for Korean women in Japan in relation to social movements. Jung Yeong-hae (1986) focused her research on women of second- and later-generations who were involved in the anti-fingerprinting movement, which flourished in the 1980s. Jung (1986) explained that for Koreans of more recent generations, racial discrimination by the Japanese was not the only form of oppression that concerned them; they also sought liberation from the oppression experienced within their families, which were dominated by their fathers, often violently. Drawing on the case study of Yang Yong-ja, a young Korean woman in Japan, Jung Yeong-hae observed that the anti-fingerprinting movement was not only a protest against racial discrimination but also implied a demand for liberation as 'individuals' from a patriarchy that oppresses women and children. Ryang, an anthropologist, examined a process of decolonization and self-identification as North Korean overseas nationals by women in the Chongryun community. Based on her research on first-generation women learning the official language in Chongryun-operated institutions, she asserts that women's emancipatory identity was constructed in connection with their positive redefinition of patriotic motherhood within the limits of a nationalist discourse (Ryang 1998). According to Ryang, the internalization of the North Korean nationalist discourse of emancipation through literacy education allowed them to secure their position in the public life of Chongryun. At the same time, however, the women attempted to find positive meaning in the accompanying ideologies of the 'wise mother and good wife' in order to thrive in oppressive Japanese society. The night junior high school movement in Higashi-Osaka is characterized by two points; first, its agent was primarily Korean women and second, it was based in a night junior high school – a Japanese public institution. Examining this movement will help to elucidate how it became possible for women to participate in the mainstream public domain while breaking-free from the gender structure of the ethnic organizations and family.

Outline of the survey

The aim of this study is to examine the macro and micro-structural contexts in which women got access to public life and constructed new forms of gendered ethnic identity through the night junior high school independence movement, using primary materials and women's narratives of their life stories. To that end, I conducted interviews and participant observation with stakeholders. In conducting the life story analysis, I attempted to reveal the dynamics of the new subject formations of Korean women in Japan, focusing on the correlations between collective political-social processes and personal experiences in everyday life.

Survey of organizational activities (April 2000–March 2002)

For the primary research, a wide range of information and primary sources were collected regarding associational activities and networks of Korean women in Japan, including the women's divisions of the established ethnic organizations, in order to develop a broad overview of the collective actions engaged in by Korean women in Japan.

Subsequently, a survey and interviews were conducted individually with women who were central to the organizations. The survey questionnaire was designed to elicit information about the background and purpose of establishing organizations, descriptions of activities, organizational structure, attributes of members (including gender, generation, place of origin and age group) and external organizations with which they have cooperative relationships. Individual interviews were conducted to glean more detailed and nuanced descriptions. Fieldwork and interviews were conducted at various events, social club activities, study meetings and social gatherings that were held in Korean neighborhoods in Osaka, Kyoto, Tokyo and Kanagawa in order to develop an understanding of women's grassroots activism. I was able to make contact with more than twenty Korean women's organizations. Of these, eleven were identified as comprising predominantly Korean women and maintaining constant operations under official names. These organizations will be discussed in Chapter 2. In the course of analyzing this data, the night junior high school movement in Higashi-Osaka was identified as one of the first 'autonomous' social movements led by first-generation Korean women in Japan. I therefore decided to conduct in-depth research into this movement.

Survey on the Taiheiji Independence Movement (March 2002–2012)

In researching the social movement that arose surrounding the night junior high schools in Higashi-Osaka City, qualitative data was collected through various methods, including life stories of the women involved, interviews with key stakeholders, participant observation and primary sources. The collection of life stories as well as participant observations were conducted during an intense period from January to March 2003. The participant observation was conducted in the classroom, at graduation ceremonies, alumni meetings, school recitals and expositions for the Taiheiji Night Junior High School and Chōei Night Junior High School, as well as classes in Uri Seodang (a learning institution for Korean women), and Sarangbang day care home (a service center for older Korean women). During my stay in Higashi-Osaka, I had lunch with the women most weekdays and participated in recreational activities at Sarangbang day care home and joined classes in Uri Seodang, Taiheiji Night Junior High School or Chōei Night Junior High School in the evening. I also attended numerous other events, including student council events, conventions by Kinki Yakan Chūgaku Seitokai Rengō (Kinki Federation of Night Junior High School Student Councils), and public lectures at Uri Seodang. Chōei Night Junior High School, Taiheiji Night Junior High School, Uri Seodang and Sarangbang are located in the Sannose district of Higashi-Osaka City, all within walking distance of one another.

Introduction

I am a third-generation South Korean living in Tokyo and had not had much to do with the Korean community in Osaka until I commenced this research. The first step of the research was therefore to have conversations and build relationships with the women in the community. My intention was to acquire firsthand experience of the deep human relationships that characterize Korean neighborhoods, as well as the ethnic culture and customs by sharing meals, attending classes, attending Korean women's informal gatherings, local festivals and engaging in a myriad of other activities while conversing in a mixture of Korean and Osaka dialects. To deepen my understanding of the world in which these women live, I regularly visited places where Korean women gather, such as Korean eateries, public baths, parks, cafes and childcare centers. Resource gathering continued after April 2003 and sporadic site visits were made for follow-up interviews with stakeholders of the movement as well as teachers' union and government officials. Additional participant observation was conducted when I was able to accompany a number of women who were studying at the night junior high schools in Kansai on a visit to a literacy education institution in South Korea as part of a literacy exchange project in October 2008.

The interview approach employed in the life story collection and interviews was semi-structured, with no predefined set of questions; participants were asked to share their stories freely, from their life in Korea, migration to and life in Japan, to their enrollment and experiences in night junior high school leading up to the independence movement. The interviews were conducted primarily in Japanese, and partially in Korean. At the beginning of the interview, the purpose of the study was explained and questions were posed to the participants. Having said that, the participants were free to speak as they wished about their personal life experiences, how they became involved in the movement, what they felt during the movement and their reflections on their time in the movement. This approach allowed the women to express their experiences and thoughts in their own voices as much as possible. The life stories were recorded through note-taking, and recording when permission was granted by the participant, and later reconstructed for analysis.

Research participants were contacted and recruited using snowball techniques, based on referrals from the movement participants and supporters. Life stories were collected from fourteen women who played central roles in the movement. Although that is no doubt a limitation of this book, the objective of the study is not to detail all of the permutations of the Taiheiji Independence Movement, but rather to explore the processes through which these women became autonomous agents of social change.

Narratives are constructed by a narrator in interactions with a particular interlocutor – in these cases, with 'me', a third-generation South Korean woman from Tokyo. Hence, they differ from life histories – fixed and formulated accounts of a life. Each narrative is unique; different stories will be told depending on who the narrator is conversing with. Narratives are not only comprised of what is spoken; factors that are not expressed in words, such as when, where, to whom and in what context the narrative is related have considerable influences. With these limitations in mind, the research presented in this book examines the narratives of women who were involved in the Taiheiji Independence Movement in a particular social-historical context and explores the new relationships that emerged between the women and the society as well as the new subjectivities that were formed in the performance.

It is worth mentioning that the greatest challenge was probably the care required in building relationships with the movement and research participants. I was fortunate enough to be generally accepted as a young fellow countrywoman and was able to enlist their cooperation. During the research, I was privileged to hear the stories of women who have been involved in diverse engagements – especially the first-generation women who blazed a trail for the rest of us – as a Korean woman, an 'insider', so to speak. It must be noted, however, that Koreans in Japan are not all the same. The research was therefore particularly sensitive to differences in their membership of ethnic organizations, their different hometowns in the Korean Peninsula, different nationalities and the deep human relationship that are specific to local Korean communities. Some women did not feel comfortable with me precisely because I was a Korean woman, and at the same time, a mother, a researcher and a graduate student because the latter roles deviate significantly from the gender norms that ordinary Korean women had internalized, especially the older ones. Occasionally my primary school age son accompanied me to my research field (primarily because I could find no one to care for him; but also because I wanted him to have the opportunity to communicate with first-generation Korean women). Older Korean women were generous to us. However, once I was told to 'go home', reflecting the belief that married women should stick to domestic matters. Although perhaps somewhat 'negative', these experiences were also quite valuable for this study to understand their moral system and how difficult it was for these women to study in night junior high school and to commit to the independence movement.

One of the points of departure for this study was the realization that it was not easy to learn the ways of life of other Korean women in Japan since, for the most part, Korean women in Japan today use Japanese names and have thus become invisible in Japanese society. Another point was a growing sense that there was a need for research on the Korean women's movements in Japan from the unique perspective of the intersection of ethnicity and gender, rather than simply as an aspect of Japanese women's movements or Korean ethnic movements because there are significant differences in the underlying conditions of Japanese and Korean women in Japan. For example, I grew up in a new residential area with few Korean neighbors in Yokohama and was educated in the Japanese school system. I was not involved in ethnic organizations when I was in school. I am a typical Japanese-born Korean in that sense. Yet I am also perhaps somewhat different from the 'ordinary' Korean women in Japan in having lived in North America and France for several years, including overseas study experience. My interactions with first-generation Korean women was limited to my two late grandmothers. I grew up in a nuclear family and either went to stay with my grandmothers or they would come to stay with us several times a year. Having a glimpse into my grandmothers' lives provided me some insight into what it is like to live in Japan as a foreigner without adequate communication skills in Japanese. Like most first-generation Korean women in Japan, my grandmothers spoke little Japanese and were illiterate. The one who lived in Tokyo used to travel on a train line to the station nearest to us in Kanagawa. She traveled on the slower local train so that she could carefully watch the scenery out of the window, because she could not recognize station names. As she could not read or write her own name, she would use symbols such as a circle to mark her belongings. In any case, my grandmothers rarely went out, for they were busy with housework. My mother used to listen to them speak in Korean but spoke back in Japanese. My mother often told me that she could not even imagine how hard it must have been for my grandmother to come to Japan at a young age with almost no knowledge of the language to join my grandfather who had migrated first. Looking back, it seems that they remembered a great many things in fine detail as they could not rely on written notes and signs. In any case, my understanding of first-generation Korean women was based only on my encounters with my grandmothers. Therefore, when I first heard about the Taiheiji Night Junior High School Independence Movement, I was very surprised to learn that there were first-generation women studying in Japanese public school and who had fought for their rights to do so. I felt compelled to meet them and learn about their social movement.

Although my interest and motivation for studying the activities of Korean women in Japan were rooted in my own personal experiences, my pre-existing knowledge and experiences were in fact not very useful for my research. As my research progressed, it became increasingly clear that there was much greater variety in the circumstances of Korean women in Japan than I had previously understood, and that they each had a different history. The absence of personal experience in social movements both positively and negatively contributed to my understanding. On the one hand, I was able to have straightforward discussions based on shared experiences of patriarchal family life in accordance with unspoken cultural codes. On the other hand, it took a long time to come to understand the structure of the ethnic organizations and their strict gender order. Overall, though, my non-involvement in ethnic organizations and not being a local member of the Korean community in Osaka did not present any major obstacles to this research; rather, it seems to have helped to establish a sort of neutral position.

At the research sites, although I was regarded as a 'fellow countrywoman' who resides within the boundaries of the ethnic group, I was also an 'outsider' in the Korean community in Osaka. Furthermore, as a speaker of standard Japanese, I was referred to as a 'person who came from Tokyo', a city with which Osaka locals have a strong rivalry. In short, I was positioned both within and outside of the boundaries that define multitudes of differences in ethnicity, generation, geography and profession, depending on the situations. This was an intriguing experience in it itself, as

Introduction 41

evidence of the fact that there is not one constant, axiomatic identity of Korean women in Japan.

Structure of this book

This book is structured as follows. First, Chapter 2 examines Korean women's movements in post-war Japan from perspectives of ethnicity, nation and gender. The collective activities of Korean women in Japan will be analyzed in terms of organizational autonomy and family / gender roles, drawing on sociological theories of women's agency as well as the intersectionality of nation and gender. This analysis is aimed at highlighting the uniqueness and significance of the Taiheiji Independence Movement and subsequent developments.

Chapter 3 focuses on the dynamics of the social movement sector and discusses the multidimensional subaltern counterpublics that have been created at the local level. Specifically, the initial formation of the Taiheiji Independence Movement and its process of development will be analyzed in the context of the interactions of various minority rights social movement groups in Kansai. A variety of anti-government movements have proliferated historically in Kansai. In this context, the Taiheiji Independence Movement was initiated by Korean women in Japan to fight for a place for learning, strongly influenced by community-based Korean people's movements as well as citizens' movement that demanded the expansion of night junior high schools.

Chapter 4 moves the focus of analysis to the micro level to examine the life courses of individual Korean women in Japan. In particular, the analysis will focus on the journeys of Korean women in Japan, from illiteracy and lack of schooling to their enrolment in night junior high school at middle-age and older. This chapter reveals the implications of individual actions of entering night junior high school from the aspect of the family gender role and bargaining with patriarchy while highlighting the issues of illiteracy and exclusion from the public domain that are all too common among first- and prewar born second-generation women.

Chapter 5 analyzes the subjective narratives that women present concerning the Taiheiji Independence Movement, to reveal the characteristics of the oppositional subjects who developed out of their efforts and ascertain what the movement meant for the participants as individuals. This examination begins with the underlying conditions that led to the formation of a subaltern counterpublic by Korean women in Japan at night junior high schools. It is followed by a discussion of the new political subjects formed through the movement from three dimensions: public and private domains and ethnic community.

Chapter 6 focuses on interactions within the subaltern counterpublic of Korean women in Japan; that is, the interactions among Korean women of different generation. The formation of women's inter-generational solidarity will be explored using the concept of social-cultural mediation, based on the participant observation at Sarangbang, a livelihood support facility that is also a 'daytime home' for the women. This is a social space that lies in the middle of the public and private domain. The chapter will demonstrate that the intergenerational solidarity that is formed there and the associated mutual utilization of the ethnic resources is a contributing factor to the subject formation of Korean women in Japan in the host society.

The final chapter discusses the characteristics and possibilities of Korean women in Japan as agents of social change, in light of the movement that took place in night junior high schools in Higashi-Osaka. The chapter also outlines the implications for the theory of subaltern counterpublics that follow from this analysis of the independence movement in Osaka, from the perspective of the formation of multidimensional transnational social space.

2 Between ethnic rights and women's rights movements

Korean women in Japan have been creating unique types of social movements since the early 20th century through their active engagement in a wide spectrum of areas. Their unique perspectives and interests have gone largely unnoticed, however, as they have been overshadowed by broader ethnic rights movements. The broad-based Korean people's movements in Japan are represented by two organizations, the Korean Residents Union in Japan ('Mindan'), which supports South Korea, and the General Association of Korean Residents in Japan ('Chongryun'), which supports North Korea. These two organizations actively participate in the national politics of their respective 'homelands' while simultaneously demanding improvements in the legal status and living conditions of Koreans in Japanese society. Since the 1970s, led by ethnic Koreans who were born in Japan, their focus has increasingly turned away from a focus on their 'homeland' and towards conducting human rights campaigns as members of Japanese society.

Despite this dramatic shift in the focus of Korean ethnic movements, the activities of Korean women in Japan have remained generally unchanged, in the sense that they continue to be carried out by women's groups that belong to male-dominated ethnic organizations. This structural subordination of Korean women's liberation movements to broader male-dominated ethnic rights movements continued despite the broad changes in gender relations being wrought in Japanese society by the rise of the women's movement. Japanese society in the 1970s was transformed by the women's liberation movement, which denounced the gender division of labor, the objectification of women in the media and the male dominance of intimate relationships as well as social and political power. However, there was a huge disparity at the time between the political and economic status of Japanese and Korean women in Japan, and therefore no common ground that would enable them to develop solidarity with one another. It was not until the 1980s, when some Japanese feminists turned their attention to the broader Asian region, that there began to be some cooperation between Korean women's rights movements and Japanese women's rights movements, based on an acknowledgement of the disparity between the two groups of women.[1]

In other words, for most of the 20th century, Korean women's social movement activities and organizations in Japan were marginalized in terms of both ethnic movements and women's movements. It was not until the 1990s that the collective actions of Korean women in Japan took definite shape and emerged as autonomous agents in the movement sector. The independence movement that was formed at a night junior high school in Higashi-Osaka City is a typical example of this new development in Korean women's social activism.

As discussed in Chapter 1, this chapter will use the autonomy of women's movements and women's roles in the ethnic group/nation as a framework for analyzing Korean women's social movements in postwar Japan, focusing in particular on their organizational structures and the characteristics of the participants' subjectivity. I have been conducting research on collective actions of Korean women in Japan since 2000, but in this book I will limit discussion to those campaigning entities that have what may be called a formal organization – that is, those that have a public name as well as a clearly defined objective and description of activities (Table 2.1).[2] The organizations in question vary widely in scale, form and whether there was an intentional women's liberation agenda or not. Regardless of such differences, I will treat any organizations whose chief requirement for membership was to be a Korean woman who lives in Japan in an across-the-board manner. It should be noted, however, that my research was limited to the Kanto and Kansai regions; there may be movement organizations in other areas of which I am not aware. It is therefore worth stressing that the aim of this chapter is not to systematically survey all of the movement organizations created by Korean women in the postwar Japan; rather, the objective is to identify and examine the female subjects who were formed by these social movements from the perspectives of gender and ethnicity. For this goal, I will explore their interests based on the specific social situations in which they were positioned, complexity and ambivalence in their relationship with Korean ethnic rights movements, and their strategies to participate in political life.

Analytical framework

This chapter will employ Molyneux's theory of the autonomy of women's movements and Yuval-Davis and Anthias' theory of women's participation in ethnic and national processes. Molyneux (1998) defined organizational autonomy as an analytical dimension for women's collective actions and identified three ideal types of direction in the transmission of authority: 1) independent movements, 2) associational linkage and 3) directed mobilization. Here, 'autonomy' refers to how the objectives, priorities and actions of women's movements are authorized. In the 'independent movements'-type, women formulate their own organizations, goals and activities. There is no higher authority than the members of the organization, and they are not subject to the control of any other political actors. The 'associational linkage'-type is characterized by women's organizations with a certain level of autonomy which opt to form alliances with other political organizations that share basic values and objectives on a range of issues. They are not subject to direction from higher authorities and women themselves have control over the organization and its agenda-settings. In the 'directed mobilization'-type authority and initiative lie outside of the women's organizations, which are subject to the control of a higher-level organization.

The directed mobilization-type of organization is historically the most common type of women's social movement organization, and can be further divided into three scenarios. (a) Women are mobilized for a more general goal unrelated to women's specific interests, such as overthrowing the government. (b) Women's interest are given consideration as long as they fit within the overarching objectives of the higher authority's social reform agenda. For example, socialist or nationalist movements may support women's rights on the condition that they do not interfere with achieving the higher goal. However, the interests of women are defined by their higher authorities. (c) Women are mobilized for purposes that may directly conflict with the vested interests of women in pursuit of, for example, nationalist or religious interests.

Yuval-Davis and Anthias have developed a theory of the inter-relationship between nation and gender, problematizing the gender structure upon which women's collectives are formed. They have highlighted that, not only have women been treated unequally to their male counterparts, they have also had reproductive roles imposed

Table 2.1: Major movement organizations composed of Korean women in Japan

Name	Year of establishment	Base	Members	Objectives	Activities	In-house publication	Organizational structure	Cooperative relationship
Zainihon Chōsen Minshu Josei Dōmei (Korean Democratic Women's League in Japan), Nyeomaeng	1947	Nation-wide organizations	Women affiliated with Chongryun	Promotion of friendship and solidarity of fellow countrywomen	Social club activities, support for ethnic education, mutual aid, human rights campaigns	Choseon Nyeoseong	Affiliated organization of the General Association of Korean Residents in Japan, Chongryun	Nihon Minshu Fujin Kyōgikai (Japan Democratic Women's Council), Chōsen Josei to Rentaisuru Nihon Fujin Renrakukai (Japan Women's Liaison Group for Solidarity with Korean Women)
Zainihon Daikanminkoku Fujinkai (Korean Residents Union in Japan Women's Association), Buinhoe	1947	Nation-wide organizations	Women affiliated with Mindan	'To become wise wives and mothers and be ethnically cultured, to contribute to the development of the motherland, world peace and international goodwill' (Cited from the mission statement)	Social club activities, mutual aid, exchanges between Korean and Japanese women, human rights campaigns		Affiliated organization of the Korean Residents Union in Japan, Mindan	Nikkan Josei Shinzen Kyōkai (Japan-Korea Friendship Women's Association)

Kodomo o Mimamoru Omoni no Kai (Omoni Society for the Protection of Children)	1974 (Dissolved in 1995)	Kawasaki	Mothers of Korean schoolchildren in Japan	Anti-racial discrimination campaigns	Exchanges, human rights education, anti-discrimination campaigns		Independent organization	*Seikyūsha, Minzoku Sabetsu to Tatakau Renraku Kyōgikai* ('Mintoren', Council for Combating Discrimination against Ethnic People in Japan)
Zainichi Kankoku Minshu Joseikai (Korean Women's Society in Japan for Democracy), Yeoseonghoe	1986	Tokyo, Osaka, Tokai	Former members of the *Zainichi Kankoku Seinen Dōmei* (Korean Youth Alliance in Japan)	Democratization of South Korea and Korean reunification, heightening of ethnic consciousness and protection of interests of fellow Koreans in Japan, anti-nuclear/anti-war and peace movements, solidarity among domestic and international women's associations	Study meetings, cultural activities	*Minshu Josei* (Tokyo), *Porappi* (Osaka)	Related organization of the *Zainichi Kankoku Minshu Tōitsu Rengō* (Federation of South Koreans in Japan for Democracy and Unification)	Korean Women's Association United (South Korea)

Table 2.1: continued

Name	Year of establishment	Base	Members	Objectives	Activities	In-house publication	Organizational structure	Cooperative relationship
Chōsen Joseishi Dokushokai (Korean Women's History Reading Society)	1984 (recessed since 1992)	Tokyo	Women affiliated with Chongryun	Studying the history of Korean women	Study meetings	*Josei Tsūshin*	Independent organization	
Mearihoe	1991	Kyoto	Parents of Korean schoolchildren	Promotion of human rights and ethnic education for Korean schoolchildren in public schools	Social gatherings, operation of children's clubs (transmission of language and culture), ethnic education in public schools, promotion of multiculturalism	*Meari*	Independent organization	*Zenkoku Zainichi Gaikokujin Kyōiku Kenkyū Kyōgikai* ('Zengaikyō', National Foreign Residents Educational Research Council)
Jūgun Ianfu Mondai					Investigation, publication of information			Korean Council for the Women Drafted

Name	Year founded	Location	Members	Activities	Publication	Type	Affiliation/Goal
Uriyoson Nettowāku (Military Comfort Women Issue Uri Yeoseong Network)	1991 (Dissolved in 1998)	Tokyo metropolitan area	People with experiences of ethnic movements	Fact-finding and early resolution of the military comfort women issue, subjectivity of Korean women in Japan	resources, hosting of conferences and study meetings regarding military comfort women	*Allim*	Independent organization	for Military Sexual Slavery by Japan ('Chongdaehyup'), Women's associations aimed at resolving military comfort women issue in Japan
Chōsenjin Jūgun Ianfu Mondai o Kangaeru Kai (Korean Military Comfort Women Issue Study Group)	1991	Kansai	Subsequent-generation Koreans	Fact-finding and early resolution of the military comfort women issue, subjectivity of Korean women in Japan	Publication of information resources, hosting of conferences and study meetings regarding military comfort women	*Mirinae Tsūshin*	Independent organization	Korean Council for the Women Drafted for Military Sexual Slavery by Japan ('Chongdaehyup'), Women's associations aimed at resolving military comfort women issue in Japan
Gurūpu Chame (Sister's Group)	1998	Tokyo, Kansai	Subsequent-generation Koreans	Self-help organization of Korean women in Japan	Hosting of workshops and public lectures, operation of a hotline	*Hotline Jamae*	Independent organization	
NPO Uri Seodang	1994	Osaka	Alumni of night junior high schools	Self-directed learning group and activity hub for Korean women in Japan	Operation of a night-time learning institution		Independent organization	Chōei/Taiheiji night junior high schools

Table 2.1: continued

Name	Year of establishment	Base	Members	Objectives	Activities	In-house publication	Organizational structure	Cooperative relationship
Korean Christian Church in Japan National Christian Women's Association	1948 (Its predecessor *Fujin Dendōkai* [Women's Mission Society] was founded in 1926)	Nation-wide organizations	Female church members	Attainment of a position and rights of women in church	Missionary work, creation of a nursing care centre, visits to Korea, anti-discrimination campaigns	*Gogae*	An organization of the Korean Christian Church in Japan	Korean Church Women United (South Korea)

upon them (Yuval-Davis and Anthias 1989). Minority women have experienced oppression at the intersection of ethnicity and gender – which has typically meant that when they sought relief from racial discrimination by participating in nationalism movements, they were circumscribed by the gender norms embedded in the nationalist movements. In the case of Korean women in Japan, the 'wise mother and good wife' was sometimes upheld as the ideal gender presentation as the political situation changed very rapidly from pre-modern society, through colonial rule with imposed modernization to post-colonization and continuing modernization. Although gender roles such as wife and mother serve to confine women to the private domain, social movements that incorporated the 'wise mother and good wife' ideology could provide a means to help women to participate in politics while avoiding conflict with men's organizations.

While it is likely that there are other determinants of the characteristics of women's social movement organizations than their autonomy from male-centric ethnic rights movements and from family gender roles, this chapter is limited to examining how Korean women in Japan turned the gender order and gender roles into social issues and transformed themselves into autonomous agents. As shown in Figure 2.1, four combinations are possible by combining the dimensions. I will discuss Korean women's social movements in Japan based on these four typological categories.

Organizations led by Korean women in Japan

Ethnic rights movements under patriarchyy

Social movement organizations characterized by the 'wise mother and good wife' ideology are largely subject to external constraints. The two main examples are *Zainihon Chōsen Minshu Josei Dōmei* ('Nyeoseong dongmaeng', Korean Democratic Women's League in Japan, hereafter Nyeomaeng) and *Zainihon Daikanminkoku Fujinkai* ('Buinhoe', Korean Residents Union in Japan Women's Association). *Nyeomaeng* and *Buinhoe* both consist of ordinary Korean women living in Japan. These were the first women's organizations to be founded after Korea's independence from Japan.[3] Both have strong connections with nation-wide ethnic organizations of Koreans in Japan: Nyeomaeng operates under the umbrella of the General Association of Korean Residents in Japan (*Chongryun*)[4]

Figure 2.1: Analytical framework of movement organizations

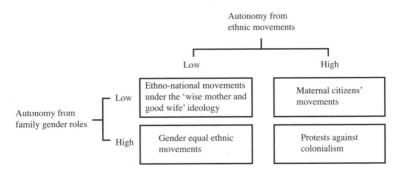

and Buinhoe operates under the umbrella of the Korean Residents Union in Japan (*Mindan*).[5] As can be surmised from their connection with the ethnic organizations, the development of organizational activities of Korean women in Japan have been influenced by the post-independence division of the Korean Peninsula much like their parent organizations.

Nyeomaeng defines itself as an organization that encompasses and represents Chongryun-affiliated adult women. Buinhoe does the same for Mindan-affiliated women. In addition to the women's organizations, the lower branches of Chongryun and Mindan include a wide array of organizations, including ones for youth, students and entrepreneurs. While Chongryun and Mindan make overarching decisions, their subordinate organizations act as promoters of the movements, carrying out activities that are pertinent to the characteristics of their members in line with the decisions made above.

Let us explore the process of the formation of Nyeomaeng and Buinhoe. According to Kim Young and Kim Pu-ja (1993), the first Korean women's organization in Japan was born as Arakawa Shibu Fujobu (Arakawa Fujobu, Arakawa Chapter Women's Section) of the League of Koreans in Japan (Choryun, the predecessor of Chongryun) in Arakawa, Tokyo in February 1946. Arakawa Fujobu operated mainly in the hamlet of Koreans formed in Arakawa and ran various operations including evening classes to teach Hangeul in preparation for 'returning home' under the slogan: 'restoration and enlightenment of national identity of Korean women in Japan'. Arakawa Fujobu's activities were not limited to regional activities, though; it also fought against the Japanese government and GHQ for rights in a joint effort with Choryun. Following the establishment of Arakawa Fujobu, women's chapters were created across the country. The policy to create women's organization named 'Alliance of Korean Women in Japan' was formulated at Choryun's Seventh Central Committee in August 1946. In October 1947, Zainihon Chōsen Minshu Josei Dōmei (The Democratic Korean Women's League in Japan) was formally founded at the central assembly held in Tokyo. The founding statement noted that 'us Korean women have lived an unspeakably miserable life' and continued to declare that 'Korean women in Japan unite under the Democratic Korean Women's League in Japan, to become a wing of the League of Koreans in Japan, a democratic front for unification of Koreans, and carry through the mission with which the Koreans are tasked, from the perspective of women' (cited in Kim and Kim 1993: 11). The statement loudly sent a message that they were going to improve women's status while participating in ethnic liberation activities.

The first lines of Nyeomaeng's mission statement reads:

> We will ensure the all-encompassing liberation of Korean women in Japan in the political, economic and social aspects. We will commit to construction and development of a progressive democratic nation. We will promote international goodwill and contribute to the attainment of world peace. (Kim Young 2009: 112)

The process of constructing Korean women as nationalist subjects is quite explicit here. The organization aimed to contribute to Korea's postcolonial nation-building while simultaneously advocating for improvements in women's status in Japan. The action agenda included: obtaining equal rights to vote and to hold elected office for men and women aged 18 and older; establishing women's right to engage in economic activities and women's autonomy; eliminating state-licensed and unlicensed prostitution and human trafficking; eradicating abuse, violence and all other discrimination against women that trace from the feudal customs of the domination of men over women; eliminating discrimination in education; rigidly enforcing monogamy; eliminating the feudal tradition of forced marriage and encouraging free marriage; simplifying ceremonials; incorporating scientific research on domestic life into the education of girls (Kim and Kim 1993: 12). As we can see, Nyeomaeng explicitly advocated gender equality at the time of its inauguration.

It is worth noting that the formation of Nyeomaeng was highly influenced by events in Korea; the mission statement was directly adapted from the official platform of the Federation of Korean Women, the predecessor to the South Korean Democratic Women's League in the Korean Peninsula (Kim and Kim 1993: 12). The first meetings of the Mindan-affiliated Buinhoe were similarly organized in Arakawa in Tokyo and Fuse in Osaka, both places where large populations of Korean residents lived. Buinhoe's Tokyo headquarters was established in 1947 by Oh Ki-moon, an active campaigner of Mindan who, following the promulgation of the Alien Registration Ordinance, decided to organize the wives of Mindan's executives.[6] Meanwhile, several other alliances were formed by Mindan-affiliated women in Arakawa, as well as in other areas of concentrated Korean settlement in Kyoto. These alliances were recognized by Mindan's central body in 1947 (Kim and Kim 1993: 15–16). The 'wise mother and good wife' value, enlightenment and cultural advancement, development of the motherland and international goodwill were included in Buinhoe's mission statement at the beginning and remain unchanged to this day (Zainihon Daikan Minkoku Fujinkai 1999; Zainihon Daikan Minkoku Fujinkai Tokyo Chihō Honbu 1993).

Buinhoe's central general headquarters was formed in June 1949 at the general headquarters of Mindan. Buinhoe's organization was, in comparison to Nyeomaeng, driven more explicitly in response to the higher organization and by individual activists' efforts. Its objective was to engage in activities with an even stronger will and patriotic spirit than men while upholding their 'duties as women' (Kim and Kim 1993: 18). The organization's statement of purpose includes the following passages:

> Family is the basic unit on which national societies are built. There must be a direct link between politics and housewives. Indeed, it is the power of housewives that takes the members of the nation of the time to success...The Eastern custom of dominance of male over female hinders the path of women and girls and even tramps on the beauty of women and girls...Some women even seem to be losing essential qualities of women, quite simply neutralizing them in their enthusiasm to demand equal rights between men and women. (Kim and Kim 1993: 17)

The approbation of housewife might be seen as an attempt to clearly differentiate themselves from Nyeomaeng which aspired to socialist power. However, when considered in the context of the respect for family and criticism of male domination expressed in the organization's statement of purpose, it seems clear that they were aiming to improve the status of women, who had been subjugated by feudal customs, by embracing the norms of modern families. A majority of the Korean women in Japan at that time was from poor farming families in Korea – therefore uneducated – and they had their hands full just supporting their poverty-stricken families. Buinhoe's emphasis on 'home,' and 'housewife' as well as its slogan to become wise mothers who could appropriately educate girls and take responsibility for nurturing the next generation of citizens was revolutionary at a time when it was widely believed that women should remain ignorant. In the context of the time, the idea of a 'wise mother and good wife' appeared to be a progressive ideology that would emancipate women from 'feudal' families and promote gender equality.

Both Nyeomaeng and Buinhoe started as grassroots mutual aid groups formed in Korean neighborhoods but in both cases the formation of organization was subject to a formal approval by the male-dominated ethnic organizations. The initiatives undertaken by women at the local level were overlooked as they were absorbed into the national organizations. As the criticisms of androcentrism gradually disappeared, both organizations started to play a role of supporting male-centric Mindan and Chongryun, acting literally as wives who help their husbands. While women threw themselves into the heated confrontation between Chongryun and Mindan that arose from the division of their homeland, their daily activities became primarily focused on cooperating in mobilization for demonstrations, working behind the scenes and collecting donations and petitions. Participating in protests with a nursing child on one arm while leading another child by the hand, they became an overwhelming presence.

The ambiguity of women's subject-positions in social movements at that time is quite clear in the description above. Despite the strong initiative clearly demonstrated in, for example, Nyeomaeng's straightforward advocacy of women's liberation at the time of its formation, after their formal incorporation into the larger ethnic-based movement organization they were gradually reduced to 'directed mobilization'-type of organizations that abided by the dictates of the male-dominated parent organizations. One of the reasons that the criticisms of androcentrism faded away was that there was an ever-increasing emphasis on the cohesion of the ethnic organizations at the expense of all else in response to the oppression of the occupying U.S. Army, the Japanese government and continuing racial discrimination, coupled with the outbreak of the Korean War and the 'red purge' within Japanese politics and social movements (Kim Young 2009: 116).

On top of these external factors, there were also numerous internal factors that contributed. These included the sheer lack of resources that would have been required for the development of autonomous movements; as mentioned, a substantial majority of Korean women in Japan at the time were illiterate and economically dependent on the men in their families. Moreover, the gender norms that excluded women from the public domain made it especially difficult for them to participate in public politics, except under the auspices of male-dominated organizations. For instance, a woman who served as the Assistant Director for a chapter of Buinhoe recalls: 'It was because there is Mindan's backing, we can face the Japanese with pride of being Korean. It was actually the women who were underpinning Mindan behind the scenes.'[7] Hence, while it may appear at first glance that the women's associations were following along in the ethnic-liberation movements led by men, on deeper reflection it becomes apparent that it was because women had no other option; in the context of the time, women were considered to be mere appendages to men, and it was therefore extremely difficult for women to represent themselves.

Within the framework of the ethnic-rights movements organized by Korean nationals living in Japan, women pledged allegiance to their national 'homelands' and tried to contribute to the nation-building in the Korean Peninsula. Certainly, to some degree, women could enhance their position within the ethnic organizations by making a contribution to the nation-building movement.

The commonalities between Nyeomaeng and Buinhoe include their centralized power structures, their daily engagement in mutual aid and social activities and that their activities and workshops provide the foundation for their efforts towards the unification of women. Currently, Nyeomaeng has a central headquarters in

Tokyo and forty-seven prefectural headquarters. Beneath them are approximately three hundred chapters, each with their own sub branches. Under the organizational goal to 'protect and nurture the ethnic consciousness through the generations', Nyeomaeng conducts activities to bring Chongryun-affiliated women together and promote friendly relationships. Its core activities include providing a place for fellow countrywomen to interact, activities to assure and support ethnic education for children and mutual assistance in various matters, including ceremonials. Regional chapters run hobby, study and sporting clubs as well as clubs to learn Korean culture such as folk music and dance, traditional instruments and cooking.[8] Nyeomaeng is especially focused on supporting ethnic education bodies under Chongryun. For example, *omoni* (mothers) associations of ethnic schools are closely connected to Nyeomaeng and play a role in the ongoing operation of ethnic schools through petitioning municipalities and international institutions, holding bazaars and charity events, and providing labor.[9]

Buinhoe also has a central headquarters in Tokyo and forty-five regional headquarters at the prefectural level, with 320 municipal-level chapters under them. Its mission statement stipulates three main principles: to make a great mother and an appropriate wife for Korean people in Japan, to contribute to the enlightenment of and cultural enhancement of Korean women in Japan and to contribute to the development of the motherland, world peace and international goodwill. Its day-to-day activities are very similar to Nyeomaeng's. Buinhoe's activities have gained so much momentum that they overwhelm the parent organization. Buinhoe was heavily involved in campaigns to discourage Koreans in Japan from returning to North Korea, refusing fingerprinting and securing local suffrage.[10] Belonging to this women's organization also meant joining together with South Korea's women. For example, Buinhoe sent representatives to the Korean Women's International Network when it was launched by the South Korean Ministry of Gender Equality in 2001, with the aim of building a network of the South Korean women living around the world and encouraging them to make contributions to the South Korean nation (Ministry of Gender Equality, Republic of Korea, 2001).[11]

Turning now to an analysis of Nyeomaeng and Buinhoe positions on family gender roles, we see that both associations require their members to be adult women. As mentioned, both Chongryun and Mindan have various affiliated organizations, including ones for youth, students and entrepreneurs. As the umbrella organization and the representative body for external relations, both Chongryun and Mindan make decisions on behalf of all of their members. Their vertical structures combined with the categorization of subordinate organizations into women and youth indicate that these ethnic organizations are modeled on the patriarchal family. As one member of Nyeomaeng commented, 'Chongryun is an organization for men, so it would be more fitting to call it "General Association of Korean *Male* Residents in Japan" than "General Association of Korean Residents in Japan".'[12]

The membership eligibility is specified as 'adult women' in both Nyeomaeng and Buinhoe. More specifically, though, they actually mean all women whose husbands are Korean men living in Japan, regardless of ethnic background, age and generation. The inclusion of Japanese women in both organizations on the basis of being married to Korean men highlights the androcentrism of these nationalist movements.[13] The organizational structure aims to enlist young women as members of youth or student associations first, and then move them to the women's organizations when they get married to Korean men. In the context of a domineering pro-marriage ideology, Korean women in Japan have been burdened with biological reproduction responsibilities. This, in turn, has meant that single Korean women who have passed the so-called marrying age have tended to be marginalized, including being excluded from opportunities to be involved in ethnic organizations.

The family positions 'wife' and 'mother' are the central to the ethnic activities in both Nyeomaeng and Buinhoe. In particular, the role of *omoni* (mother) constitutes the very core of organizational operations. The expectation for Korean women in Japan has been that they will marry a fellow countryman, give birth and raise a child – more specifically, a son who will succeed his father as head of the family – and devote themselves to serve their husbands' family. Women have been responsible for protecting the family domain, performing reproductive labor including household chores, child-rearing and nursing care while providing emotional and financial support for husbands who are themselves subjected to racial discrimination in the Japanese labor market.

These women's associations have not, however, always succumbed to the demands and expectations of their male counterparts; there have been a number of cases in which they insisted on women's rights. One early example of this is the case of Arakawa Fujobu, the predecessor of Nyeomaeng, which played an active role in improving the position of women by running evening classes and intervening in family issues such as domestic violence and the conflicts typical of relationships between daughter-in-law and mother-in-law in the typical living arrangements of women in Korean families. Later, when Nyeomaeng was officially founded, gender equality was boldly included in the platform for action. For women who had long suffered from the multilayered discrimination of colonialism and patriarchy, this action by Nyeomaeng was indeed a ray of light. It made them acutely aware that women are constitutive members of ethnic society.[14] It also provided a justification for their extra-domestic activities.[15]

However, as Nyeomaeng worked with Choryun to promote ethnic rights, gender rights activism gradually receded into the shadows. Nyeomaeng was celebrated as 'one of the two crucial wheels to drive patriotic movements' (Zainihon Chōsenjin Sōrengōkai 1991: 43) and positioned as an important partner of the men in the nationalist movements. Any criticism of the gender order within the collective body was treated as a threat to solidarity which could increase the organization's vulnerability. The common pattern that Enloe summed up as 'not now, later' (Enloe 1989: 62) is repeated in this instance, as the concerns of the ethnic group override the specific concerns of women.

'Patriotic motherhood' was expected of women by the collective that Chongryun represented. This ideology emphasized the importance of giving birth to and raising children who will contribute to the nation-building of North Korea and Chongryun communities. Nyeomaeng has focused most of its efforts on providing support for ethnic schools. It is widely understood that the operation of ethnic schools is largely attributable to the selfless contribution of women in collecting donations, recruiting new students and preparing and serving school lunches. Women's activities are highly recognized in Chongryun; but in many respects this simply reinforced the 'wise mother ideology and good wife'. To many first-generation Korean women in Japan, surrendering themselves to the roles of patriotic motherhood was seen as an opportunity to be part of the liberation movement to dispel the humiliation suffered from colonialism (Ryang 1998).

In comparison, Buinhoe's objectives at the time of its establishment were three-fold: 'family', 'culture' and 'economy,' all of which emphasized the roles of women as mothers and wives. The 'family' objective urged them to 'endeavor every day to maintain peaceful and happy families, to become wise and great wives and mothers' even while seeking to break with 'the family system that follows the old feudal customs'. The 'culture' objective criticized the moral code of women's obedience, yet at the same time called for women to master the knowledge of Hangeul, history, art, hobbies, food, clothing and housing to 'establish the images of decent mothers and wives'. The 'economy' objective addressed participation in consumers' co-operatives and credit associations as well as establishing workplaces with child care centers (Zainihon Daikan Minkoku Fujinkai, 1999; Zainichi Daikan Minkoku Fujinkai Tokyo Chihō Honbu 1993). Buinhoe has also been an active participant in Mindan's anti-Chongryun campaigns, as well as participating in human rights campaigns such as the fingerprinting refusal movement and local suffrage movements. All of these facilitated women's contribution as 'omoni' (mothers) in the ethnic community.

Both Nyeomaeng's and Buinhoe's participation in the political domain is different in form from men's, emphasizing their 'omoni' (mothers') identities. Under the 'great omoni' discourse the self-sacrifice of women for their ethnic communities and families was taken for granted. The exclusion of Koreans from Japanese society created additional demands for women to act as 'mothers' of the community, further increasing their burden. It is important to recognize, however, that there are also Japanese women's organization that define women first and foremost as mothers.[16] Regardless of ethnicity, the public domain in Japan used to be much more male dominated than it is today, and hence the possibilities for women to campaign as autonomous subjects in social movements was quite limited.

There was, however, another case in which women became active Korean nationalists without adopting the 'wise mothers and good wives' ideology. At Chongryun-operated ethnic schools in the late 1950s, the girls and women began to wear Korean-style clothing (*hanbok*) designed by Korean women as school uniforms. This trend arose of their own volition, independently of Chongryun. Since this coincided with a time of growing patriotism, as Chongryun strengthened its ties with North Korea, the adoption of *hanbok* by both students and teachers of ethnic schools might be viewed as an attempt to visually represent the women's nationalism. This women's initiative was eventually overruled, however, as Chongryun's executives tightened their control on women's activities (Han Tonghyon 2006). Once again we see a case in which the autonomous initiatives of women were undermined as if they had been brought under the control by an androcentric organization.

Gender equal ethnic organizations

In this section we will examine Korean women's organizations that have little autonomy from male-dominated ethnic organizations but relatively high autonomy from family gender roles. The specific body that will be examined is the Zainichi Kankoku Minshu Joseikai ('Yeoseonghoe', Korean Women's Society in Japan for Democracy), which sought gender equality within the ethnic rights movements.

Yeoseonghoe is a women's organization and a 'member organization' of the Zainichi Kankoku Minshu Tōitsu Rengō ('Hantongryun', Federation of Koreans in Japan for Democracy and Unification). Hantongryun is an organization of South Koreans living in Japan whose primary goal is the democratization of South Korean society and Korean reunification. Hangtongryun is the successor to the Kankoku Minshu Kaifuku Tōitsu Sokushin Kokumin Kyōgikai ('Hanmintong', Conference for the Restoration of Democracy in South Korea and the Promotion of Unification), which split from Mindan in 1973 following a conflict over Park Chung-hee's military dictatorship. Hanmintong was founded to promote democracy and was renamed Hantongryun during organizational reform in 1989. At the time of the schism in Mindan, democracy-leaning women who had been suspended for opposing the dictatorship in Buinhoe's Tokyo headquarters also left Buinhoe and joined Hanmintong.[17] Zainichi Kankoku Seinen Dōmei ('Hancheong', Korean Youth Alliance in Japan) is another member organization of Hantongryun. Hantongryun, Yeoseonghoe and Hancheong primarily campaign in urban areas with high concentrations of Korean residents.

There was a fifteen year gap between the schism that split Mindan and the formation of Yeoseonghoe. The backstory to the independent formation of Yeoseonghoe is therefore worth exploring. In 1986 in South Korea, a police officer was charged over the sexual torture of a female university student involved in the labor movement in the so-called Kwon In-sook case. Kwon In-sook's accusation came to symbolize state violence against women and fueled women's resistance against sexual assault. In South Korea, social movements have long been dominated by the so-called 'earnest desire of the Korean people' for democratization and the reunification of the Korean Peninsula, and the subordination of women was left to be dealt with later. The successful conviction of a police officer in a society in which the gender norms tended to impede female victims of sexual crimes from pressing charges was a huge step forward for the women's liberation movement in South Korea. This was a society in which the rural development campaigns and other 'modernization' projects of the military dictatorship, had made unmarried women in rural areas work in manufacturing plants to assist export promotion. Following the democratization movements of the 1970s, intense resistance to the state control of female laborers arose in the 1980s. As the resistance grew, sexual violence at home and in the workplaces also became targets of criticism and the women's liberation movements achieved considerable social influence.

Women's issues had long been suppressed within Hanmintong, beneath the issue of national reunification and democratization. The Kwon In-sook case provided an opportunity for it to be brought to the fore. A group of likeminded women from Hanmintong set up Yeoseonghoe to pursue women's liberation in Tokyo in November 1986 and in Osaka the following year.

In contrast to Hanmintong's vertical organizational structure, Yeoseonghoe's organizations have horizontal relationships. There are about ten to twenty active members in each of the Osaka and Tokyo branches of Yeoseonghoe, with a majority being second-generation married Korean women. It aims to achieve five goals: democratization of South Korea and Korean reunification, women's liberation, protecting the interests of Koreans in Japan, peace-building on the Korean Peninsula and in the world, and solidarity with similar organizations in democratic countries.[18] Yeoseonghoe is an associated organization of Hantongryun and is thus an 'associational linkage' type organization in Molyneux's typology.

One important point that should be made here is that Yeoseonghoe formed a joint relationship with a women's movement organization in South Korea; the Korean Women's Association United. Sharing a philosophy of women's emancipation with an organization of women in the homeland enabled Yeoseonghoe to ensure its autonomy from male-dominated organizations such as Hantongryun and provided justification for its movements while avoiding confrontation. In other words, Yeoseonghoe solved the dilemma of 'either-or' choices between the traditional ethnic liberation movement and the women's liberation movement by developing solidarity with women in the home country. This made it easier to engage in gender-related issues, such as gendered division of labor, sexual violence and military comfort women.

Yeoseonghoe shares Hantongryun's political objectives of Korean reunification and advancing the interests of Koreans in Japan. But it differs from Hantongryun in explicitly advocating for the liberation of women – and that is a significant departure in both theory and objectives. Yeoseonghoe openly criticized Hantongryun for clearly dividing its activities according to gender, with men holding all of the decision-making power and women being forced into a variety of subservient roles.

With a traditionally male-dominated organizational structure, male members of the Hantongryun-affiliated youth group were sometimes accepted into the adult organization Hantongryun as full time paid staff, but it was difficult for their female counterparts to remain in the organization no matter how substantial their contribution was. Rather, female members were encouraged to marry their male counterparts and then support their husbands by dedicating themselves to their families.[19] The formation of Yeoseonghoe can be seen as an open challenge to these conventions by women, triggered by the women's liberation movements in South Korea.

Yeoseonghoe is thus intrinsically critical of the gendered division of labor and the 'good wife and wise mother' ideology. In this regard it is quite distinct from Nyeomaeng and Buinhoe: its members are not defined by family gender roles; its objective is to be involved in social activism as individuals, not simply as mothers or wives. At the same time, Yeoseonghoe's position on social and political issues other than women's liberation, that is, Korean reunification and issues concerning the rights of Koreans in Japan, are aligned with Hantongryun. In other words, except for its advocacy of women's liberation, the organizational autonomy is rather low; it remains largely reliant on Hantongryun. Yeoseonghoe often participates in events hosted by Hantongryun. It participates in the ceremonies of the global Korean unification movement in conjunction with Hantongryun, and its in-house publication seems to present the same views as Hantongryun. In this sense, Yeoseonghoe can be regarded as an ethnic rights movement by women who seek gender equality. In the 1990s, when a huge wave of support for military comfort women swept across South Korea, it sought to mobilize support in Japan through various efforts, including the translation of materials published about the campaigns in South Korea. In the 2000s, it was representative of Korean women in Japan participating in the gender politics of South Korean society as part of an international network of Korean women, an initiative of the South Korean government's globalization efforts.[20] Hence, Yeoseonghoe appears to have a strong association with both South Korean society and the broader Korean society. Its engagement in the political struggle for the reunification of the Korean Peninsula exhibits strong characteristics of the 'long-distance nationalism' of diasporas (Anderson 1992, 1998) and in many respects it appears to be detached from the concerns of ordinary Korean women in Japan.

There are, however, important regional differences on this last point. For example, Osaka Yeoseonghoe works in cooperation with the Korean Council for the Women Drafted for Military Sexual Slavery by Japan ('Chongdaehyup'), an organization that campaigns on behalf of military comfort women, while also seeking to improve the situation of Koreans in Japan. Part of these efforts includes a survey of several hundred women living in Korean communities, seeking to better understand their situation.[21] The horizontal relations between the regional branches becomes quite apparent when we compare differences between them. For example, whereas the Tokyo Yeoseonghoe maintains close ties with Hantongryun, the Osaka Yeoseonghoe gradually distanced itself from Hantongryun while also creating a space in which fellow countrywomen can freely assemble in Ikaino. It is actively working for women's emancipation in the Kansai region through hosting public seminars and participating in the Women in Black movement, a silent vigil originated by Israeli women who dressed in black in protest at their country's violence against Palestinians, and which has now spread around the world. Osaka Yeoseonghoe and its successor Café Nabi,[22] while maintaining its base in Ikaino, an area with a large Korean community, is helping women to emerge as transnational activists for women's liberation by facilitating solidarity among women's grassroots movements in Japan, South Korea and North Korea.

Maternal citizens' movements

For movements that are characterized by high levels of autonomy from other movement organizations but low autonomy from family gender roles, I will examine a case of political participation based on grassroots activism by mothers of Koreans in Japan.

The 1970s saw development of movements by second-generation Koreans in Japan who were born postwar in Korean neighborhoods in metropolitan cities including Osaka and Kawasaki, to demand the elimination of discrimination. Until then, the Korean people's movements in Japan had been underpinned by a sense of belonging to the nationalist communities comprising first-generation Koreans and associated with vertically structured national bodies. In contrast, the postwar-born second-generation Koreans had relatively little interest in the politics of the Korean Peninsula but contested their identities as 'foreign residents', emphasizing their membership in and attachment to local Japanese society. In Kawasaki in 1970, Paku-kun o Kakomu Kai (Civil Group to Support Park) was created by young Koreans and Japanese citizens who supported the legal struggle waged by a young second-generation Korean man, Park Jong-seok, who had received a letter of acceptance for employment at Hitachi Software and had then been notified that this offer was withdrawn after Park informed Hitachi of his Korean nationality. He won his case in the Yokohama District Court in 1975. In the process of the legal struggle, Minzoku Sabetsu to Tatakau Renraku Kyōgikai ('Mintōren', Council for Combating Discrimination against Koreans in Japan) was created in 1974. As a national platform of Korean civil rights movements, it has actively sought to eliminate discrimination based on national and ethnic differences in areas ranging from education to the right to public service employment, employment in private companies, alien registration and eligibility for public housing. These new social movements by young Koreans born in Japan were facilitated by the proliferation of new types of social movements in Japan during the 1970s, in which class was no longer the primary basis of the conflict as it was in the traditional labor movements.[23]

New movements led by second-generation Koreans emerged simultaneously in a number of Korean neighborhoods across Japan. These movements helped to create new civic subjects at the local level through negotiations with the administration. In the process the focus of movements shifted from the national-level to local-level politics and many independent groups sprang up across the country, giving rise to various loose networks such as Mintōren.

Kodomo o Mimamoru Omoni no Kai (Mother Society for the Protection of Korean Children, hereafter 'Kawasaki Omoni no Kai') was created from the social gathering of Korean mothers who sent their children to Sakuramoto Nursery School in Kawasaki in 1975. The nursery school is operated by Seikyūsha, which is a social welfare corporation managed by the Korean Christian Church in Kawasaki for the purpose of providing ethnic education to Korean children in Japan. Seikyūsha's nursery school addresses Korean children by their Korean names, while the majority of Koreans in Japan use Japanese names. Inspired by the school's programs, the children's mothers began to organize social gatherings in which they studied the problems of human rights and discrimination as well as the histories of Japan and Korea and engaged in cultural activities such as traditional dance. Most of the mothers were second-generation women who were hard-pressed to make ends meet and had never participated in social movements. Having seen their children using Korean names, they decided to identify themselves with their Korean names as well, to embody the ideal of 'living ethnically rich lives'. When the children were targeted for racially motivated bullying in local public schools or denied the use of Korean names, the mothers stepped in and negotiated with the teachers and PTA (parent-teacher association). Kawasaki Omoni no Kai gradually began expanding its scope of activities to include campaigning to improve the human rights of local Koreans. Among other things, it organized a protest against JACCS, a Japanese leading consumer credit card company, for discriminating against Koreans in issuing credit cards (Kawasaki Kodomo o mimamoru Omoni no kai 1995; Song 2007).[24]

A similar grassroots movement was formed by mothers of Korean children in Kyoto in 1991. Mearihoe (*meari* means 'echo'), officially named Nishikyo-ku Zainichi Jidō Seito Hogosha no Kai (Parent Association of Nishikyo Ward Korean Schoolchildren) is a parent

association of Korean children who attend Japanese public schools.[25] Its main activities include:
1. regular monthly meetings to promote fellowship among parents
2. children's clubs for ethnic education, to teach language and culture
3. campaigns for equal educational opportunities for foreigners within the school education system.[26]

It has petitioned the Kyoto City Board of Education to demand that Korean names be used, that the dates of birth on graduate certificates be presented in the Gregorian calendar rather than the Japanese imperial era and to object to flying the Japanese national flag and singing the national anthem at their children's graduation ceremony. It raised various issues in meetings of the Zenkoku Zainichi Gaikokujin Kyōiku Kenkyū Kyōgikai ('Zengaikyō', National Foreign Residents Educational Research Council), which consists of teachers of public schools. It also participated in meetings with an advisory body composed of Kyoto City residents of foreign nationality. In addition, in 1997, it was involved in preparing a report by Japanese NGOs to be submitted to the United Nations Committee on the Rights of the Child.

As with Kawasaki Omoni no Kai, the core members of Mearihoe are postwar-born second- or third-generation women who were educated in the Japanese school system. Its members had experience participating in various Korean youth clubs during their high school and university years, such as Korean culture study clubs, to learn the culture and language of Korea. Despite actively taking part in ethnic rights movements when they were young, they had typically withdrawn from activism in the public domain after marrying and having children, as each day became a struggle to make ends meet. Seeing their children discriminated against at public schools, however, made them realize the need to create an environment in which the ethnicity of Korean children is duly respected. Since they were personally educated in the same school system, they are acutely aware of the importance of children using their Korean names and learning the Korean language and culture to nurture their self-esteem. The women therefore began, from the perspective of mothers, negotiations with schools, local parents and the educational authorities with a focus on the issues of children's ethnic rights.[27]

While both Kawasaki Omoni no Kai and Mearihoe were in part inspired by movements such as Seikyūsha and Korean youth clubs, in both cases, the role of 'mother' lies at the foundation of the organization. They were both formed by mothers of Korean children at schools and were built upon the everyday interactions between mothers through their children. In response to shared issues they initiated actions to transform the social situation for Koreans in Japan. A study of Hispanic immigrant women in the United States revealed a very similar process in which women who were generally confined to the domestic sphere became socially active members of their local communities through the organization of collective actions in a variety of areas relevant to their everyday lives, including their children's education, family health care and housing. The politicization of women based on 'motherhood' represents a specific kind of citizenship beyond any category of the public domain which cannot be readily explained by conventional notions of citizenship based on rights and obligations or from a simple legal perspective alone (Coll 2010: 74). The cases of Kawasaki Omoni no Kai and Mearihoe represent a different form of political participation from men: political subjects who might be categorized as maternal citizens.

From the perspective of gender norms, the emergence of new types of social movements based upon the experiences of women as mothers exposes the magnitude of the role as mothers imposed upon Korean women in Japan and the corresponding limitations placed upon their political participation. As discussed in Chapter 1 and at the beginning of this chapter, nurturing the next generation of the ethnic group, i.e., biological and cultural reproduction, is a role for which women have been made heavily responsible (Yuval-Davis and Anthius 1989). In Japan, where the myth of ethnic homogeneity continues to prevail and multicultural policy is scarce, the rights of children from minority groups to be educated in their ethnic language and culture within the public education system has not been recognized. Therefore, unless they are sent to private ethnic schools, children's education in their ethnic language and culture is only in the home, which means, essentially, that mothers are almost solely responsible. A member of Mearihoe whom I interviewed is critical of the division of housework or childrearing between men and women; but, she says,

Korean men are in most cases self-employed because of widespread discrimination in Japanese society and that naturally strengthens the bond of the community, or the family. So women who are married to Korean men not only have to dedicate themselves to supporting their husbands and family members as housewives but also bear the added burden of being responsible for their children's ethnic education. Although I knew it was wrong that *omoni* (mothers) alone were responsible for parenting, I had to act as a traditional woman as a temporary solution since I could not keep my children from growing up. However, I am in a dilemma because I don't want my children to copy me.[28]

Being driven by their responsibilities and identities as mothers, Kawasaki Omoni no Kai and Mearihoe are similar to Nyeomaeng and Buinhoe. All of these organizations are based in the experiences of Korean women in Japan being substantially defined by family gender roles. The women of Kawasaki Omoni no Kai and Mearihoe, however, in contrast to the others, are critical of the 'wise mother and good wife' ideology and the gender norms that confine women to the family domain. Organizationally, however, it was because all of their members were mothers and no men were present, that women could take the initiative and pursue unique campaigns as individuals with child-rearing responsibilities.

It is worth noting that campaigns intended to address mothers' concerns often wane as children grow up. However, Mearihoe is an exception, and is taking a new turn. Drawing from its history in promoting human rights in education, some members have become committee members of Kyoto-shi Gaikokuseki Shimin Shisaku Konwakai (Kyoto City Discussion Group on Policy on Foreign Citizens) and Kyoto-shi Jinken Bunka Suishin Konwakai (Kyoto City Discussion Group on Promotion of Human Rights and Culture). The former is an organization formed to study and deliberate on a variety of matters regarding foreign citizens and identify the issues that the city should address in order to promote the participation of foreign citizens in municipal politics and to create a 'multiculturally harmonious community'.[29] This is an instance in which many years of grassroots activism that emerged from the concerns of motherhood developed into more generalized political participation, eventually creating new civic actors in the context of multicultural symbiosis. While Kawasaki Omoni no Kai was dissolved in the mid-1990s, Song Puja, a founding leader, continues her activism by performing monologues about the lives of Koreans in Japan as well as being director of Korea Museum in Tokyo (Song 2007).

Emergence of Korean women as autonomous social actors

Finally, I will examine social movement organizations that formed independently of existing ethnic organizations and relatively more independently of family gender roles.

Chōsen Joseishi Dokushokai ('Dokushokai', Korean Women's History Reading Society) was established in the mid-1980s as an assembly of second-generation women who had attended Chongryun-affiliated ethnic schools. It was started by a group of women who were skeptical about Chongryun's dependence on the North Korean government and the 'wise mother and good wife' ideology. They began to hold regular gatherings separately from the organization to discuss issues concerning women. As the name suggests, Dokushokai (History Reading Society) sought to gain a deeper knowledge of the gender challenge inherent to their ethnic culture by reading *Korean Women's History* produced by Ewha Women's University, a leading institution of women's studies and movements in South Korea. The group began to produce Japanese newsletters as a mouthpiece for expressing their concerns. As an informal network, Dokushokai was not itself geared toward campaigning,[30] but the newsletter brought together women who were campaigning as non-Chongryun-affiliated individuals and from organizations such as Yeoseonghoe under the common cause of women's liberation. This informal network of women led to the establishment of Jūgun Ianfu Mondai Uriyoson Nettowāku ('Yeoseong Net' Military Comfort Women Issue Uri Yeoseong Network) in the 1990s.[31]

Yeoseong Net began as a meeting arranged by Dokushokai, of women who were interested in the issue of military comfort women. As mentioned above, this issue had sparked major debates in South Korea in the early 1990s. Formally inaugurated in 1991, Yeoseong Net's stated objectives were to establish the facts and to pursue early resolution of the military comfort women issue in Japan, specifically addressing its effects on Korean women in Japan. The forum it hosted in Tokyo to hear Kim Hak-sun, the first women to have come forward as a former military comfort woman in South Korea, speak about her experience attracted the attention of both the women's liberation movement and the mass media, setting the stage for a high-profile and broad-based campaign to question Japanese society on this issue. As this campaign gathered momentum, the Jūgun Ianfu 110-ban (Military Comfort Women Hot Line) was established by Yeoseong Net, in conjunction with Nihon no Sengo Sekinin o Hakkiri Saseru Kai (Association for the Clarification of Japan's Postwar Responsibility) Chōsenjin Jūgun Ianfu Mondai o Kangaeru Kai (Association to Think through the Comfort Women Issue) and Yeoseonghoe to collect information from people, mainly former military personnel. It conducted meetings, intensely petitioned, and translated campaign resources from Korean and overseas research into Japanese.[32]

The ethnic rights movement by Koreans in Japan since the 1970s has advocated extending citizenship rights and identifying themselves as members of Japanese society, rather than the divided state of the Korean Peninsula. They were primarily carried out by people in Japan with South Korean nationality, though. Yeoseong Net, in contrast, is remarkably diverse in terms of both nationality and the campaign experiences of its members. This may at least in part be because the establishment of Yeoseong Net in the early 1990s coincided with the end of the Cold War, which in some respects enabled Koreans in Japan to stand somewhat outside of the political situation of the Korean Peninsula and in part because of the rising prominence of second-generation women who have completed higher education and have either attained economic independence or have continued to be politically active while raising children.

The most significant characteristic of Yeoseong Net is that it included women from a broad spectrum of organizations and with vastly diverse experience in social movements. It included members of Dokushokai, as well as activists who had seceded from Yeoseonghoe. Many of its core members did not fit into the androcentric ethnic movement organizations and were searching for a new approach to social activism. Its membership included women who had studied abroad in the United States and South Korea as well as women from Korean ethnic schools in Japan and Japanese schools. This broad diversity led to the development of a global network and expansion of activities beyond the boundaries of the state.

Yeoseong Net worked in cooperation with Chongdaehyup of South Korea and Japanese women's liberation movements, but its campaigns were conducted from the perspective of 'Korean women in Japan' who differentiated themselves from both 'women of the motherland' and Japanese women. Yeoseong Net used the Korean traditional *saekdong* pattern as an expression of the diversity of its members and the harmony of different individuals working together.[33] The heterogeneous linguistic and cultural backgrounds of its members is reflected in the organization's name, which is a mix of Japanese, Korean and English words. It is worth noting that *Uri Yeoseong* means 'fellow countrywomen' in the Korean language.

Another important characteristic of Yeoseong Net is that it also raised the dual oppression of race and gender experienced by Korean women in Japan in conjunction with efforts highlighting the abuse endured by military comfort women. As we have seen, the network was launched by women who were struck by the similarity in the structure of oppression of Korean women in Japan and the military comfort women who spoke out about their experiences as victims of sexual violence during the colonial era. Awareness of this issue is expressed in the statement: 'The issue of military comfort women is an "issue that uncovers the basis of the identity"[34] of us Korean women in Japan.'[35] Yeoseong Net's campaigns were completely reliant on the initiative of its member. However, differences between members in their approaches to the issues of Korean women in Japan and the colonial era military comfort women became increasingly apparent, so some of the members established new campaign structures.

The Yeoseong Net members began to be active in different organizations with distinct themes while maintaining a loosely connected network. They played active roles in creating a variety of organizations which include both Japanese and Korean women in Japan as well as people of other nationalities, languages and cultures. These organizations include Zainichi no Ianfu Saiban o Sasaeru Kai (Support Group for the Lawsuit of Korean Former Comfort Women Resident in Japan) to support Song Sin-do, a former Korean military comfort woman living in Japan; Gurūpu Chame (Sisters' Group), a self-help organization focused on the issues faced by Korean women in Japan; and VAWW-NET Japan (Violence Against Women in War-Network Japan), an organization that worked on the issue of wartime violence and organized the Women's International War Crimes Tribunal in December 2000, a civil tribunal to bring those responsible for the systematized military sexual slavery of Japan to justice. Yeoseong Net was dissolved in 1998, as the members moved in different directions. Yeoseong Net fulfilled its part as a nodal point for Korean women in Japan, while the members' personal networks continue today.

The solidarity among Korean and Japanese women activists may be considered to have resulted from macro-level political changes in women's liberation movements in Japan, exemplified by the Asian Women's Association, a transnational feminist organization which campaigned against the economic globalization and postcolonial structural inequalities in cooperation with women in South Korea and the wider Asian region.

Finally, let us explore the night junior high school independence movement in Osaka, which also picked up momentum in the 1990s. The school in question, Chōei Night Junior High School, was situated on the fringe of an area with a dense Korean population. Since opening its door in the 1970s, the vast majority of its students had been first-generation and prewar-born second-generation Korean women. These women had been of school age when Korea was a Japanese colony and had missed out on schooling opportunities due to poverty, colonial domination and the common belief that women did not need to be educated. Consequently, they were therefore unable to read and write and had faced many difficulties in their lives. After reaching middle or older age, they finally had the opportunity to enter night schools and begin learning to read and write in Japanese.

The Taiheiji Night Junior High School Independence Movement was born in response to the Higashi-Osaka City Board of Education's decision to establish an extension class within the premises of the neighboring Taiheiji Junior High School and forcefully relocate half of the students without consultation. The educational quality of the class was poorer in every respect: it had fewer classrooms and fewer teachers for it was not officially a night junior high school. The women who were affected by this decision commenced a campaign, proposing that their rights to an education should be seen as postwar compensation. During this campaign, which began in the spring of 1993, women petitioned both the municipal and prefectural boards of education, staged a sit-in and collected signatures from 50,000 people. The campaign ended in the spring of 2001, following the opening of a new independent Taiheiji Night Junior High School, but their spirit and network carries on today, continuing to serve as a local activity hub for Korean women in Japan.

Among the other achievements of this prolonged campaigning, a self-directed learning institution, Uri Seodang, was founded for women who had been forced to graduate from school due to imposed limitations on the length of schooling. Another was the establishment of Sarangbang, an organization that runs a day care home and day care service. This was a response to the aging of the graduates of night junior high schools. Both Uri Seodang and Sarangbang act as nodes where Korean women who fought the night junior high school independence movement meet and interact with more recent generations of Koreans – both descendants born locally and newcomer Korean women. Uri Seodang has been incorporated as an NPO that represents the interests of Korean women in Japan at the local level, advocating on their behalf on issues of identity and other local concerns.

Yeoseong Net and Taiheiji Night Junior High School Independence Movement both linked the socio-historical perspective of the colonial legacy to women's perspective. These postcolonial movements are associated with a global movement that gained momentum in the 1990s following the collapse of the Soviet Bloc. This was a movement to hold former colonial powers to account for unresolved post-war problems. Similarly, both Yeoseong Net and the Taiheiji Independence Movement address the 'current problems' of Korean women who were illiterate because they were denied educational opportunities before the war and multiplicity of oppressional structure to which Korean women have been subservient. However, whereas Yeoseong Net linked this issue to aspirations for women's liberation, gender discrimination was not an explicit part of the campaigns by the Taiheiji Independence Movement. We will return to this in a later chapter. The important point to note here is that both of these movements posed a question to Japanese society about the Korean women who had been made invisible and disempowered by androcentric ethnic rights movements and the Japanese women's movements turning a blind-eye to racial discrimination. Regardless of their differences, these two movements which emerged almost half a century after the end of WWII played significant roles in enabling Korean women in Japan to establish the foundations of autonomous social movements in the public sphere. The new perspectives opened by these two movements have passed on to newer movements.

Conclusion

In this chapter I have analyzed the movement organizations established by Korean women in postwar Japan in terms of their background, structure, membership and activities. My focus has been on their relationships with other organizations and their autonomy from gender specific roles. Analyzing the formation of different organizations chronologically using the typology of women's movements suggested by Molyneux reveals a clear shift from directed mobilization to associational linkages and finally to independent movements. We have also observed a transition in their orientations to family gender roles, from strong manifestations of the 'wife' and 'mother' identities to participation as individuals who are also female. This particular development, however, has not been linear or homogenous; we see various movements of each type being actively pursued today. With this in mind, I will now outline my argument.

First, an analysis focused on women's social movement organizations provides a new perspective which relativize the male-dominated ethnic rights movements. Previous studies of Korean people's postwar social movements have focused on ethnically motivated collective actions in which nation-states are the axis of confrontation. As the postwar Korean people's movements confronted the nation of Japan, the conceptual equation of nationality with ethno-national identity permeated both the Japanese authorities and the majority of Korean residents in Japan (Kashiwazaki 2000). In the context of a Japanese national policy which only permitted one of two options – either assimilation or exclusion – Koreans in Japan have developed unique citizenship movements from the perspective of residents with foreign nationalities. These movements emerged during and after the 1970s, demanding equal rights with Japanese citizens while insisting on their ethnic identity as 'foreign residents'. Applying T. H. Marshall's (1992) notion, citizenship movements in Japan for Korean people started with civil rights and then expanded to social and political rights. This expansion of rights movements helped to strengthen their political relationships with the respective municipalities, however not with the government of Japan (Higuchi 2000). Among other things, Koreans in Japan have little opportunity to directly affect public politics due to their lack of voting right. Through campaigning over the Alien Registration Act, ethnic education, the right to employment in the public service, and admission to public housing, their resistance contributed to the transformation of public authorities, ranging from municipalities to the nation-state. The shift in the type of movements was also reflected in kinds of research undertaken to understand the needs and issues facing Korean people in Japan as a marginalized minority against the nation-state. A dichotomy between the host nation-state and an ethnic minority is only relevant, however, when focusing on politics in the public sphere. Such an approach disregards the issues in the private sphere, and thus hinders recognition of the roles that women have traditionally played. For those Korean women's groups that maintain close connections with broad-based ethnic organizations, an analytical approach that neglects structures of gender inequality can only yield superficial evaluations and will not fully capture the specificity of women's participation in politics.

The questions are: What were the contextual circumstances that led to the formation of Korean women's social movements in Japan? What were the interests that were pursued during the movements? What did they mean for the individual participants? And, what impact did they have on the social movement sector? An investigation into these questions requires that research be conducted at a deeper level than just Koreans in Japan versus the nation-state, taking into consideration social categories such as nation-states, ethno-national communities and families as well as the structures of gender inequality in the mainstream public sphere where social movements are active.

Second, Korean women's organizations were not completely independent of androcentric movement organizations. They were therefore subject to the strong influences of the structures of gender inequality in the ethnic society until at least the 1980s. One of the reasons for the changes in social movement organizations that began in the latter half of the 1980s was changes in the macro structure surrounding Koreans in Japan. The accepted discourse of an ethnic identity based on either North or South Korean nationality began to lose ground in the wake of a new influx of South Koreans beginning in the 1980s. This accepted norm was further problematized by the end of the Cold War. There was also a crisis of the nation-state in the late 1980s, during which women who had been harboring doubts about patriarchal organizations began to create counterpublics, where they could voice their opinions freely across national and organizational boundaries. All of this was facilitated by changes that had been occurring in the social movement sector at roughly the same time. From the 1960s, small-scale and horizontally networked movements started to emerge, initiated by individuals. This spurred a great diversification of movement organizations. In traditional mass movements addressing issues of class or race, it was generally accepted that addressing women's issues would weaken the movement. These changes enabled Korean women in Japan to more easily establish solidarity with other women and create autonomous networks that extended beyond questions of nationality and organizational membership, facilitating the formation of a subject-position of women who sought to transform the social structure through movements.

Third is the generational factor. Second- and later-generation women who have a command of the mainstream language spoken in the host society started to express their discontent about ethnic and gender discrimination openly in the public sphere via the Japanese media. Yeoseong Net was largely composed of second- and third- generation women with higher education while the Taiheiji Independence Movement consisted of first-generation women who had learnt Japanese reading and writing at night junior high school. The latter will be discussed in detail in the subsequent chapters but it should be mentioned here that Yeoseong Net became a bridge between women's movements in South Korea and their counterparts in Japan by capitalizing on their multilingual abilities in Japanese, Korean and English. Furthermore, they became active participants in the movement for the global solidarity of women which aims to eradicate wartime violence.

Finally, changes in the nature of women's liberation movements in Japan was also an important factor. The type of movements that were engaged in both domestic women's issues and issues of the political-economic gap across Asia within the context of postcolonial feminism, such as the Asian Women's Association, were radically new. This provided a foundation for developing solidarity among ethnically mainstream women's movements in Japan and those on the fringes of the Japanese nation-state, such as Korean women in Japan.

3 Counterpublics and the Taiheiji Independence Movement

Resistance against local power politics

Chapter 2 analyzed the postwar organizations of Korean women in Japan from the perspective of their autonomy from ethnic rights organizations and traditional gender roles. We saw that, on the one hand, the Taiheiji Night Junior High School Independence Movement in Higashi-Osaka shares some characteristics with conventional Korean women's movements in Japan, specifically in that it arose within the framework of 'racial' discrimination. On the other hand, it differs from the rest in that it was independent of traditional ethnic rights movements and that the women who founded it were fighting for the right to study, not as 'mothers' or 'wives' but, simply as people with human rights. Let us now explore the processes that brought Korean women in Japan to the point of initiating this relatively autonomous social movement.

This chapter will examine the Taiheiji Night Junior High School Independence Movement. We will explore its relationship with other social movements, especially ethnic rights movements and the night junior high school expansion movements in the Kansai region. We will focus in particular on the effects of its interactions with the broader social movement sector.

First, I will provide a brief account of the independence movement. In the 1990s, a sharp increase in the number of students in public night junior high schools in Higashi-Osaka City became a local political issue. A majority of the new students were Korean women. The Municipal Board of Education ordered that some of the students move to an extension class at a neighboring junior high school. This was a temporary arrangement, though, with substandard facilities and an insufficient number of teachers, all of which presented impediments to study. Deeming these circumstances unsatisfactory, the students started a social movement demanding that the public education authority turn the extension class into a regular, standard night junior high school.

Among other things, the students considered the move to be an act of racial discrimination. Their social movement raised highly political issues between Japan and Korea at the local community level, highlighting postcolonial discrimination against Koreans in Japan. They appealed for the rights of Koreans in Japan to receive an education, relating it to the postwar compensation. The movement ended in 2001, after eight years of action, with the formal opening of Taiheiji Night Junior High School.

Grassroots social movements had been gathering momentum in the Kansai region for some time prior to this one. A social movement sphere had formed as various groups began actively opposing the administrative authority. Groups of people who were marginalized because of their place of origin, class or racial category became increasingly active and influential in the Kansai urban space. Resistance to the hegemonic power had gradually built momentum over a variety of issues integral to everyday life, such as housing, education and work. These subaltern counterpublics included members of the urban lower strata, the human rights movement by buraku (descendants of outcast communities), day laborers and people from marginalized regions such as Okinawa and the Amami Islands; ethnic rights movements by Koreans in Japan and their descendants; and the night junior high school expansion movements. They had achieved varying degrees of success in terms of the redistribution of resources and acknowledgement of their divergent, non-mainstream identities.

The night junior high school movement in the 1990s built upon the oppositional social space that had grown out of multiple minority movements. At the same time, it highlighted the identity of Korean women in Japan as political actors who had historically been invisible, yet who played a role in the 'multiplicity of publics' that formed through the solidarity among social movements.

In the next section, I will provide an overview of the historical formation of minority social movements in the Kansai region. I will inquire into how these social movements generated counterpublics that influenced the transformation of social structures. Then I will introduce the ethnic rights movement and the night junior high school expansion movement, which each had a significant effect on the Taiheiji Independence Movement. After that, I will discuss the process by which the Taiheiji Independence Movement arose. Finally, I will examine the Korean women's subaltern counterpublic from the perspective of its interaction with diverse social movements.

Minority movements in Kansai

During the early capitalist industrialization of Japan, the metropolitan areas of the Kansai region required a huge influx of workers to satisfy the labor demands. These demands were met by relocating people from Imperial Japan's conquered territories: the Korean Peninsula, Okinawa, and the Amami islands. This mass migration reshaped the urban landscape, resulting in concentrated settlements of Okinawans, Koreans and day laborers appearing in various parts of cities such as Osaka, Kobe, Nara and Kyoto. These settlements were typically in the heart of the urban space, alongside communities of buraku, who had been present since before the Meiji era. The specific needs and perspectives of the minority communities were ignored by urban planners, though. Residential segregation is particularly notable in Osaka, where ghettos arose in barracks and illegally occupied pieces of land and buildings. Those areas are visually quite distinct from other areas in the city. For example, single male day laborers and homeless, Koreans, and Okinawans are heavily concentrated in the Kamagasaki (also known as Airin) district in Nishinari Ward of Osaka Prefecture; Ikuno Ward, Higashinari Ward, Nishinari Ward, Higashi-Osaka City and Taisho Ward, and have formed their own communities.[1] Since infrastructure and social services had been neglected in these areas, the collective actions by minority groups were primarily local movements demanding social and community services. In other words, these were grassroots community movements petitioning municipal and prefectural administrative organs for improved living conditions.

Mizuuchi (2005a, 2005b) discusses the issue of social exclusion and inclusion in postwar urban Osaka, focusing on administrative responses to minority group campaigns. He suggests that the movements initiated in Osaka by buraku, Koreans, Okinawans, and day laborers all nurtured distinctive identities that were inseparable from their residential areas. This blending of ethnic or class-based identities with local community-based identities formed unique social agents in the protests against public authorities. A new kind of 'public' was created through the confrontation between the 'public authorities' and the 'people' as the latter calls the former to account for their discrimination.

First, in the case of the buraku liberation movement, barrack residents in the war-affected areas began to call for improved living conditions in the mid-1950s. They demanded public housing and the provision of a communal water supply system for squatters. They were undeterred by police crackdowns on protests, continuing their sit-ins and other protest actions. Their perseverance was rewarded as low-rent public housing units began to be constructed on a massive scale. Their success provided a model and motivation for subsequent struggles to demand public housing in response to poor living conditions. They demonstrated that their lifestyle of squatting and barrack-style housing was directly attributable to social discrimination, which was in turn a resounding criticism of the government's negligence for failing to improve living conditions of the underclass. By highlighting that disadvantage directly flows from administrative discrimination, they succeeded in achieving both concrete improvements in their living conditions, and a recurring budget-allocation for anti-discrimination measures.

The greatest concentration of migrants from Okinawa settled in the swampy lowlands of Taisho Ward before the war, creating a high-density residential area of small housing units and barracks. This '*kubunguwā*' (meaning 'sunk land' in the Okinawan dialect) came to symbolize the place of Okinawans at the lowest point in Japanese society. In the 1970s, young Okinawans, especially second-generation migrants, began a campaign demanding improvements in the poor residential environment and an end to employment discrimination. This campaign was sparked by a group of teachers of Okinawan origin, who were, in turn, inspired by the buraku liberation movement.[2] The younger Okinawans perceived their substandard living environment and employment situation to be a direct result of discrimination through a structure of domination by mainstream Japanese authorities. From this perspective, the Kansai Okinawa Kaihō Dōmei (Kansai Okinawa Liberation Alliance) began negotiating with Osaka City to eradicate discrimination. Among their successes was compensation for forced evictions.

The problem of day laborers and homeless people is concentrated in the so-called 'skid row', the Kamagasaki (or Airin) district. There had been a large migration of single men into this area, beginning during the rapid economic growth of the 1950s, and surging in the 1960s with the construction boom for the Osaka World Exposition. Unlike the buraku and Okinawans, these single male day laborers sought only cheap and temporary lodging and employment, rather than permanent public housing. The administration's residential policy aimed at permanent living arrangements, however, and was irrelevant to their lifestyle and needs. Hence, administrative intervention was very limited, including the expansion of private sector lodging houses. Single male day laborers criticized the businesses, gangs and police that maintained the structures of labor exploitation – expressing their frustration and anger through riots – rather than demanding social resources such as public housing. The direct action taken by day laborers brought about links with other labor movements and student movements, resulting in the formation of a united front in the Bōryoku-tehaishi Tsuihō Kamagasaki Kyōtō Kaigi (Kamagasaki Solidarity Congress for Expelling Violent Recruiters) in the 1960s.

Finally, Kansai is home to a large number of Koreans. They had been participating in labor disputes since before the war. After the war, they campaigned against the public authorities over issues such as alien registration, the oppression of ethnic schools, deportation and the Korean War (Yang Young-hoo 1994). As we will discuss in later chapters, the Hanshin Education Struggle (1948) arose in reaction to the forced closure of ethnic schools. It was a watershed in the education sector as an ethnic rights protest against the public authorities and influenced the Taiheiji Independence Movement. The night junior high schools where this movement occurred are located around an area with a high concentration of Koreans, across the eastern region of Osaka City through to Higashi-Osaka City. Adjacent to Higashi-Osaka City is Ikuno Ward, where a quarter of the population are of Korean origin. The place name 'Ikaino'[3] has become emblematic of the areas of concentrated settlement of Koreans in Japan.

Koreans in Japan also experienced poor living conditions. However, unlike other minority groups, their situation was not conducive to making demands on Japanese authorities for improved living conditions. In the first place, many of them were intending to return to Korea as soon as possible after the war, and in the second place, they became 'foreigners' following the denationalization of the 1952 Peace Treaty.[4] They therefore invested their efforts in establishing and expanding their own institutions to meet their needs, ranging from finance, insurance, and education to mass communication. Thus, they survived the postwar hardships through mutual assistance from fellow Koreans, rather than demanding government action.

There was a significant change of direction in the 1970s, when second-generation Koreans in Japan began to assume that they were permanent residents and started campaigning for the protection of their rights and interests. This new movement demanded the removal of the Nationality Clause from public housing, child allowance and pension eligibility criteria, as well as eligibility for public office jobs. In campaigning to strike the nationality criteria from public housing eligibility, they found allies among several buraku liberation movement organizations that were closely involved with the Dōwa Projects (social integration projects) since many Koreans lived alongside the buraku in the designated 'social integration' districts. Similarly, the movement to demand the rights to ethnic education was influenced by the 'liberation education' movement which sought to end discrimination against the buraku people in the education system, and resulted in the opening of Japan's first ethnic class in a public elementary school in Nishinari Ward in the 1970s.

It is clear from this brief summation of Mizuuchi's study that throughout the postwar period, minority groups in the Osaka region have increasingly raised their voices in protest against the discrimination that they experience in the public domain. Mizuuchi argues that specific identities such as the buraku, Koreans and Okinawans are closely associated with their places of residence, and this gives rise to local resistance movements, as evidenced by their struggles to demand better living conditions in local communities. The important point for present purposes is that these social movements by minority groups have been successful in their struggles for improved housing and educational opportunities by mutually supporting and influencing each other. In particular, the buraku liberation movement, which had begun before the war, had accumulated significant social movement resources in the forms of theories, methods and human networks, and were influential on other minority rights movements.

Conventional research has focused on the antagonistic polarized relationship between Japan's mainstream society and its oppositional minority groups. For a more accurate understanding, however, it is necessary to examine not only the relationship between the mainstream majority and a particular minority but also the interactions among different minority groups. In fact, the multiple, multi-dimensional 'subaltern counterpublics' that have formed in opposition to the mainstream society constitute one holistic social movement.[5] In fact, in the Kansai region, at least, the marginalized minorities have been the primary constituents of the 'publicness' in the urban space through confronting the public authority. That publicness, which overlaps with what Fraser refers to as 'a multiplicity of publics', is an alternate civil space created by the interactions of different minority movements intersecting with diverse factors including race, locality, class, and with one another.

The Taiheiji Independence Movement developed in the 1990s in the public sphere that had been formed through the interactions of the social movements of the different minorities of the Kansai region. It added a new element to the mix of identities involved – Korean women in Japan – further increasing the diversity of the public sphere.

Korean community in Osaka and ethnic rights movements

At the end of 2010, there were approximately 127,000 people of South Korean or Chosun nationality in Osaka, accounting for about 60% of the total number of registered foreign residents, which sits around 212,000.[6] Ikuno Ward, located in the east of Osaka City, has an especially high concentration of Koreans, having been as high as a quarter of the total population, and still accounting for more than 20%.[7] In Higashi-Osaka City, where the Taiheiji Independence Movement took place, the number of South Korean and Chosun nationals was around 13,000, comprising about 80% of the registered foreign residents in the city.[8]

It is no surprise, then, that first-generation and prewar-born second-generation Korean women have always constituted a significant proportion of the students in night junior high schools in Kansai. Accordingly, the Taiheiji Independence Movement is characterized as a Korean ethnic rights movement.

Chōei Night Junior High School is located within this area of concentrated Korean settlement (Figure 3.1). In the late 1980s it had the largest number of students of all of the night junior

Figure 3.1: Osaka's Ikaino District and location of night junior high schools

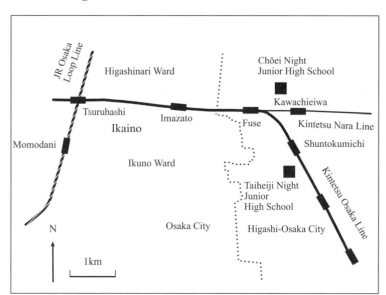

Source: Created by the author.

high schools and admitted the largest number of Koreans in the country. When it was opened in 1972, Korean students comprised less than 20% of the student body, but their numbers skyrocketed, reaching 97% only two years later (Chōei Chūgakkō Yakan Gakkyū, 1989: 222). Many Korean students heard about the school by word of mouth and began commuting from across Higashi-Osaka City, Ikuno Ward and Higashinari Ward in the adjacent Osaka City.[9]

Let us look at the background of the Koreans in particular areas of Osaka. Prior to the war, the Hanshin area rapidly industrialized, and experienced a huge demand for cheap labor. In Osaka, Hanshin's central city, there was a surge in construction with the expansion of urban infrastructure, including transportation systems and harbors, creating a demand for large numbers of construction workers. Meanwhile in Korea, under Japan's colonial rule, a large number of farmers had their farmland confiscated by the colonial authorities and were reduced to tenant farmer status. The farmers' poverty was further aggravated as vast quantities of Korean rice were appropriated and shipped to Japan following the Rice Riots of 1918. Many Korean farmers went bankrupt and left the land, traveling to northeastern China and Japan in search of a better life. Osaka became home to many migrants from Jeju Island after a direct shipping route opened in 1923. A significant proportion of people who originated in the Korean Peninsula were employed as unskilled laborers in Osaka's spinning mills and small factories (Sugihara 1996, 1998).

The typical pattern of migration was that men migrated to Japan first, and women and other family members followed. However, in the Kansai region, quite a number of female workers migrated to Japan by themselves to work as female divers or in spinning mills in Kishiwada or Sakai (Yang Young-hoo 1994; Kim Chan-jung 1980; Sugihara 1998). By the end of 1942, approximately 410,000 Koreans had settled in Osaka Prefecture, making it the city with the second largest population of Koreans in the world, after Keijo in Korea (Higuchi 2002: 61). The areas where most Koreans lived typically lacked basic infrastructure such as sewerage and electricity. Japanese people would generally not accept such living conditions for themselves.

As discussed above, residential segregation is prominent in the urban areas of Kansai. The area where Koreans have settled extends across the eastern part of Osaka Prefecture, and is widely perceived to be an ethnic social space. In Ikaino District, which lies on the eastern side of Tsuruhashi Station on the Osaka Loop Line, there is a high concentration of Korean restaurants, stores carrying Korean foods, miscellaneous goods, bedding items, furniture and books, as well as real estate agencies and finance businesses. Many layers of ethnic networks have developed, including ethnic organizations such as Chongryun, Mindan and Hantongryun. There are also Christian, Buddhist and other religious-ethnic organizations as well as provincial associations, which are social groups for people from the same hometown. Chongryun-affiliated elementary, middle and high schools have been established across the eastern part of Osaka City to Higashi-Osaka City. Businesses are commonly small scale and run by family members, often engaged in vinyl and plastic processing, collecting recyclables and needlework. Korean women can be found all over the city, working in small home offices, stores and eateries. In parks, you find middle-aged and older women exercising in groups in the early morning and men sitting in circles and playing board games during the day.

Ikaino is a place that satisfies the basic living needs – whether political, economic, educational, religious, cultural or financial – for Koreans living in Osaka. This virtually self-sufficient society formed through mutual efforts to overcome their alienation from mainstream society and their general lack of public services.

A series of active ethnic rights movements have formed in Ikaino. Among the various issues addressed through social movements – including alien registration, deportation, fingerprinting and suffrage – education was an especially important domain for social activism. The biggest protest movement in postwar Osaka is probably the Hanshin Education Struggle (1948). This was a protest against the oppression of ethnic schools by the Japanese authority, which at the time was under the Supreme Commander for the Allied Powers. There was a nationwide protest, but Osaka was the site of especially fierce resistance. The Hanshin Education Struggle is regarded as the original ethnic rights movement in Osaka. Following in its footsteps, the Taiheiji Independence Movement was dubbed the 'Second Hanshin Education Struggle', highlighting the continuity of its protest against the public authority. A summary of the Hanshin Education Struggle will therefore provide useful background for our discussion of the Taiheiji case.

Immediately after WWII, a large number of schools were established by Koreans across Japan to teach the Korean language in preparation for their children's return to Korea. In Osaka, there were more than eighty elementary and middle schools providing Korean education to over 10,000 students in 1947. At that time, Choryun had strong connections with the Japanese Communist Party and both the occupying U.S. Army and the Japanese authorities were hostile to the ethnic schools under its umbrella. In January 1948, as tension increased between the U.S. and the Soviet Union, a circular was issued by the Director-General of the Education Bureau requiring that all Korean children of school age attend a public or private elementary or junior high school approved by the prefectural agency. Korean schools were ordered to close down as of 15 April and make their students enroll in public schools.

The Korean schools responded with a joint statement declaring that these measures were 'designed to destroy the autonomy of ethnic education and extinguish the language, history and culture of Korea'. They petitioned the education authorities and, on 23 April 1948, more than 15,000 Korean schoolchildren and parents assembled in front of Osaka Prefectural office to demonstrate against the government's decision. When negotiations between the demonstrators and the Osaka Prefectural Government reached a deadlock, around 4,000 Koreans poured into the prefectural office and 179 were arrested. A Korean boy was shot dead by the police, which indicates the intensity of the struggle (Yang Young-hoo 1994: 77–88; Higuchi 2002: 160–163; Pak Sam-sok 1997: 158–160; Uri Hakkyo o Tsuzuru Kai 2001: 63–67). The women who participated in the Taiheiji Independence Movement are old enough to have firsthand memories of the Hanshin Education Struggle.

Since the 1970s a string of community-based movements have emerged, led by second- and subsequent-generation Koreans. These movements have encompassed a broad spectrum of interests and issues, from cultural activities such as literary publishing, social gatherings and the Ikuno Minzoku Bunkasai (Ikuno Ethnic Culture Festival)[10] to programs to address more practical needs, such as establishing ethnic classes in public schools and providing assistance to elderly and disabled people. The Korean people's movement in Kansai has had some remarkable successes in the education sector, especially in terms of promoting ethnic education for Korean schoolchildren in Japan. Organizations were created around local children's societies such as Takatsuki Mukuge no Kai (Takatsuki Mukuge Society) and an association was created for Korean ethnic instructors in Japan: Minzoku Kyōiku Sokushin Kyōgikai ('Minsokukyō', the Association for Ethnic Education Promotion) (Kashiwazaki 2002b). Furthermore, in Osaka Prefecture, as of 2010, classes teaching Korean language and culture as extracurricular studies are offered in more than 170 public schools to approximately 28,000 students.[11] These classes are taught by Japan-born Koreans. The aim is to teach Korean language and culture to Korean schoolchildren, to nurture their ethnic identity, and to fight against racial discrimination in schools. At the same time, negotiating with the various layers of government over ethnic education is to engage in the politics of redistribution and demand acknowledgment of their Korean identity. From this perspective, the Taiheiji Independence Movement can be seen to have advocated for basic human rights and for recognition of the identity of middle-aged and older Korean women in Japan through a specific struggle in the education sector.

Night junior high school expansion movement

Abolition of night schools and expansion movement

The Taiheiji Independence Movement arose in the wake of a widespread citizen's movement that had swept across the country from the late 1960s, particularly vigorously in Kansai. This was a grassroots movement calling for the continued, and expanded, operation of public night junior high schools to guarantee an education for people who, for a variety of reasons, had not previously had the opportunity for schooling or to learn literacy skills. Participants were drawn from a wide cross section of the general public, as well as teachers of night junior high schools, researchers and activists. The movement aimed to redress the social exclusion of the urban underclass, with the night junior high schools as a focal point.

Public night junior high schools[12] are public educational institutions that provide classes at night. They were established in order to guarantee the rights to an education for people who could not complete their education when they were school age. They are operated by the local boards of education and will reward a certificate equivalent to graduating from a full-time junior high school upon completion of the designated curriculum.

The first public night junior high schools were established in 1947, when the 6–3 compulsory education system was introduced. The new compulsory education system could not address the long-term absenteeism due to poverty, which was quite common for some time after the war. In order to accommodate students who had to work or help their families in other ways at this time, an 'evening class' was offered in a junior high school in Ikuno by the voluntary effort of like-minded teachers, without authorization or administrative support. Kobe, Yokohama, Kyoto, Nara, Hiroshima, Tokyo, Nagoya and Fukuoka soon followed suit, opening similar night junior high schools. The Ministry of Education remained circumspect, though, on the grounds that these programs were not recognized under the School Education Law.[13] Hence, although there were 87 night junior high schools teaching some 5,208 students by the mid-1950s, these numbers declined to 21 schools and 416 students by 1968.[14] There was increasing pressure to close the schools from the Ministry of

Education as well as the Ministry of Labor, which was concerned that school-age children were not attending full-time junior high schools because they were working. The government's position was that the literacy problem had already been resolved when the postwar recovery gathered momentum and Japan entered a period of rapid economic growth.[15] In 1966, the Administrative Management Agency recommended abolishing these schools on the grounds that they had been a temporary arrangement, were not covered under the School Education Law, and the idea of working during the day and going to school at night was at odds with the principles of compulsory education. This recommendation appeared to make their closure inevitable.[16]

One night junior high school graduate, however, started a campaign in 1967 that ultimately reversed this decision. Infuriated by the Administrative Management Agency's recommendation, which ignored the needs and rights of illiterate people, Takano Masao began a campaign to not only resist their closure but to demand that the service be expanded. The campaign began when he screened the self-produced documentary film *Yakan Chūgakusei* (Night Junior High School Students) in various locations in 1967.

Takano was a war orphan repatriated from China. At the age of 17, he was taught to write by a Korean man who worked as a garbage collector in Ueno, Tokyo. He says that when he entered a night school in Tokyo at the age of 21, he discovered a 'society without discrimination' and found 'comrades' for the first time (Takano 1993). Arguing that 'being deprived of literacy is equivalent to being deprived of air', Takano walked across the nation, screening his documentary. The film attracted an audience of almost 10,000 people when it screened in Osaka, serving as a catalyst for a massive citizen's protest. In fact, this proved to be the turning point. From this point forward, the suggestions that night schools should be abolished were put to rest and the momentum changed direction. A new night class was opened in Tennōji Junior High School in 1969, and ten new schools were established in 1970 through movements led mainly by the Yakan Chūgaku o Sodateru Kai (Night Junior High School Development Association). Of the first twenty new night junior high schools opened across the country at this point, eleven were located in Osaka Prefecture.[17]

Thirty citizens' groups were involved in establishing night junior high schools in the ensuing years and twenty-eight 'self-directed night schools' were established by citizen volunteers who chose not to wait for the public school system to respond to their needs.[18] These self-directed night schools operate throughout Japan. Student numbers range from ten to several hundred people who gather at venues such as community centers to study.[19] The operational approaches of self-directed night schools vary depending on local circumstances; some do not aspire for national recognition whereas others reward graduate certificates from a municipal junior high school with which they are affiliated after completion of a specified curriculum.[20] There are also a number of 'literacy classes' run by the Buraku Liberation League and other volunteers in Kansai. These classes are taught by teaching staff, students, the general public and other movement supporters. Operating funds are raised through membership fees, donations and rummage sales.

The Japanese government has not addressed the social exclusion of illiterates based on the claim that 99% of the population is already literate; but citizen's movement assert that there are one million illiterate people. As citizen's movements continued their efforts to fight for the neglected 1%, nation-wide linkages were formed (Matsudoshi ni Yakan Chūgakkō o Tsukuru Shimin no Kai 2003; Yakan Chūgaku Zōsetsu Undō Zenkoku Kōryūshūkai 1986, 1994, 1997). The Yakan Chūgaku Zōsetsu Undō Zenkoku Kōryūshūkai (National Exchange Meeting for Night Junior High School Expansion Movement) has met every year since 1982.[21] Since the late 2000s, citizens' movements have lobbied lawmakers to initiate legislation concerning night junior schools. In 2015, the Ministry of Education expressed a new policy which aims to establish at least one night junior high school in every prefecture (Ministry of Education 2015: 155). There were several distinct parties involved in the citizen's movements in support of night junior high schools: citizens, teachers, students, human rights lawyers and politicians, all of whom campaigned for the expansion of the night schools. This social movement collected the voices of different marginalized minorities. The students of night junior high schools come from many different minority groups with various backgrounds and places of origin. Among them, though, Korean women accounted for a majority of the students until the early 2000s and have had a substantial influence on the citizen's movements campaigning for night junior high schools.

Diversity of students at night junior high schools

As of 2015, there were thirty-one public night junior high schools across the country, mostly in metropolitan areas and the Kanto region, with 1,800 students enrolled.[22] Until the mid-1960s, most of the students who studied at night junior high schools had been unable to attend school during the postwar chaos, either due to economic conditions or because they had been repatriated from one of the colonized territories, such as China. During the 1970s, the student numbers increased; however, the demographics were different. Now students were primarily people of diverse origins who did not speak Japanese as their native language, such as repatriates, Koreans in Japan, war-displaced people left in China, refugees, Japanese migrants returned from South America and their descendants and other newcomers. There was also an increase in Japanese who had quit school because: they suffered from discrimination against the buraku, or sheer poverty; they refused to go to school owing to family circumstances or bullying; or they had not acquired the standard of academic skills necessary to graduate from junior high school. Figure 3.2 depicts changes in the number of students throughout Japan by place of origin as reported by Zenkoku Yakan Chūgakkō Kenkyūkai. It is clear that Koreans in Japan constituted the largest group until the mid-1990s, after which the number of newcomers other than Koreans grew.

The Zenkokoku Yakan Chūgakkō Kenkyū Taikai (National Night Junior High School Study Conference), an annual conference held every year since 1954, first addressed the issue of repatriates from China in the 1970s. A subcommittee was tasked with addressing 'problems regarding education of foreigners' at the 23rd conference in 1977. This was the first time the issue of Koreans in Japan was addressed. The first subcommittee meeting discussed the following topics: that Korean students enrolled at night junior high schools were primarily elderly women who experienced a variety of obstacles to learning, including night shifts, health and challenges associated with old age as well as various problems regarding the use of their real names and sometimes having to work.[23] The relevance of the curriculum of night junior high schools to the diverse student bodies was the main topic of the 27th conference held in 1981 (Zenkoku Yakan Chūgakkō Kenkyū Taikai Jikkō I'inkai 2004). Night junior high schools are significantly more

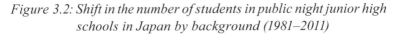

Figure 3.2: *Shift in the number of students in public night junior high schools in Japan by background (1981–2011)*

Source: Created by author based on each year's edition of *Zenkoku Yakan Chūgakkō Kenkyū Taikai: Taikai Shiryō*, (National Night Junior High School Study Conference: References).

Note. The data broken down by background of origin prior to and including 1980 was not available. The reference statistics did not use the category 'Koreans in Japan' for 1981–1989. Correspondingly, the number of 'students of foreign nationals living in Japan' (a significant part of which is inferred to be Koreans in Japan) is applied.

diverse than full-time junior high schools in terms of nationality, life history, academic skills and age. Such diverse student bodies reflect contemporary Japanese society. Nevertheless, as shown in Table 3.1 and Figure 3.3, Koreans in Japan accounted for almost half of the total students of night junior high schools across the

Table 3.1 Number of students of public night junior high schools in Japan by prefecture and background (1993)

	Tokyo	Kanagawa	Chiba	Kyoto	Nara	Osaka	Hyogo	Hiroshima	Total
South Korean or Chosun nationals	43	4	0	59	43	1,134	95	20	1,398
Japanese	92	13	7	21	99	421	47	18	718
Repatriates	172	2	1	0	54	291	5	12	537
Returning immigrants	12	11	7	0	19	20	0	0	69
Other nationals	36	5	2	15	45	64	10	9	186
Refugees	21	6	5	0	0	19	6	0	57
Total	376	41	22	95	260	1,949	163	59	2,965

Source: Created by author based on *1993-nendo dai-39-kai Zenkoku Yakan Chūgakkō Kenkyū Taikai: Taikai shiryō* (*The 39th National Night Junior High School Study Conference 1993: References*).

Figure 3.3: Students of night junior high schools in Japan at the time of the start of the movement: Percentage by background (1993)

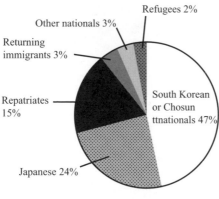

Total: 2,965

Source: Created by author based on *1993-nendo dai-39-kai Zenkoku Yakan Chūgakkō Kenkyū Taikai: Taikai shiryō* (The 39th National Night Junior High School Study Conference 1993: References).

Figure 3.4: Students of night junior high schools in Japan at the time of the start of the movement: Percentage by age group (1993)

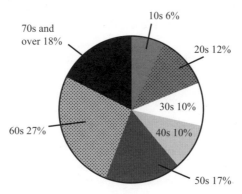

Total: 2,965

Source: Created by author based on *1993-nendo dai-39-kai Zenkoku Yakan Chūgakkō Kenkyū Taikai: Taikai shiryō* (The 39th National Night Junior High School Study Conference 1993: References).

Figure 3.5: Students of night junior high schools in Japan at the time of the start of the movement: Percentage by gender (1993)

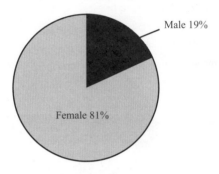

Total: 2,965

Source: Created by author based on *1993-nendo dai-39-kai Zenkoku Yakan Chūgakkō Kenkyū Taikai: Taikai shiryō* (The 39th National Night Junior High School Study Conference 1993: References).

country in 1993, when the Taiheiji Independent movement began. Furthermore, in Osaka, approximately 60% of the students were Koreans. By age group (Figure 3.4), students in their 60s accounted for the highest proportion with 27% while combined, the age groups over 50 comprised around 60% of the total. As for gender, women constituted an overwhelming 80% of the students (Figure 3.5). These data demonstrate that middle-aged and older Korean women in Japan constituted the majority of students of night junior high schools.

Many of the students enrolled in night junior high schools have experienced unfair treatment and discrimination or are lacking in self-respect because they did not complete primary education or were illiterate.

> The night junior high schools…started as bona fide teachers created a temporary place to study, having heard the earnest voices demanding education from people who had been discarded from the mainstream education system, were stripped of access to literacy and speech and had their livelihoods threatened. (Yakan chūgaku zōsetsu undō zenkoku kōryūshūkai 1997: 205)

Building on this perspective, the movement appealed for constructing, expanding and improving the night junior high schools. It demanded that the government guarantee access to an education on the grounds that the right to education is enshrined in the Constitution of Japan.[24] Furthermore, campaigners claimed that night junior high schools are a form of postwar compensation, referring to the fact that there was a proportion of Koreans and repatriates enrolled. While there was little progress in public compensation for war victims, returnees and Koreans in Japan were defined as victims of imperialism and the colonial policy of the prewar Japanese government.[25]

The Buraku Liberation League has focused on the link between illiteracy and social exclusion in their quest to run literacy classes in the Kansai region.[26] As mentioned, the night junior high school expansion movement was influenced by the buraku liberation movement in both theory and practice. Takano Masao, who led the expansion movement, encountered the buraku liberation movement when he was hosting screenings of his self-produced film *Yakan Chūgakusei*. Having learned of the harsh discrimination against buraku communities, and deeply moved by the *Suiheisha Sengen* ['Levelers' Declaration], proclaimed at the National Levelers' Association Inaugural Conference in 1922, he decided that he would refuse to accept mere sympathy; a call for recognition of his human rights and independence would be the pillars of his social movement (Takano 1975, 1993).[27] The human rights movement for night junior high school students has benefited significantly from the buraku liberation movement. The movement in Nara Prefecture in the mid-1970s to demand the establishment of night schools was inspired by the literacy classes run by the buraku liberation campaigners who had identified 'emancipation from discrimination' as the goal of 'learning'. The Nara campaigners thus regarded night junior high schools as hubs for anti-discrimination, liberation education and activism.[28]

The independence movement, which arose in 1993, had been preceded by the Kokusai Shikijinen Suishin Higashi-Osaka Renrakukai (International Literacy Year Coordinating Committee Higashi-Osaka Liaison Meeting), which was formed by the Chōei Night School Student Council, Higashi-Osakashi Kyōshokuin Kumiai (Higashi-Osaka City Teachers Union) and Hagusa and Aramoto literacy classes. Its aim was to pursue social integration issues in 1990, the International Literacy Year. My point is that the student movement in Higashi-Osaka did not arise spontaneously; it was built by linking different citizen's movements that had formed around the core issue of 'literacy'.

The movements' aim was not assimilation into mainstream society through improved academic career and literacy skills. Instead, it sought the literacy and speech skills necessary to produce a counter-discourse that could challenge mainstream society. This path had already been pioneered by earlier social movements in Kansai. However, while drawing on their predecessors' theories and resources (both human and organizational), the Taiheiji Independence Movement's demands were rooted in the historical experiences and living conditions of Korean women in Japan.

Dynamics of Taiheiji Independence Movement

Chōei Night School and extension class

The Chōei Junior High School Night Class was opened in 1972. It was the third night junior high school in Osaka Prefecture, following Tennōji and Kishiki Night Junior High Schools. All three arose out of citizen's demands. When it opened, it had three classes and 63 enrolled students (34 men and 29 women), including 12 Koreans (less than 20%). By 1974, there were 151 Koreans, comprising 97% of the 156 students enrolled. Koreans have continued to make up the vast majority of students enrolled in this school ever since (Figure 3.6). The average age of the students was 37 at the beginning. By 1982, it was 58.[29] In the 1990s, the student body reached about 400, which was more than the number of full-time students. At this time, Chōei had the largest student body of any night junior high school in Japan. Most of them were middle-aged and older Korean women. At that time, the night junior high schools in Osaka City were concentrated in the southern part of the city – but many students opted to commute to Chōei Night Junior High School in the inner city, an easy commute by bicycle from Ikuno Ward and Hiagshinari Ward.

Facilities were inadequate for the surging number of students. This began to disrupt the after-school activities of the full-time students who shared the premises. In the late 1980s and early 1990s the municipal board of education received numerous requests to open another night junior high school in Higashi-Osaka City. The

Figure 3.6: Shift in the number of students in Chōei Night Junior High School

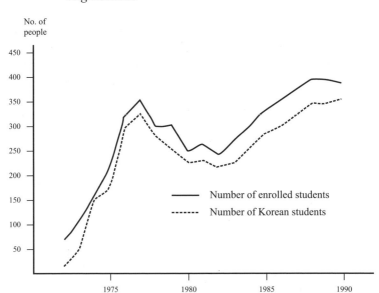

Source: Created by author based on *Otona no chūgakusei* (Adult junior high school students) for 1972–1988 and *Zenkoku Yakan Chūgakkō Kenkyū Taikai: Taikai shiryō* (National Night School Study conference: References) for 1989–1990.

Kinki Yakan Chūgakkō Renraku Kyōgikai (Kinki Liaison Council of Night Junior High Schools) and the aforementioned Shikiji Renrakukai lodged most of these requests, but the problem was not immediately resolved.

The issue took a major turn, however, when a newspaper article titled 'Students overflow at night junior high school (Yakan chūgaku afureru seito)' appeared in the *Sankei Shimbun* Osaka Edition in June 1992. The article reported that the number of students enrolled in Chōei Night Junior High School was 'an unprecedented outnumbering of daytime students'. Furthermore, it reported that the students were 'mostly Korean people who were not able to receive an education owing to the war or economic reasons' and went on to report that one of the causes of the increasing number of students was the significant proportion of 'repeaters' who failed to graduate in three years due to old age. It highlighted that the huge student numbers were straining the facilities, which was affecting the daytime students' club activities and PTA (parent-teacher association) meetings. It also reported that the PTA of the full-time students and the school principal had formally requested that the municipal board of education provide a separate building for the night junior high school.

Following the article's publication, the PTA and the municipal board of education both expressed increasing concern over the growing number of students at the school, leading to discussions about how to resolve the situation. It is worth examining what exactly they were concerned about, though. Graduates and teachers of night junior high schools pointed out to me that the article's focus on the fact that most of the students were Koreans seems to have been what provoked most of the local residents, especially the parents of the students of the school that shared the premises. In short, the broad-based contempt for Koreans in Japan appears to have been the main driving force behind the sudden turn of events.

The city council soon raised the student numbers as an urgent issue requiring immediate attention.[30] The following year, in February 1993, with the new school year in sight, the Higashi-Osaka City Board of Education set forth a policy to 'open the Taiheiji extension class in April to adjust the school size' and 'restrict the admission of non-residents'. In April 1993, an extension class was offered at Taiheiji Junior High School, located a little over one kilometer south of Chōei Junior High School and a restriction was imposed on inter-city commuting. Of the 378 students enrolled in the night school at the time, 121 who lived south of the Kintetsu Line were transferred to the extension class. They were joined by 58 new students. Thus the 'Chōei Junior High School Night Class Taiheiji Extension Class' began with a total of 179 students in 1993.

The government decided to create a separate extension class with no regard for the students themselves. The measure was abrupt and ill considered. The biggest problem for the students was that the new extension class was in substandard facilities. There were only three classrooms available for more than 180 students. Students were crammed into the classrooms, and overflowed into the corridor where desks were set up. There was no parking provided for bicycles nor a dedicated entrance. They could not use the sporting grounds at night because there were no lights. They were not allocated a school nurse or a vice principal. The extension class was a temporary fix. The standards for an independent school were not applied. The forced relocation of Korean women students to this substandard facility was a blow to their pride and self-respect. Despite the government's denials, this treatment appeared to be simply another instance of discrimination inflicted upon women who had been long regarded disdainfully by their local community.[31]

Birth of the independence movement

The first student council meeting after the extension class opened was flooded with a myriad of complaints. The meeting demanded that the board of education designate the extension class an independent night junior high school. Improvements to facilities could be expected if it was designated an independent school, as well as the appointment of a vice principal and the provision of a sick room. Above all, though, the Korean women wanted their 'equal rights to study' to be acknowledged by the municipal board of education. Hence, the students of Chōei Night Junior High School and the Taiheiji Extension Class started a movement calling for the extension class's independence. The Korean students called this the 'Second Hanshin Education Struggle'. This association with the resistance movement against state power from fifty years earlier confirmed the ethnic frame of the new movement.

The first- and second-generation Korean women who comprised the large majority of the students took a variety of actions, including submitting requests to the municipal board of education, distributing flyers, petitioning and organizing meetings. Television news programs and newspapers began to feature Korean women proudly claiming their 'rights' before the municipal board of education. What follows now is an account of the development of the movement based on teachers' records,[32] newspaper reports and interviews that I conducted with people who were either studying or teaching at the night junior high schools at that time.

In September, the students launched a three-week campaign to demand independence for the extension class, more classrooms, additional teachers and removing the restrictions on non-city dwellers. Seitokai Rengō also collected 50,000 signatures, mainly from students, and submitted a request to the prefectural board of education. The municipal board of education replied at the end of the month that all of these items were 'difficult'. Moreover, they declined to negotiate directly with the students. The students responded with a sit-in (the photo on the front cover). For four days, from the 4th to 7th of October, around 40 students held a sit-in, wearing printed shirts that read, 'We need more teachers', 'We need more classrooms' and 'Independence for Taiheiji', taking turns during working hours, between 8 am and 5 pm. Their teachers and students of other night junior high schools supported them. So did human rights activists, ethnic heritage class instructors at public schools, younger Korean students and local Korean residents. The Seitokai Rengō, Minsokukyō, the Buraku Kaihō Osaka Fumin Kyōtō Kaigi (Buraku Liberation Osaka Resident Joint-Struggle Council) and the Nikkan Mondai o Kangaeru Higashi-Osaka Shimin no Kai ('Nikkan Shimin no Kai', the Higashi-Osaka Citizens' Group for Considering the Problems of Japanese-Korean Relations) all expressed solidarity. Korean restaurants in the neighborhood delivered food. Participants sang *Arirang* (Korean folk song) and called out in unison '*Igyeora*' (meaning 'Win').

The Higashi-Osaka City Board of Education refused to negotiate directly with the students, but agreed to a meeting with the Shikiji Renrakukai on the 8th of October. More than 200 people crowded into the Yaenosato Labor Hall venue, including students, teachers, Seitokai Rengō and people involved in literacy classes.

The crowd called for 'independence of the Taiheiji Extension Class', 'more classrooms', and 'additional teaching staff'. At an associated rally, the students chanted: 'Please do not bully us anymore. Give us love and more teachers.' 'Please understand our pain of having been deprived of words.' 'We are finally able to read. We want to learn more. Please remove the enrollment restriction.'

After two and a half hours of negotiations, the municipal board of education promised to escalate the request to convert the extension class to an independent school to the Osaka Prefectural Board of Education, the authority concerned with the constitution of night junior high schools and teaching staff. The prefectural board responded that, they would talk to the city and make a decision with due consideration of the situation once the city had formulated a plan, but the prospect was 'unlikely under the current circumstances'. Among other things, they concluded that the construction of new classrooms for the Taiheiji Extension Class was not feasible due to space limitations within the facility. Ultimately, no agreement was reached.[33]

The students continued their campaign to publicize the plight of the night junior high schools. In November 1993, the Chōei and Taiheiji held a combined five-day event 'Night Junior High School Festival' to reach out to the local community, to foster wider understanding and to highlight their predicament.[34] A few month later, in February 1994, the Osaka Prefectural Board of Education announced several new conditions of night junior high schools in Osaka Prefecture. First, they stipulated that applicants would not be admitted if acquiring Japanese language and literacy skills was the primary purpose of enrollment. Next, they declared that admissions would be the responsibility of the municipal board of education in an effort to manage enrollments more efficiently. They also set a maximum length of study at nine years, with a transitional rule of three years.

Nine-years appears at first glance to be a sufficient period of study. However, the learning progress of Korean women in Japan can be very slow for a number of reasons. First, some of them are quite elderly, and many of them are busy with household chores and work. Learning takes more time for those people who did not even finish elementary schooling yet are jumping into the junior high school curriculum. Plus, they are frequently absent due to their own ill-health or because they are responsible for caring for family members. Chōei Night Junior High School therefore had a considerable number of students who had been enrolled for more than ten years when the movement started.

With assurances that they would list the independence of the Taiheiji Extension Class as an agenda item, the municipal board of education pressured students who had been enrolled for more than fourteen years to graduate. Consequently, 53 students of Chōei Night Junior High School, some of whom had been studying for up to eighteen years, accepted graduation in March 1994, believing in the independence of the extension class.

However, at the time of their graduation in the spring of 1994, the extension class was not yet independent. The Higashi-Osaka City Board of Education submitted the 'request for an independent school' to the Osaka Prefectural Board of Education on the 27th of March 1994. Hence, it was practically impossible for the extension class to open as an independent school on the 1st of April, the start of the

Photo 3.1: Classroom in Uri Seodang

Source: Taken by the author

school year in Japan. This led to substantial disappointment, anger and distrust among students, and generated more enthusiasm for the movement. The students adopted a range of protest strategies against the municipal board of education. For example, the graduation ceremonies from 1995 and 1998 could not be conducted because they were boycotted by students who were being forced to graduate in accordance with the maximum length of schooling proclamations. These boycotts, however, were quite painful for the Korean women, who had envisioned graduating with congratulations by close family and friends. Letters of protest addressed to the municipal board of education were full of emotions. 'We cannot give up like this. Nor are we going to just sit by in silence. Without independence of Taiheiji, there will not be graduation. We do not come to school for what they call fun or as a pastime.'[35]

Until April 2001, when the independent school finally opened, the student council remained in a difficult situation. Their campaign had achieved no tangible progress despite continued appeals to both the municipal and prefectural boards of education. In fact, as we have seen, the municipal board of education's initial response was to introduce more stringent criteria, such as compelling students who had been in school for 'too long' to graduate. Some students began to complain that they 'cannot study because of the movement'. Student council meetings were regularly bogged down in arguments over the movement's policies. The students inevitably began asking themselves why they ought to study at night junior high schools and how it related to their position in Japanese society.

While they continued pressing the government to create an independent school, they faced an immediate problem of how to educate those Korean women forced to graduate. Supporters of the movement addressed this issue by creating a self-directed educational institution, which they named Uri Seodang (meaning 'our village school'), within the Chōei Night Junior High School (Photo 3.1). Built on a theme of 'learning from learners', Uri Seodang offered a bidirectional interaction in which younger Koreans and Japanese students learn from the experiences and wisdom of the older Korean women, and in turn teach the older women language and literacy skills, rather than the uni-directional model of students learning from teachers. Uri Seodang provided lessons at two locations: Chōei and Taiheiji Night Junior High Schools, each of which was attended by about twenty women who had been active participants in the independence movement. The students of Uri Seodang continued their strong commitment to the independence movement even after being forced to graduate. This commitment spilled over into other aspects of their public life, such that when an incident occurred in which a student of Uri Seodang was verbally abused by a transportation officer, the students ran a protest campaign.[36] As we can see, Uri Seodang is not only a learning institution but is a more generalized institution protecting the interests of Korean women in Japan. It is managed by a governing body consisting of Japanese and Korean members with a public subsidy provided under the lifelong learning framework. Teaching is provided by Japanese teachers and Korean ethnic instructors.

The period from 1998 to 1999 marked a change in the movement after a prolonged stalemate. New negotiations with the government were brokered by Minsokukyō and the Shikiji Renrakukai. During discussions with the latter, especially, the responsibilities of the Higashi-Osaka City Board of Education were gradually clarified. This encouraged renewed efforts to press the prefectural board of education to create an independent school. In April 2001, after eight years of struggling, Taiheiji Night Junior High School opened its door. The Taiheiji Independence Movement came to a fair end with this victory.[37]

Figure 3.7: Correlation chart of 'subaltern counterpublics' around Korean women in Japan

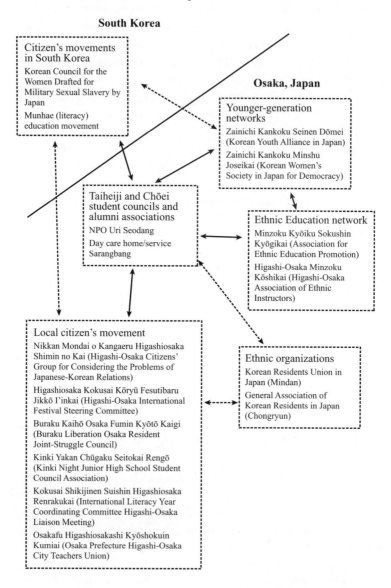

Source: Created by author based on interviews with people involved in the movement and primary sources.

Interaction of various movements and subaltern counterpublics

While students were the direct actors in the Taiheiji Independence Movement, it was also supported by teachers and a variety of social movement organizations. These included the Seitokai Rengō, the teachers' union, as well as solidarity between Japanese and Korean citizens, ethnic organizations and buraku rights campaigners. The Taiheiji Independence Movement brought together a multiplicity of publics centered on Korean women in Japan through the organic interaction of many different social movements from various localities. Figure 3.7 illustrates the subaltern counterpublics of Korean women in Japan with the night junior high schools at the core. Let us now examine the ways that different social movements were involved in the Independence Movement.

First, Seitokai Rengō and the Shikiji Renrakukai played important roles. The former is a federation of student councils of night junior high schools throughout the Kinki region. The latter formed in recognition of the International Literacy Year in 1990 by literacy classes associated with buraku liberation, the Higashi-Osaka City Teachers Union and the student council of the night junior high school. From its inception, the Shikiji Renrakukai operated as a network representing the interests of students and persistently demanding that the municipal board of education should open a second night junior high school in Higashi-Osaka City. The Higashi-Osaka City Teachers Union also played a crucial role in negotiations with the board of education.

The citizen's group Nikkan Shimin no Kai also played a key role in negotiations with government agencies. Nikkan Shimin no Kai was inaugurated in 1977, to protest an incident in which a Korean man from Higashi-Osaka City was incarcerated for political offences while studying in South Korea when the country was governed by a dictatorship. Nikkan Shimin no Kai has a history of active campaigning from the citizen's perspective, focusing primarily on the politics of the Korean Peninsula and the human rights of Koreans in Japan. Its activities include rescuing political prisoners in South Korea, seeking revisions to the Alien Registration Act, providing support to workers in labor disputes with Japanese firms operating in South Korea, and defending the human rights of foreign residents. Gōda Satoru, a representative of Nikkan Shimin no Kai, was a Christian priest who had been building connections with the government through citizen's movements since the 1970s. He was thus able to negotiate with the government in the Taiheiji Independence Movement and became the first representative of the self-directed learning center Uri Seodang.

Korean ethnic organizations, particularly the networks of ethnic education, such as the Higashi-Osaka Minzoku Kōshikai (Higashi-Osaka Association of Ethnic Instructors) and Minsokukyō, were also outspoken advocates of the Taiheiji Independence Movement. The movement drew the attention of later-generation Koreans as 'the fight of *halmoni* (grandmothers)' and became a locus for ethnic solidarity that transcends generations. Uri Seodang and the day care home Sarangbang, both created during the Taiheiji Independence Movement, attracted numerous younger women who were involved in Hancheong and Yeoseonghoe (the Korean Women's Society in Japan for Democracy) to participate as volunteer teachers and paid staff. The dominant ethnic organizations Mindan and Chongryun were not directly involved in the movement, but were nevertheless forces for the government to reckon with as they were connected to other groups that were involved, including Nikkan Shimin no Kai.[38]

Other local social movement organization also endorsed the Independence Movement. These included: the Buraku Kaihō Osaka Fumin Kyōtō Kaigi (Buraku Liberation Osaka Resident Joint-Struggle Council), a federation of twenty-seven organizations including the Buraku Kaihō Dōmei Osaka Furen (Buraku Liberation Movement Osaka Prefectural Association), Rengō Osaka (the Osaka Local of Japanese Trade Union Confederation) and JICHIRO (All-Japan Prefectural and Municipal Workers Union) Osaka Prefectural Headquarters.

As mentioned, the independence movement came to an end upon the achievement of its objective in the spring of 2001. Uri Seodang, though, an offspring of this movement, has continued its activities as an educational institution for Korean women in Japan and as an agency that advocates for their interests. Since 2002, it has organized exchanges with literacy education bodies in South Korea. There is also a social movement in South Korea, Anyang Civil University,[39] campaigning for literacy education for adult women who were not educated because of the Korean War or poverty. Its objective is '*munhae*', meaning liberation from oppression through literacy. Older women in South Korea and Korean women in Japan have much in common; they both experienced colonial rule and war and they both face problems of illiteracy because they are female. Uri Seodang, in conjunction with the night junior high schools in Kansai, has been conducting Japan-South Korea literacy exchanges with Anyang Civil University located on the outskirt of Seoul.[40]

As we can see, the success of the Taiheiji Independence Movement can be attributed to the interaction and mutual support of a variety of social movement organizations based in Kansai. I will now present this conclusion in terms of the theory of subaltern counterpublics. Under the banner of seeking independence for Taiheiji Night Junior High School, Korean women in Japan became politically active, highlighting the unjust racial discrimination which persisted at the roots of their local community. In the course of their campaigning, these women voiced their experiences of ethnic and gendered identities to the local society for the first time in their lives. They raised objections to the social structures that oppressed Koreans in Japan, making demands upon the government as political subjects entitled to civil and social rights. Through this movement, Korean women in Japan who had long been invisible – hidden within families, ethnic organizations and local communities – manifested as social actors for the first time. The sight of *omoni* (mothers) and *halmoni* (grandmothers) fighting in public for their rights shook-up the conventional images of Korean women in Japan.

The mutual interaction between diverse social movement organizations was a critical component of this movement. The public sphere is a conceptual domain composed of multilayered social spaces (Hanada 1996: 30–31). The public sphere where Korean women are social actors is an open, multidimensional and mutable social domain that varies from the dominant ethnic communities in a number of ways. Whereas a public sphere can be defined as a space of discourses that are generated from people over a common set of interests, a community, especially an ethnic community, is a space that shares substantive values and culture and expects singular belonging and loyalty. Whereas community integration is mediated by patriotism and solidarity and requires assimilation/exclusion, a public sphere is an open space that allows multidimensional relationships between diverse organizations and groups (Saitō 2000: 5–7). The social space created through the night junior high school independence movement is but one of multiple subaltern counterpublics; it plays a part in an oppositional public sphere that has been formed by the interactions of multiple movement organizations seeking to enhance the human rights of various minorities in Kansai and Korea. It is, in this sense, a translocal transformative counterpublic.

From a gender perspective, Korean women were situated in social structures in their ethnic community and family that consider men to be superior, which provided very little scope for them to engage in political activities. In the Independence Movement, ethnicity facilitated the formation of a collective identity as Korean women in Japan. Although the perspective of women's liberation may not be readily apparent, the movement domain created around night junior high schools empowered women to be political actors for social change without the usual constrictions of the patriarchal system because of the absence of Korean men.[41] There were many Japanese men involved in the movement, whether as teachers or advocates, but it never occurred that Korean women were subordinate to these men, possibly because ethnicity was more significant than gender in this instance. It appears that it was because the Taiheiji Independence Movement kept a distance from the dominant ethnic organizations that it was able to empower women to become actors in civil society. We might then conclude that Korean women in Japan essentially achieved some degree of liberation from the patriarchy despite the fact that the liberation of women was not addressed by their movement.[42]

4 Life course: Illiteracy and Night Junior High School

Korean women at night junior high school

The previous chapter examined the development of Taiheiji Night Junior High School Independence Movement from the perspective of the interactions between a variety of minority group social movements in the Kansai area. This chapter will explore the life stories of individual Korean women who participated in the Independence Movement, investigating the factors that formed this movement from the micro perspective. An overwhelming majority of the first-generation and prewar-born second-generation Koreans in Japan who study at night junior high school is female. I will therefore analyze issues of illiteracy and school non-attendance in their early life, which is common among these generations of women, examining the life courses leading up to their enrollment in night junior high school in middle age or later. I will focus particularly on the race and class status that have carried over from the colonial to the postcolonial era as well as the gender factors.

Middle-aged and older Korean women accounted for a majority of the students of public night junior high schools in Osaka until the 1990s. Many of them began studying at night junior high school in their late fifties to seventies. Night junior high school was their first schooling experience. Although education was institutionalized in Korea under colonial rule, education was not compulsory there as it was in 'Japan proper' and few people in rural villages could afford to go to school. Thus a significant proportion of the population was illiterate and never attended school. Koreans who migrated to Japan were excluded from learning opportunities due to poverty and work. Nevertheless, poverty and racial discrimination are not sufficient to explain the high rate of illiteracy among those women or their decision late in life to enter night junior high school to address this situation.

Tonomura Masaru estimated that only 10–20% of Korean women in Japan from the 1920s to 1930s could read and understand or had received an education compared to 50–70% of their male counterparts (Tonomura 2004: 80–82). On the Korean Peninsula, in 1930, approximately 64% of Korean men and 82% of women were illiterate (Tonomura 2004: 78). More recently, a 2004 survey by the Zainichi Korian Kōreisha Fukushi o Susumeru Kai (Osaka Association for Advancement of Welfare for Senior Koreans in Japan) of 300 Koreans in Japan over the age of seventy, found that 86.5% of the men could read Japanese passages, but only 29.4% of the women surveyed. If they were strictly tested for comprehension of the passages, no doubt these figure would decline.[1] This study clearly indicates a considerable gender gap in the literacy of Koreans in Japan.

The high rates of illiteracy of Korean women in Japan can be attributed to a gender order which places women second to men and its interaction with the racial and class order that has been shaped since the colonial era. As part of the household survival strategy, men assumed the role of breadwinners while women were expected to perform unpaid work such as household chores, child rearing and nursing care. Scarce educational resources were invested in sons but not daughters. Exclusion from educational opportunities significantly disadvantaged Korean women in their daily lives. Enrollment in night junior high school was an action which they decided for themselves as individuals. Hence, the Taiheiji Independence Movement was a reflection of the multitude of experiences and emotions that those women had accumulated over many years.

I conducted life story research with women who participated in the Taiheiji Independence Movement. Their narratives represent the life courses of Korean women in Japan. The life course, as defined by Iwakami (2003: 34), is 'the trajectory that ties together the various roles an individual pursues through their lifetime'. Humans are born in a particular society and they take on and play a variety of roles as they struggle through life and society. Life course research does not concern the 'lifecycle' point of view in which a biological condition, specifically aging, automatically triggers a switch to the next phase. Life course research uses individuals rather than families as the unit of analysis and focuses on how individuals have lived their 'roles', regardless of whether they were actively chosen or passively accepted. Moreover, life course research emphasizes how individuals struggle through life as they interact with society while being subject to the norms imposed by social-historical circumstances (Iwakami 2003: 32–36). The life course approach is helpful in analyzing the illiteracy and lack of schooling of Korean women in Japan as well as their decision to enter night junior high school late in life.

This chapter analyzes the life stories I collected for the period from October 2001 to June 2005 from fourteen Korean women who vigorously participated in the Taiheiji Independence Movement or were perceived to have done so, with the cooperation of Uri Seodang, a learning organization for elderly Korean women in Japan. The profiles of the research participants are set out in Table 4.1. I also conducted interviews with night junior high school teachers, activists, subsequent-generation Korean women in Japan, as well as officials in the Higashi-Osaka City Board of Education and Department of Health and Welfare.

The chapter will explore the gender factor and its intersection with racial and class factors in light of the life stories of the women who took part in the movement. The alienation of women from the public sphere and their illiteracy-associated dependence on family will also be examined. Finally, I will explore the reasons for their enrollment in night school later in life by focusing on changes in the gender relations within the family and 'bargaining with patriarchy'.

A remark should be made here on the use of the names of the research participants. In sociological research, it is common practice to use aliases to protect the privacy of participants. I have followed this convention in the papers I have previously published. However, during the prepapration of this book, I received a request to use real names from Uri Seodang, an organization formed by these women and their supporters, on the grounds that there was special meaning for the women engaged in Taiheiji Independence Movement to do so under their Korean names – their 'real names'. Koreans in Japan generally use Japanese names rather than their Korean names in daily lives for fear of discrimination. Most of the women who participated in my study had lived most of their lives behind Japanese names so as to go unnoticed as much as possible. Thus, identifying themselves by their Korean names during this movement connoted their defiance of the local community's oppressive norms – they were going to reclaim 'their own names'. Having considered

Table 4.1 Profile of research participants

Full name	Generation	Year of migration to Japan	Age of migration to Japan	Schooling prior to night junior high school	Age of enrollment in night junior high school	Activity in student council	Work status at the time of the movement
Oh Bok-deok	First	1941	18	None	68	Class representative	Home-based piecework
Park In-seok	First	1945	13	None	55	President of the student council, secretary and other student council officer	Home manufacturing
Shin Yun-jeong	First	1948	27	*Seodang* (Korea)	72	—	—
Park Yun-gyeong	First	1938	16	*Seodang*, evening classes (Korea)	58	President of the student council, President of the alumni association	Home manufacturing
Im Yong-gil	First	1931	8	Evening classes (Japan)	57	—	Home-based piecework (product finishing)
Kim Jeong-rye	First	1939	21	None	61	—	Home-based piecework (umbrella manufacturing)
Kang Woo-ja	Second	N/A	N/A	One year in elementary school	53	President of the student council, President of the Seitokai Rengō,	Garment piecework
Jin Soon-nam	First	1932	6	None	59	Class representative	Home-based piecework (rubber)
Lee Geo-ryeon	First	1940	18	None	62	President of the student council	—
Lee Gap-saeng	First	1942	18	*Seodang* (Korea)	67	—	Mechanic

Life course: Illiteracy and Night Junior High School

Chung Nam-seon	First	1928	12	Evening classes (Japan)	60	—	Part-time shoe manufacturing
Kim Ok-ryeon	First	1940	19	Regular school (one year), evening classes (Korea)	70	—	—
Song Wol-seon	First	1948	22	Chongryun's literacy class	70	—	—
Ahn Gwi-soo	First	1932	8	None	70	Vice-President and President of the Seitokai Rengō, President of the alumni association	

the politics surrounding the names of Koreans in Japan, plus the fact that the real names of my research participants have already been exposed by mass media reports, I decided to honor their request and use their real names in this book.

The gender factor in illiteracy and non-attendance at school

The participants were aged in their late sixties to late eighties, with those in their eighties accounting for the majority at the time of the life story research. All were first-generation except for one second-generation Korean born prewar. When they enrolled in night junior high school, five were in their fifties, five in their sixties, and four were in their seventies. When the Taiheiji Independence Movement was initiated in 1993, a large number of them were in their seventies.

Seven of them – that is, half of the participants – were originally from Jeju Province in Korea. Four were from Gyeongsang Province, two were from Jeolla Province and one was from Chungcheong Province. Most of them came from farming families. They migrated to Japan at between six and twenty-seven years of age, but most of them (ten) were less than twenty years of age. They migrated for work or education purposes or to join other family members, with the exception of one who was a refugee from the Jeju April 3 Uprising (1948).[2] All fourteen participants either were or had been married, including those widowed and divorced. This is indicative of how significant the marriage system is in the social status of Korean women in Japan.

At the time of the research, five lived alone and the rest lived with others, typically either their husband or a son and his wife. Four of those who lived alone had at least one of their children's families living in close proximity and had some interaction on a daily basis. Eight out of fourteen had engaged in home-based piecework, part-time work or helped in home manufacturing. Their jobs were typical of the Korean neighborhood in Osaka, such as making shoes, bags, rubber goods or clothing. Most first-generation Koreans in Japan were excluded from the national pension system due to the Nationality Clause; therefore, many of my research participants struggled to make a living and continued working into old age. Hence, they barely managed to attend night school because of the numerous difficulties they had to deal with, including paid work as well as caring for family members and their own health issues.

They typically spoke Korean in their local dialect rather than the 'standard Korean' spoken around Seoul and Pyongyang as their mother tongue. Although they had all lived in Japan longer than they had in Korea, their level of comprehension of Japanese language varied widely; some were capable of only the most basic conversations. The first-generation women were distant from the mainstream Japanese society despite spending their lives in Japan for several reasons: harsh living conditions, swamped by daily work left them no time to learn Japanese; there were no provisions for Japanese language education for Koreans by the Japanese government; and residing in Korean neighborhood and practicing family-centered living provided few opportunities to engage with native Japanese.

A large proportion of first- and second-generation women who were of school age during the colonial period are unable to read and write Japanese even if they can speak it. It is not uncommon to find cases in which they were never taught to read and write either Japanese or Korean. The one participant who was born in Japan has higher communication skills in Japanese than Korean; nevertheless, her schooling was limited to only a short period in elementary school due to poverty and her reading and writing abilities are inadequate at times.

Being illiterate inevitably means being dependent on others – even on those who discriminate based on gender or race – to read what is written, explain the meaning of texts and to write on one's behalf, even simple messages and personal letters. Illiterate people are unable to publicize the issue and plight of illiteracy in written forms for the very reason that they cannot read and write. It has even been claimed that women do not need to learn to write since all that is expected of them is to stay home and do domestic chores, not go 'outside' to work. In reality, of course, many women worked long hours for low wages but are not recognized as contributing to earning a living.

Eight of the fourteen participants in my research attended some kind of educational or learning institution before night junior high school. Of those eight, three had attended private traditional schools in Korean known as *seodang*,[3] which taught reading and writing Hangeul as well as arithmetic. One participant who went to elementary school during the Japanese empire in Korea attended for less than one year. Five learned Hangeul or Japanese in evening classes or Choryun / Chongryun's literacy classes. The other six did not have any formal education at all. Many of them missed out on school because they were women, and therefore were excluded from opportunities to learn reading and writing. Let us picture this in their life stories.

Oh Bok-deok was born into a farming family in the South Jeolla Province in the early 1920s. She has three brothers and three sisters.[4] The brothers who are more than ten years older than her went to *seodang* and elementary school, while her younger brother, who is five years younger, went to elementary school. Neither she nor any of her sisters had the opportunity to go to school.

> In the whole village, there was only one girl that went to school. She was a daughter of the village head and her family [was so rich that they] even had a clock in their house. I can never forget her name and that field day.
> – Did you learn Hangeul?
> I used to ask my little brother about studies. As for Hangeul, I didn't go to school but *oppa* [older brother] and *unni* [older sister] taught me and my friends at home. Our parents didn't want us to go to school. They don't want girls to study. Girls don't need to study. They looked down on us all.

The first-generation women mostly came from poor families in rural villages in Korea. For as long as she can remember, Oh Bok-deok was expected to contribute important labor to help with domestic chores and farming work. After she married, she had six children of her own and spent several decades tending to household duties, raising children, caring for her husband's family while attending to family business or doing home-based piecework to alleviate hardship, even if only slightly. The gender norm that women do not need education that leads to social and economic improvement because they are expected to devote themselves to the family has denied women learning opportunities. Women were kept from learning to write for the sake of maintaining the male-dominated family system.

The following comments were collected during the life story interview. 'Men were sent to school in Korea but women weren't allowed to because they would write sad letters to their family if they learned how to write.' 'If women learned how to write, they might write home to complain.' 'It would cause trouble for the family.'

Women who are described as 'having no home in three worlds' obey male family members throughout their lives as a daughter, a wife and then a mother and are in a subordinate position within the husband's family. Oh Bok-deok says women who were barred from going to school were envious of girls who studied at school and she cannot forget the field day she watched from far away. They have kept strong desires to go to school hidden away for several decades. However, later in life, they happened upon night junior high schools and decided to try to realize that dream of studying.

In both Korea and Japan, it is expected that women should play an active role in the private domain while men should do the same in the public domain. A family in Korea is a social group organized based on male lineage and which obliges women to be subject to men. Women's social status is established through their family, which is formed around men. In addition to unpaid domestic labor, women from poor agricultural households and lower-class families in cities had no choice but to also engage in wage labor (Lee Hyo-jae 1997, Moon Ok-pyo 1997). Thus women had neither time nor money for education. As a result, they remained illiterate and suffered great inconveniences in their everyday lives as well as low self-esteem.

Kim Pu-ja analyzed the prewar education system from the perspectives of race and gender. In colonial Korea, elementary education akin to Japan's was developed in the 1920s and the 'institutionalization of schooling' progressed. However, it was different from Japan in that education was not compulsory and racial inequality was institutionalized such that Korean children were charged higher tuition rates than their Japanese counterparts. Funding for school-related expenses including tuition fees, textbooks, school supplies and travel expenses was hard to come by, especially for families in rural villages. Meanwhile in Japan, the compulsory education system was established and the children of Koreans in Japan were granted eligibility in the 1930s. However, there were conditions: an application was required for enrollment and a school had to have sufficient room to accommodate Korean children. In other words, despite establishing a modern education system in both Korea and Japan after Japan's annexation of Korea, Koreans were shunned from educational opportunities through deliberate racial inequality. When combined with the male supremacy that characterized pre-colonial Korea, Korean women's schooling opportunities were extremely limited. In many respects, the institutionalized discrimination of the modern education system meant that the inequality became even more extreme than when *seodang* was the main educational institution (Kim Pu-ja 2005).

Although they were denied an education by the convergence of the hierarchy, racism, class and gender distinctions, the women who participated in my study expressed no anger about not being able to go to school. That was 'just the way things were' in the context of the time governed by the Confucian order in which parents' decisions were absolute. The women had themselves internalized the gender norms of the time and thus have no perspective from which to view their lack of schooling opportunities as 'discrimination against women'. For example, in the case of Park In-seok (born in the 1930s, from Jeju Province), her older and younger brothers learned classic Chinese scripts at *seodang* but she and her older sister were not allowed to attend *seodang*. Writing belonged to men and in the words of Park In-seok, 'a man is not a man if he can't write'. According to her, this is true particularly for the eldest son because they have a role in *jesa* (Korean memorial service), which requires them to inscribe with ink ancestors' names on spirit tablet made of paper called *jibang*. This is just one example of how women internalized a gender norm that associates literacy with masculinity.

Alienation in the host society and dependence on family

Having said that, internalized gender norms and a desire for literacy are two different things. Park In-seok migrated to Japan at the age of thirteen to go to school, expecting to be able to rely on her sister. She at first thought of entering the first year of a regular school but later decided not to do so, after having heard that 'Koreans are made fun of and doomed to have a miserable experience'. Despite hoping that the chance of going to school would be better in Japan than in a rural village in Korea, she gave up on the idea in the face of racial discrimination. Park In-seok enjoyed looking at signs around town, television and newspapers 'and yet could not read'. She said:[5]

> Until I went to night junior high school, I wasn't able to write and what I did was '*darōyomi*' [reading by guessing].[6] I couldn't piece together or understand [the meaning when looking at words] but tried to guess and remember them together as a set. My sister subscribed to a newspaper even though she couldn't read.

Life course: Illiteracy and Night Junior High School 121

– Did you not go to Chongryun's mothers' literacy class (for learning Hangeul)?

I know there was such a thing but I worked until eleven at night and had children. There was one in the neighborhood so I wanted to go though. I wanted to go back to Korea, too. I wanted to learn how to write, no matter what. I was hoping they would let me in at elementary school of *urihakgyo* [referring to Korean school run by Chongryun in Japan]. That was my wish. But when my children grew up, I was already in my mid-fifties. I thought I was finished. Then, I saw night junior high school on TV.[7] I looked at the faces [on television] and they were all Korean.

Women who could not afford to learn reading and writing used their imagination to read texts they could not read and dreamt of studying writing at school some day while sending their children to school. The inconveniences caused by illiteracy are beyond description but the foremost challenge is that they could not obtain critical information. When shopping, while monetary transaction may not pose an issue, the assessment of the quality of products is difficult since they cannot read the labels. They cannot understand mail articles, notices from the neighborhood association or letters from their children's schools without asking their husband or children. Some have had their foreign resident registration expire after accidentally throwing away the notification card because they could not read it. Others absented themselves from visitation days and parent meetings at their children's schools because they did not want their inability to write to be exposed.

Similarly, illiteracy significantly limits those women's areas of activities. Challenges include not being able to use ticket vending machines at train stations, identify their own location or distinguish between local and express trains. Going to the bathroom while being outside home is another potential issue. Not being able to read the signs makes locating a lavatory laborious. Some women have even entered the men's room by mistake. Since beyond their neighborhood is a 'different world', they become reluctant to travel far without a companion. That is to say, illiteracy strips women of autonomy, increasing their dependence, particularly on family. For instance, they need a family member to accompany them whenever they are going to an unknown place or a public office for government services.

Another issue is a feeling of alienation that arises from the inability to access knowledge about the society in which they live. 'Written words were my enemy.' 'Schools have many windows so that they can see the world well.' Those are the words Park In-seok wrote around seventeen years after she entered night junior high school. Illiteracy had hitherto segregated her from the society around her. The school that taught her to read and write was an open window onto the society in which she lived. Illiteracy not only creates inconveniences but also restricts one's potential for participating in society.

Now let us explore how my informants felt about a family-centered life. Shin Yun-jeong (born in the 1920s, from Jeju Province) had only a little learning experience of writing at a *seodang* in her early childhood. She says she did not go to school because she did not enjoy it despite coming from a relatively affluent family which was open to schooling women. She did not recognize the importance of study as a child but later became envious of her brothers who could read and write fluently. After getting married in Jeju, she migrated to Japan at the age of twenty-seven with her husband. She said she lived as a full-time homemaker who barely helped out in the family business or engaged in work outside the home since her husband ran a successful business in Japan.

> I mostly stayed inside home until I entered night junior high school. At home I had no trouble because it was only *urimal* (our language) [that they spoke]. I didn't understand Japanese... I learned Japanese by asking my husband, [pointing at and asking about] newspaper headlines and things like that. I couldn't understand TV [even though she could converse in Japanese]. I am interested in politics. My hobby is to watch live broadcasts of Diet proceedings. I asked my husband whenever I didn't understand. I was tormented that I couldn't understand. I regretted I could have gone to school when I was a child... It was located in an extension classroom but I had fun [when she enrolled in night junior high school in the early 1970s]. I enjoyed teachers' stories and social science classes. I attended all the classes, even in the rain or wind. You can't register things when you are seventy. But if you persist long enough, you can learn them eventually. I wanted to go to part-time high school (after graduation

of night junior high school) as well if I had been younger but my children objected because the school was far away.[8]

Her narrative was filled with a strong interest in the Japanese society in which she had spent her life as well as regret about not being able to read and write. Because of her desire to understand the society, the language barrier stood in her way, causing a sense of alienation and frustration.

Shift in gender role and night junior high school

The demographics of the Korean women who went to night junior high school is clearly different to the other groups who typically comprise the student bodies of night junior high school. These include the buraku (descendants of outcast communities); newcomers from Asia; repatriates from countries such as China; returned Japanese emigrants and their descendants; and refugees. The 1970s and 1980s saw a spate of public night junior high schools being opened in response to civil movements. It was in this context that a large number of middle-aged and older Korean women enrolled. Their enrollment was not, however, a specific intention or objective of the social movements. Rather, it just so happened that the period in which the night junior high schools proliferated coincided with the time when first-generation and prewar-born second-generation Korean women in Japan reached a stage in life in which they were freed from family obligations to some extent. Regardless, becoming an 'adult junior high school student' requires considerable determination. Furthermore, there was little chance that the efforts of middle-aged and older women to complete the requirements for junior high school graduation would be rewarded with greater social status or financial remuneration. This raises questions about the mind-set of the Korean women who were driven to enroll in night junior high school in their later stage of life.

Consider Park Yun-gyeong, for example. Park Yun-gyeong was born in the 1920s in a rural village in Gyeongsang Province. Her brothers went to *seodang*, but her parents could not afford to provide all eight children with standard education, so the girls did not go. Park Yun-gyeong worked on the family farm from the age of five and later attended evening classes, but only for about two years. She migrated to Japan at the age of sixteen to study but married a Korean man three months later. Since then, she had worked incessantly; providing care for her seven children as well as her husband's parents; looking after her husband's brothers; and engaging in family business, peddling and doing home-based piecework. Throughout all of this, she says, even when she was working so much that she had no time for sleep, her eagerness to study never wavered. Let's look at her narrative at length.

– Was your family [in Korea] not opposed to you going to Japan to study?

Halmae (grandmother in the Gyeongsang dialects) and mother and everyone were in Gyeongsang, but the passport (travel permit) suddenly arrived [as arranged by her brother] and there weren't many days until the travel date. I said I wanted to go but when the day came my heart began racing. I didn't tell any of my friends, except my best friend. I told her how I happened to go. We lived in the countryside. I went into town and stayed there the day before to go to Pusan. And we rode a bus and caught a train to Pusan from there. Up until then, I was with my mum and stayed at an inn with her. Next morning I parted with my mother and went with a relative. Her husband's brother was someone that had gone to Japan and come back, so she took me to Pusan...I was also going to come back in one year. I was just going to pack up embroidery work and notebooks I used for study and bring those home with me...

I married on the third month [of coming to Japan]. Like I said, I came to study but when I got here in Japan it was full of soldiers practicing everywhere. The preparation was done and I got married in April. Back then, that wasn't considered fast at all. In the old days, there were not even arranged meetings. It was just that my husband's father was a friend of my distant relative. And my older brother told this person that his sister [referring to herself] came from his hometown. Then that story reached my husband's father's ears. A young female relative came over and things like that. That's how it started (laugh). There was no introduction or whatsoever in the old days. As long as you find out about your place in Korea (referring to hometown) and surname, it's all good to go. They will know everything, like if you are a *yangban*.[9] So I didn't know his face or anything.

– Did you have a wedding ceremony in Japan?

Yes. I had my brother and sister-in-law, two children and some distant relatives as well. We wore formal kimono.

– You had a Japanese-style wedding ceremony. How did you feel about that?

Traditional Korean costume was banned then. If you walked in it, you would get water poured on you or might get your back slashed. In my hometown, apparently people thought that was my intention [to get married] when I left (laugh) although I came with an intention to study.

– Did you go to school in Japan?

No. Not a chance. When I came over, soldiers were everywhere. They practiced in the parks and rice fields and everywhere. Then slowly the war began and study was the last thing I could do. For a very long time, I wore a kimono and just lived everyday life.

– What is your husband like?

He was twenty. One year apart from me. At that time he was in a steel mill. There weren't many jobs in the mill, too. We sewed those field caps, they are called, those ones worn by soldiers, on a sewing machine as our own business. But they said there was going to be compulsory recruitment. So he [her husband] went to my brother's factory. He came to Japan when he was eleven. Now he can read and write classic Chinese scripts. He went to Japanese school. We have seven children. All of them are married. My husband is the only child. So we were desperate just to make a living. Just when the war started, we were going in and out of a bomb shelter, taking two others along. I was with my parents-in-law but my father-in-law passed away here so my husband and I went to South Korea to have another funeral... There was no choice but to work and feed ourselves because there was nothing to eat. Mother-in-law was sick, grandmother-in-law passed away and father-in-law passed during the war. Then, we cared for the sick mother-in-law for thirty-eight years. I have never been to a movie yet, not that I'm not interested either.

After the war, even men didn't have jobs. Everyone was empty-handed. So, really, as a bit of handiwork, we sewed pants or children's shoes on sewing machine. We used to bring things from Tsuruhashi but I didn't dare to ride a bicycle. Of course we couldn't afford bus fees. We started piecework, working on sewing machine at home. We asked our neighbor if there was any work for men and we were told there was some place you could work on sewing machine and that's how we started our handbags. Back then there was nothing so we made hard nylon into something like a children's diaper. We had seen something similar and he was good with machines. But then we weren't paid for it. So we had no food and we were in a mess. We had a very tough time. That continues to today. For over fifty years. During that time, it was all about food. We bought rice from different black markets and sold it to wholesale merchants. And because that's the rice from the black market, it was over when the police came. You would be taken to the police station. Everyone would go to buy it before the police came. Other than that, we bought starch and made *miso* candy and sold them wholesale. We did all sorts of things. But after doing this and doing that, nothing worked so we ended up with handbags...

He was once waiting for a ship to go back [to North Korea] but I went to stop him. I was prepared to have a quarrel. So no one [from the family] has gone. There was a time everyone thought of going back once all together because we had such a tough time here [in Japan]. Then we wouldn't have to worry about food. But I was dead set against it. Because if you calculate my age, I was already past thirty and I finally had learned that much Japanese since coming to Japan after all those years. If I went over to North Korea then, I would have to start from nothing all over again. I don't have any siblings there and although it may be called my homeland, it's actually not home at all for me.

Park Yun-gyeong's narrative includes a detailed description of migration, marriage and family-centered living in Japan. The economic insecurity she describes is typical of the lives of many Koreans in Japan who found themselves at the bottom of the economic structure as a result of racial discrimination. She gave birth to and reared seven children while caring for her husband's parents. Now she has twenty-one grandchildren. It was notable that she spoke with satisfaction about a life in which she worked herself to the bone, dedicating herself to her family as a 'mother,' 'wife' and 'daughter-in-law'. While family care work is imposed upon women in many societies, in the case of Korean women in Japan, the burden on women seems to be relatively increased by the sequence of colonial rule in Korea and racial discrimination in Japan. Under those circumstances, 'going to school' could only be a dream for her. Hence, when late in her life she found out about the

Life course: Illiteracy and Night Junior High School

possibility of attending night junior high school, she immediately took action.

> I was fifty-eight when I entered night junior high school. I didn't know about the night (junior high) school. I thought I had no luck with study and just kept working so I didn't know what was going on outside. I hear this person [pointing at the night junior high school teacher] was handing out many flyers (to promote night junior high school) but I didn't receive any of them. My son told me, a Japanese elderly lady in the neighborhood was attending night junior high school. I had no idea. I wondered where this night junior high school was. So I went to look for it on my own, then I was told to go to the Board of Education but I had no idea where the Board of Education was. I had never been there. So I asked around and looked for it. Patience has kept me going (to night junior high school) until now. Don't you think I'm stubborn? So the school knows me for twenty-five years already. But I work late everyday at home. Even after I go to school, I come home and I work again until twelve o'clock. I try to sleep a little bit after everyone has gone to sleep. So, it has been a good number of years but I haven't studied at the desk much. I never missed school though.
>
> – Was there no objection from your family?
>
> No one was against it. For me, now that my parents-in-laws passed away, the term of service was over and my children finished school, I thought it was my turn. It was my long-awaited dream. We extended the house because it was too small but there was still no space to sit down. Back then (electric) fuses used to blow so often. But even that condition was a luxury for me. You know, we are used to hardship ever since we were kids. When I started going to school, because my eldest son was getting married and things like that, I opened a small shop. So I would leave around nine in the morning with a packed lunch and go straight to school after work. It would be past nine at night when I returned home. I would check on how it was going and if it looked busy, I had no time to have dinner. I worked again and then had small dinner past ten o'clock. Now, I am healthy, all my children are independent and I own a house so my wishes came true.
>
> – Did you know there were many Korean women at night junior high school?
>
> Like I said, I didn't know anything at all. Really, I never went out. There was no TV like today and we didn't have a radio because it would

get in the way of work. I got no flyer either. I came to know everything only after I visited school and thought I had to join in with everyone and work hard.

Park Yun-gyeong enrolled in Chōei Night Junior High School in the early 1970s, shortly after the school opened its doors. When she discovered the night junior high school, she was comparatively less burdened in terms of roles in domestic work, child rearing and nursing care since her children had become independent and her husband's parents had passed away. Nevertheless, she was not completely free of housework or work outside the home when she entered Chōei Night Junior High School. She attended night junior high school for over twenty years by managing her time minutely to cope with study and household responsibilities simultaneously. I met her on a daily basis as part of the participant observation in Sarangbang, a day care home, and in fact she seemed to ensure that all of the household chores including preparing meals for her husband were thoroughly performed, returning home a number of times while she visited Sarangbang during the day and studied at Uri Seodang at night. She says that her husband is a quiet person who does not interfere with what she's doing; nonetheless, it might be said that she secured her 'freedom' to attend night junior high school by flawlessly completing her duties as a 'housewife'. More important, it seems, is her position as a 'mother-in-law', although it was not directly mentioned in the narrative. As a 'mother-in-law, she is in a position to delegate a major part of family responsibilities and roles to her 'daughters-in-law' who lived in her neighborhood with her sons, instructing them to deal with various affairs. Women face a prolonged period of life in which they are subordinate to their husband's family after marriage. However, it is also true that giving birth to sons who eventually marry and start their own families can confer a relatively comfortable position on a 'mother-in-law'. As Park Yun-gyeong's story reveals, the possibility for Korean women in Japan to enroll in night junior high school later in life is closely related to changes in their position within the family.

To begin learning at night junior high school late in life involves disadvantages that would not have been present when they were younger, such as fading memory, deteriorating health, reduced income and new duties caring for grandchildren. Class times at night junior high school are generally from around five in the evening until nine at night and the curriculum is designed on the assumption that students will attend school every week day, demanding extensive effort and self-discipline as well as cooperation from family members for older women. The older Korean women have been rising to this challenge – whatever the difficulties may be – in order to realize the dreams of 'studying at school' which they had harbored for many years.

Bargaining with patriarchy

The burden of domestic reproductive labor becomes lighter as women age. Other barriers to studying can be removed with the assistance of their children and spouses. In most cases, the greatest obstacle to studying encountered by Korean women in Japan is their husbands, because women's engagement in the public sphere is a significant deviation from the norm for women as defined by the patriarchy.

Confucianism, which was the ruling principle of Korea during the Joseon dynasty, acknowledged that men and women are mutually complementary, yet stipulated that a woman was merely a dependent member of the family formed by a man. Women were kept out of the public sphere, and indoctrinated with the belief that the only appropriate way to enrich their lives is to fulfill their family duties as a daughter-in-law, wife and mother. These gender norms were carried over from colonial Korean society directly into the lives of Koreans in Japan. From the historical perspective, although men are formally placed at the head of household, in reality, women have often been active in the public sphere through employment and other activities, especially during the colonial period when Korean men experienced a substantial diminution in their social position. Nevertheless, patriarchy has persisted as the norm, exerting a profound impact on the lives of Korean women in Japan. Hence, women seeking to enter night junior high school had to confront the patriarchy. That typically meant facing their husbands.

I will examine the negotiations that occurred between husbands and wives over entry to night junior high school in light of the concept of 'bargaining with patriarchy'. Kandiyoti (1988) is critical of the tendency to regard the term 'patriarchy'[10] as a monolithic concept of male dominance, pointing out that there are various forms of patriarchy formed by the intimate inner workings of culturally and historically distinct arrangements between the genders. Furthermore, she observes that women do not just take passive roles in patriarchal oppression, but employ various resistance strategies within a set of concrete constraints, varying according to class, caste and ethnicity/race. She calls these various resistance strategies 'bargaining with the patriarchy' (Kandiyoti 1988: 274–5). The women who participated in my research were engaged in various forms of 'bargaining with the patriarchy' as they negotiated their desires to attend night junior high school with their husbands.

All fourteen research participants were married, widowed or separated. Half of the women were either widowed or separated by the time of their entry to night junior high school – which appears to be quite significant, even after taking women's longer life expectancy into account. Moreover, of those seven, two enrolled in night junior high school within a year or two of losing their husbands.

The other seven were still married to their husbands at the time of enrollment. Of these, four had their husband's approval to enroll while three went despite their husbands' objections. This highlights that the relationship with the husband was the main hurdle that had to be overcome before these women could study at night junior high school.

The following case studies will examine how women bargained with their husbands over enrollment in night junior high school in concrete terms. As Kandiyoti (1988) argued, the patriarchal bargains put powerful influence on the shaping of women's gendered subjectivity, the potential for and specific forms of women's resistance in the face of oppression. In the case of Taiheiji Independence Movement, the women's experiences of bargaining with patriarchy influenced the shaping of their active resistance against the Board of Education on its decision to send half the students to a new but poorly equipped school. In order to facilitate understanding this bargaining process, I have included information about the couples' relationships prior to the issue of night school arising, as well as their relationships to other ethnic organizations.

Case 1: Enrollment against objection from husband

Im Yong-gil (born in the 1920s, from Jeju Province) migrated to Japan at the age of eight with her father. She attended evening classes when she was seventeen for a year and learned Japanese there. After leaving evening classes due to moving house, she attended Korean literacy class run by *aka* (communist) for three months. She married her husband at the age of twenty. Her husband had finished high school in Japan and was a hard worker but suffered from poor health. Im Yong-gil therefore helped him to earn a living with home-based piecework including attaching bases to sandals and working with a sewing machine. She entered night junior high school at the age of fifty-seven. The following is her narrative.[11]

> I wanted to go to school all my life. I found out about night junior high school from a newspaper and that's how I came to enroll in Tennōji [Night Junior High School]. I had kept it a secret from my family so I was caught by surprise when they sent documents to my house. When Chōei opened, I moved from Tennōji to Chōei. I entered Chōei when I was sixty. That was after I married off all my children. I did piecework at home with sewing machine until I was sixty-seven.
>
> At the end of every month, my husband would nag. He would make sarcastic comments such as '[by studying so much,] are you going to be a lawyer? Or do you want to be a prosecutor?' He did me a favor and went to the government office to get a certificate issued when I was going to enter Chōei. He didn't oppose it at the time of the enrollment but it was after I started going to school that he constantly complained about how I wasn't able to graduate in three years and how we were strapped for money. I kept going for five or six years but later ended up quitting night school because I was too annoyed by my husband.
>
> After my husband died when I was sixty-seven, I entered night school again. I graduated six years ago. Now I'm living alone. I'm happy. When I attended Chōei, I joined a women-only group called *gye*[12] and work was busy but I had fun. I enjoyed listening to teachers' stories and social science and math were my favorites. I couldn't make friends at night junior high school because I had work though…I attended Mindan only when they had events because I didn't understand the language. My husband was the president of the association of Koreans from our village in Jeju and attended relatives' gatherings often, too. I also dropped in more or less once a month but it was like a meeting of elite men. In Jeju, men are sent to school and do not work. Work was everything for me. It was like

my husband was working under me [as Im Yong-gil was mostly in charge of their business]. I knew some Mindan people but my network is from night school. When I went to junior high, all I did was study and couldn't make many friends. I think I only started talking with them when I came to Sarangbang. Now I'm feeling freer than ever before...I joined *gye* after I became alone after my husband's death. We are all women and we go on trips and hot springs together. There are about thirty of us.

Im Yong-gil could not freely engage in activities outside the home when her husband was alive. Not only was she busy with work but also, and more importantly, she was restricted by her husband. Her husband was actively involved in ethnic organization activities and keen on socializing with fellow Korean men. At the same time, though, he frowned upon his wife having relationships outside the home such as going to night junior high school. When she enrolled in Tennōji Night Junior High School the first time, she did so secretly in order to avoid friction with her husband. She even gave up going to night junior high school for a while, as his sarcastic remarks (among other things) were affecting their relationship. But she reenrolled in night junior high school following his death. She seems to have met many fellow Korean women at night junior high school and enjoyed interacting with them.

In another case, Kim Jeong-ye (born in the 1910s, from Jeolla Province) got married at the age of eighteen and migrated to Japan in her early twenties with her small son, expecting to rely on her husband, who had already migrated to Japan.[13] Her husband had already passed away before the interview.

My husband came to Japan first and worked at a bar. We also ran a barbeque restaurant for around three years. My husband was a big drinker. There was a time when he lost three million yen. When I was younger, I had a hard time with my husband's drinking, women and gambling. I wanted to die but when I saw the faces of my children sleeping, I couldn't do it. He worked as a [recycling] collector until he was eighty-four. Then he passed away eight years ago at the age of ninety-six. Since my husband passed, my four sons have been sending me money. The rent is about 110,000 yen. I don't receive a pension but Higashi-Osaka City gives me 10,000 yen[14] every month. I have a health condition but I'm optimistic and happy.

Life course: Illiteracy and Night Junior High School 133

– When did you get married?

When I was eighteen. It was the third marriage for my husband. I had heard he was twenty-five but he was thirty-three. He came to see my face but I didn't see him [when she was in Korea before marriage]. I didn't know it was his third marriage. I wouldn't have married him if I had known. Who would? Even when I was beaten, I took it on the chin because I didn't want to bring disgrace to my family. We had a memorial service for the first one [of his wives] for as long as sixty years. I asked [my husband] whose memorial service it was; initially, he didn't tell me. I met his children [from his first wife] who were nervous because their mother changed twice too. I found out everything after I came to Japan.

– Your husband was in Japan to begin with but came to South Korea from Japan to get married and then you came over to Japan. Is that right?

That's right. I lived at my parents' place [in Korea] for three years [after marriage]. I gave birth to my son, too. [She received] letters from my mother because my father could write. Until I was thirty-five, I put up with it [her husband]. I started to talk back when I was thirty-seven. Our children were unharmed but I didn't have friends and had a tough time. I couldn't tell my parents. I couldn't go back with a miserable face on. The war ended and a ship arrived three days after I lost my daughter. [As she planned to go back to her hometown,] a fortune-telling person told me that I was going to be all alone if I went to South Korea and I was disheartened. But I am glad I didn't go. There would have been nothing for me there.

– Did you not have a connection with Mindan? How about Buinhoe?

I am a member of Mindan but haven't done anything. I have never been to Buinhoe either. I couldn't go out when my husband was home. Not even thirty minutes.

– Did you not attend any gatherings of some sorts?

I did when ethnic schools were closed down [referring to the Hanshin Education Struggle]. I was waving flags. Mindan's refusal of fingerprinting demonstration and local suffrage movement, too. Mindan required at least one person to partake [per household] so either my husband or I went to participate.

– Did you help your husband's work?

I have never helped his work either. I just did things around the house. We attended neighborhood association meetings as a couple, too. We had to be always together as a married couple...My youngest child found out about the junior high school from a newspaper and told me about it. Chōei Night Junior High School it was. My husband got angry whenever I went to night junior high school. He kept nagging that I shouldn't be going. He went to *seodang* for a bit but never went to school and all he could do was to write a little bit of Chinese characters. He was jealous because he couldn't write. He never entered the school...If I was late coming home even just a little bit, he would be waiting outside. There was this one time he was looking inside the classroom from outside. He suspected I had another man. If I had taken him to school with me, it would have been such an embarrassment. I went to night junior high school for about twenty years but I only attended ten years' worth of classes. Because of things to do, my husband, piecework I was doing at home and also I had to draw water at five o'clock. I worked on piecework from eight to twelve every night. So I would forget so quickly at first. Finally I managed to be able to write my name and address. I could understand train ticket inspection and signposts. My husband would say 'lucky you, you can read'. Because I wasn't allowed to go outside alone, it was always two of us. At his deathbed, he said 'I have put you through a tough time'. The funeral was done at the temple across from our place, the Japanese style. We didn't have many Korean acquaintances. I was surprised there were so many Koreans like me in Japan when I went to night junior high school.

In this case, there was a tendency for the husband to control the wife, forcing her to stay inside the home. While the husband enjoyed socializing with his fellow Korean men, the wife was obliged to live in isolation, forbidden from having contact even with fellow Korean women. Under such circumstances, it could not have been easy to decide to go to night school. Nevertheless, she continued to attend night junior high school undeterred by her husband's various interferences. Although her husband was also mostly illiterate, attending night junior high school together was apparently not an option. It can be assumed that, for first-generation Korean men in Japan, who had internalized the idea that men and women should be treated differently and that men are superior to women, it was difficult to accept that they would be studying side by side with women, especially at a night junior high school where the vast majority of students were Korean women. In a sense, women who did not have to constantly prove their superiority were thus able to study at night junior high school without having to be concerned about the opinions of others. In this sense, women might be seen as being freer than men.

In our next case study, Kang Woo-ja identifies herself as an 'almost-first-generation second-generation'. Kang Woo-ja is the eldest daughter of five siblings. Her father died when she was little. She attended only one year of elementary school. She spoke Japanese fluently, having been born in Japan, but her reading and writing abilities were limited until she studied at night junior high school.

Kang Woo-ja helped her mother raise five children, supporting her financially by giving up school and instead working for a Japanese farmer. She regarded this to be the duty expected of the eldest daughter and was content that her younger siblings could go to school. Her mother had grown up in a wealthy family in Korea, but never learned to write, bound by the custom that 'women should be kept inside the home'. According to Kang Woo-ja, her mother believed that 'any person ought to be able to read and write, regardless of whether you are male or female' and regretted that poverty had prevented her from being able to provide an education for Kang Woo-ja.

After getting married, she gave birth to and raised four children. She continued to engage in garment piecework at home. Her husband was a first-generation Korean man who took great pride in his Korean culture. However, he looked down on his wife and 'constantly referred to her as "a mere woman"'. Therefore, Kang Woo-ja lived quietly, as if holding her breath inside her home. She enrolled in night junior high school at the age of fifty-three, but says that her husband's protest lasted for two years from then.

> I might sound insincere but I like studying. So when my daughter entered school, I studied with her. She didn't like that and got upset sometimes. I persistently kept asking her what she learned at school until I understood while I did the '*matome*'.[15] I learned Chinese characters this way. I studied so much then; it would be impossible to learn that much now...The multiplication table and things like that as well. The one thing I just couldn't get was fractions. My husband wasn't bothered by that sort of thing. He often taught me Chinese characters. I couldn't read newspapers so I would ask him what it meant and he would tell me.

– What was he like when you were going to enter night junior high school?

When I was going to enter, my husband said that there was no need to go to night school because he could read newspapers. And how starting school now wouldn't be any help. My husband didn't know about night junior high school. He probably thought it was an extension of the day school classes. Another thing is that night school wasn't well thought of. I knew why once I went there though. They were looking at it with prejudice. Korean women gathered together at night; everyone is prejudiced against that kind of things. To my mind, it was not a place for gathering but a place to study because I like studying.

– And then how?

I had a major illness...When people are lying in hospital bed, thinking what they would regret the most if they were to die, they would probably think they hadn't married off their children or things like that. For me, it wasn't about that. I regretted so much that I didn't get to go to school. I wanted to go to school. I wanted to attend a graduation ceremony. That was my earnest thought. Like I said before, my husband opposed me going to night school. Having that happened, I pleaded again that I wanted to go because I wanted to go to high school. I even asked everyone to persuade him. My daughter's husband would tell him 'father, mother wants to go, please allow her to go'.

Having been unable to go to school as a child, Kang Woo-ja tried to learn how to write whenever there was an opportunity. When the illness caused her to reflect upon her life, her regret that she 'could not go to school' could no longer be repressed, and that led to her deciding to enroll in night junior high school after she was released from the hospital. Her husband who had willingly helped her learn some basic reading skills, was opposed to her studying properly at night junior high school. Presumably this was because such an action deviates from the norm for 'women'. Until then, she had spent her life worrying about her husband's opinions; however, when it came to night junior high school, she was determined to follow through her decision. After two years of conflict with her husband, and with help from her children and their spouses she finally managed to persuade her husband to let her enter school. Kang Woo-ja's is a case of a woman who had lived as a loyal spouse for decades before revolting against him to pursue her freedom as an individual after contemplating the meaning of her life in her later years.

Case 2: Enrollment after husband's death

Cases in which there was no conflict with the husband can be grouped into those in which the husband had passed away before enrollment and those in which there was simply no conflict. Needless to say, there is a significant qualitative difference between the two. Let us consider Jin Soon-nam (born in the 1920s, from Gyeongsang Province) as one case of the former.[16] At the age of six, Jin Soon-nam moved to the San'in region where her sister lived with her husband's family. At the age of ten, after working as a live-in nanny in a Japanese temple, she moved to Osaka where her father's relatives lived. In Osaka, she worked in plastic processing, ice making and garment manufacturing before marrying at the age of nineteen. After marriage, she and her husband started running a rubber factory. She continued working until she was seventy years old. She had three children who all attended a university of science and technology. Her husband was enthusiastic about education for his children, based on his view: 'we are *Chosun saram* (Koreans) but I do not let anyone take my arms'.[17] Her husband had attended *seodang* but Jin Soon-nam had no schooling experience at all, either in Korea or Japan. At the age of fifty-nine, with her husband's sudden death serving as a catalyst, she decided to enter night junior high school when a friend asked her to join her.

> I didn't even know how to hold a pencil because I had never gone to school in Korea or Japan. Up until then, whenever I needed to read something, I asked my sons. They must have felt sorry their mother didn't understand. How I came to enroll in night school was, when I suddenly lost my husband and went crazy (not knowing what to do), someone I knew was attending night junior high school and took me along, asking me to 'just drop in'. I am really grateful for night junior high school. I was surprised that a world like that existed when I went there for the first time. I was puzzled when I first walked in. It didn't feel like a Japanese school. Meals were provided, too. Until then, all I did was work and I never went outside the house. I had just one friend. I had already given up that I wasn't meant to

go outside and that women are supposed to stay at home. I was told that when women step outside, their laughter shouldn't be heard from three doors down.

There are a lot of women who do go out. My older sister was free because her husband passed away early. She told me 'you know, your life gets shortened for sure [by marriage]'. I thought that's the way it was supposed to be so I didn't feel that was hard. Work was very busy and I had to finish them off, otherwise couldn't make it to the deadline...After my husband's passing, I went to school for ten years while working on rubber on a piecework basis. I missed many classes because of sickness though. My sons were happy. They encouraged me, 'mum, that's great' and 'our mother now understands arithmetic'. My daughter-in-law also bought a Japanese alphabet book for me. Mathematics was my favorite. I was very happy when I began learning division and multiplication. I liked music, too. I felt the happiness of going to school at the age of fifty-nine. I wasn't embarrassed of anything at all. It was like a dream. I was at school for about ten years but I properly attended classes only less than half of that period. I had fun making a lot of friends. They were eager to learn and everyone was nice. All the teachers were nice, too.

The couple had a good relationship when her husband was alive. Even so, she had internalized the norm that women should not assert themselves, thus trying her best not to cause any friction with her husband. It appears that she probably would have restrained herself from enrolling if she had learned of the night junior high school when her husband was alive.

Case 3: Enrollment backed by husband

Finally, I will explore cases in which the husband approved of enrolling in night junior high school. Lee Geo-ryeon (born in the 1920s, from Jeolla Province) migrated to Japan at the age of eighteen, expecting to be able to rely on her sister. She got married half a year later. She has been living as a full-time homemaker since she was relatively wealthy from the family business performing well.[18]

> My parents in Korea tried to have boys finish at least elementary school even though we were poor. Girls were to help parents. Girls are said to become impertinent if they went to school and there are a

lot of things that require children's help in farming families. I wanted to go to school. Some girls from rich families could go to school. I learned Japanese through playing with Japanese kids and things like that...After I got married, I only stayed inside the home. I didn't have any problem at all from not understanding Japanese. However, there was a time when I went to a parent meeting at my child's school, I couldn't read what was written and I felt my face turn red. I couldn't supervise homework either. But that's about it...I entered night junior high school when I was sixty-two or sixty-three. My children had grown up and I was retired. When I was asked by a friend to join her, the first thought was 'I had no idea there was a place like that'. On the very same day, I applied for admission at the government office. I didn't have a talk with my family. I had such a strong mindset that I was going to divorce if he opposed it. But everyone approved it. I was told 'it's a good thing, mother'. 'I didn't know you wanted to learn how to write that much.' One thing I'm pleased about coming to Osaka is that I could go to school...My husband was a kind person. He was a good husband. He let me do whatever I liked to do, without interfering. In most cases, people that come to night school don't have a husband. If they did, they wouldn't be able to come.

Her entry into night junior high school was unproblematic owing to the amicable relationship with her husband. Nevertheless, she was aware that she was deviating from the norm by enrolling. She considered it to be so important that she was even prepared for a divorce. Lee Geo-ryeon, who had an understanding husband, is a 'privileged' case. Cases in which there are no restrictions imposed by the husband are quite rare and her case is exceptional among Korean women in Japan who went to night junior high school. Lee Geo-ryeon's narrative reflects the confidence of a subject who creates a life for herself even while complying with the patriarchal conventions. Her easy entry into night junior high school can be assumed to have resulted from the amiable husband-and-wife relationship that she had built up with many years of effort over their marriage life.

A large proportion of the Koreans living in Osaka come from Jeju Island. If my research participants are representative, Koreans from Jeju Island account for more than half of the students of night junior high school. Jeju Island, which is located a long way from the Korean mainland, is a society in which women have traditionally actively participated in economic activities. It is therefore relatively more lenient about women engaging in activities outside of the home.[19] Some have suggested that the Korean women who study at night junior high school are those who were accustomed to freedom outside of the home because of the culture of Jeju Island. In fact, as we have seen, women had to bargain with the patriarchy about night junior high school regardless of their place of origin. This bargaining occurred within the relationships between women and their husbands. Even the women who were widowed or enjoyed their husband's support were not completely free from gender norms; they just happened to be in a more favorable position when it came to bargaining with the patriarchy. This can be seen in recurring comments that I heard when interviewing Korean women who did not enroll in night junior high school, such as: 'people who go to night junior high school are those who have already lost their husband or are lucky (that their husbands do not try to control them).' Those who did study at night junior high school are only a small proportion of the Korean women in Japan; there are a large number who 'wanted to go but could not'.

It is also important to recognize that those women who did go did not reject the family framework. Nor did they really deviate from it, even when in the face of a tempestuous relationship with their husband or other family members. We can see from their narratives that these women attempted to move their relationships in favorable directions, shielding themselves with many years of commitment to their families. Park Yun-gyeong's remark that 'it was my turn' exemplifies this. In other words, women were forming new subjects that depart from the tradition by challenging patriarchy and effectively bargaining with it. Enrollment in school does not mark the end of the bargaining with patriarchy. Attending night junior high school each day meant the assertion of their agency, countering the continuing patriarchy in a performative manner.

5 Formation of oppositional subjects

Creation of the new female subjectivity

> At first I didn't know there were so many Koreans at school and I was feeling embarrassed. Once I entered the school, none knew how to write, just like me. I have never hid [that I am Korean]. It would be more embarrassing if people found out later. However, in my neighborhood, we just used 'Tokuyama' (her Japanese name) for everything. For banking and work, we used our Japanese names only. Only my old friends call me Lee Gap-saeng. So when the teacher called me 'Lee Gap-saeng' at the night school, I was surprised that a Japanese person could read it. (Lee Gap-saeng, born in the 1920s, from Jeju)

Night junior high schools, where Korean women accounted for the majority, were places where they could address each other with their Korean names. They were, for those women, public spaces that provided a sense of comfort incomparable to any other place in Japanese society. As discussed in the previous chapter, the Korean women who missed out on schooling as children secretly nurtured a desire to learn how to write and go to school for many decades. Then, late in their lives, as they became less burdened with family duties, they decided to enter night junior high school. As they nervously stepped into the classroom on the first day at school, they saw other Korean women like themselves studying next to one another. The night school classrooms in which senior Korean women and Japanese teachers engaged in heated debates, accompanied by booing and jeering in the Korean language, were substantially different from daytime classes. In Chōei and Taiheiji Night Junior High Schools, a large majority of the students were elderly Korean women until the number of new migrant students began to increase in the late 1990s. This numerical majority was the biggest factor driving the formation of a public space led by Korean women.

There are a variety of women's groups of varying sizes in the Korean neighborhoods in Osaka. More formal ones include the women's associations under Mindan and Chongryun; the women's leagues of Korean religious organizations; the *omoni* (mothers) associations at ethnic schools; and parents' organizations for students of ethnic classes in the public schools. More informal ones include groups called '*gye*'; parenting networks among mothers; and other women's groups that develop organically in cafes and parks.[1] I will explore some of the differences between these groups and the collective body of women who formed and followed through with the Taiheiji Night Junior High School Independence Movement.

The crucial difference between the collective body of the women who initiated the Taiheiji Independence Movement and other groups is that the former carried out a relatively autonomous social campaign from a gender perspective. The characteristics of the Taiheiji Independence Movement can be summarized as follows:

1. It was a collective body that is independent of attribute categorization such as nationality- and ethnicity-based organization, and hometown or clan affiliations, and it was not governed by male-dominated organizations.
2. It was a collective body that was independent of family gender roles such as 'mother' and 'wife'.
3. It provided a space for Korean women to develop an oppositional subjectivity in the local Japanese society through anti-government campaigns.

The collective of Korean women that formed in the 1970s at night schools underwent a qualitative transition to become a movement for social change in the Taiheiji Independence Movement. While the direct goal of the movement was to improve the educational environment, it also provided a place for Korean women who had been denied the freedom to express their ethnic identities in Japanese society to demand recognition. After winning the struggle to have an independent school established, the social movement entered a new stage, engaging the subsequent generations in the assertion of ethnic identity and continuing to assert themselves in the operation of self-directed learning organizations and day care centers. This became an indication of the position of Korean women in Japan as a whole – not only those directly involved in the movement – as social actors who influence local society.

Let us investigate how the collective body of women that formed at night schools transformed to become social actors calling for redistribution of resources and recognition of their ethnic identity. When we consider the fact that first-generation and prewar-born second-generation Korean women in Japan were relegated to inferior positions due to the intersecting discriminations of race, class and gender orders within both mainstream Japanese and ethnic Korean society, the importance of this transition becomes quite apparent. It was extremely difficult for those women to create a discourse positioning themselves as socially active subjects since they were excluded and marginalized politically, economically and socially. And they were illiterate. Not being able to represent or speak for themselves, they fit the category of 'subaltern women' as defined by Spivak (1988). The Taiheiji Independence Movement was a process that facilitated the formation of 'subaltern counterpublics' by Korean women, enabling them to propose to the society at large a discourse that constructs them as socially active subjects.

This chapter will focus on the Taiheiji Independence Movement to identify the conditions that gave rise to these 'subaltern counterpublics' and to reveal the characteristics of this newly formed subjectivity. The chapter draws on participant observation, the life stories of the women who comprised the movement, and interviews with other people who were involved in the campaign. The next section will examine the link between this social movement and the human rights and literacy education offered at night schools, considering the extent to which the curriculum was a factor that contributed to the creation of Korean women's 'subaltern counterpublics'. The third section will discuss public night schools as an institution and their role in mediating between Korean women and Japanese society. The forth section will consider various aspects of the oppositional subjectivity formed by Korean women through the Taiheiji Independence Movement in terms of the public, private and ethnic spheres or realms. The final section will investigate the new civic subjectivity of Korean women in Japan formed through the independence movement in relation to multicultural politics at the municipal level.

Social space for Korean women in night schools

This section will examine the way that public schools affected the creation of the subaltern counterpublics of Korean women in Japan. The discussion will specifically focus on three points:
1. the redefinition of ethnic characteristics brought about by human rights education
2. the acquisition of the skills necessary to express oneself in the Japanese language
3. the role of the student council as a forum for discussion.

Education of the 'oppressed' and call for social change

Night schools have been places that accommodated the needs of those who could not complete their education in childhood for various reasons, including poverty and discrimination. Most of the students in these schools are members of groups that are marginalized in mainstream Japanese society such as repatriates; buraku (descendants of outcast communities); Koreans; and other migrants. In other words, night junior high schools are places that highlight the oppression and exclusion of different minority groups in contemporary Japanese society. These men and women have typically experienced unjust treatment in many facets of life including education, work and marriage – and this prolonged experience has had an effect on their self-esteem. The internalization of mainstream society's inferior image of them adds complexity to the issue.

The National Night Junior High School Study Conference (Zenkoku Yakan Chūgakkō Kenkyū Taikai) consists of people who are involved in night junior high schools, such as teachers. It operates as a place where regional and individual night schools can report on their situations and discuss solutions to various issues that are specific to their classroom environment, which differs significantly from the regular daytime junior high schools. A subcommittee tasked with addressing 'problems regarding the education of foreigners' was created during the twenty-third conference in 1977, especially to deal with Korean female students. At the time of its creation, a public debate was conducted on various issues, including teaching the Japanese language and the use of 'real' Korean names.[2]

While the demographics of student bodies varies greatly between regions, the common practical approach adopted across all night junior high schools aims to help students to establish positive identities by attending to the relationship between lack of schooling, illiteracy and social exclusion. In Kansai, where the Taiheiji Independence Movement took place, the International Literacy Year facilitated liaison between different social movements including the buraku liberation movements, Korean people's movements and the night school movements. These liaisons provided momentum for the night school movements to grow beyond the boundaries of individual schools and to move towards social transformation at the local level. Paolo Freire, a Brazilian educator and leader of the critical pedagogy movement, visited Kansai around that time, and had considerable influence on the education debate of the night schools.[3]

Freire emphasizes the possibility of people who are oppressed, dehumanized and silenced developing an ability to recognize the oppressive relationships between self and others or (self and world) and to transform these relationship through education with the cooperation of a 'coordinator' (Freire 1970). Literacy, he argues, is not just the mastery of skills of decoding writing but alters the relationship between one's self and the world. For the minority that has only been seen as an 'object', literacy is a practice that would transform them into a 'subject' who can face the world and decipher its meaning. In short, Freire's pedagogy considered teaching literacy to be a political practice, one that functions as a practice of liberation rather than a tool for oppression (Satomi 2010: 21, 34–50).

bell hooks also recognizes a relationship between literacy and women's liberation. hooks, who is critical of the women's liberation movement dominated by white middle-class women, concurs with Freire's argument in *Pedagogy of the Oppressed* that minorities transform into oppositional subjects through critically recognizing their own social status and participating in a struggle for social transformation (hooks 1994).[4] This claim is supported by my research, where we find that Korean women who were taught how to write for the first time at night school, subsequently became involved in social transformation through an independence movement. This is clearly a case which confirms the idea that literacy plays a special role in empowering minority women to take initiative to change the social status that has been imposed upon them.

Since its establishment in 1972, Chōei Night Junior High School has had the largest number of Korean students in Japan. It has set out to provide a human rights education that could directly address the students' lived experience. They have designed a curriculum in line with their self-identified goals, namely: 'creation of personal history', 'recognition of social position' and 'confirmation of identity'. For instance, Korean is offered as a foreign language subject, which is highly unusual. Topics such as 'Korean history and culture' and 'modern society' are covered in the social science classes under which students learn about the historical relationship between the Korean Peninsula and Japan, issues of discrimination and the concept of human rights. The Japanese language subject '*Kokugo*' which literally means 'national language' is replaced with '*Hyōgen*' (Expression) and literary works of Koreans in Japan are introduced. In music classes, Korean songs are used when possible and ethnic instruments are taught. The aim of the curriculum is for students to learn the history, language and culture of Korea as well as the relationship between Japan and the Korean Peninsula, including the colonial period, and to teach an understanding that the struggles that they have personally experienced – such as those arising from the Japanese discrimination against Koreans – are a social structural issue.

In order for a minority to overcome oppression, the cause of the oppression must be critically understood. That requires renouncing the negative images of themselves projected by the oppressor that they have internalized. This curriculum is believed to help students to develop self-respect and to establish a foundation upon which a new relationship with Japanese society can be built.[5] This special consideration for Korean students is a result of the ethnic education movement in Kansai (discussed in Chapter 2), a practice of ethnic education within the public education system.

Let us explore the education of the oppressed from the perspective of the use of ethnic names. The use of ethnic names is a pillar of the educational practice for Korean students at Chōei Night Junior High School. A policy was adopted in the fourth year of operation to only use ethnic names upon entering the school. This practice is sometimes confronting for students, placing pressure on those students who had only used Japanese names until then. We can see this in Kang Woo-ja's (born in the 1930s, second-generation) narrative.

I entered night school. Then, I was given a hard time by teachers A and B. You know, we were supposed to bring our certificate of residence[6] that has our real name on it. I was asked what my real name was. I simply said it was Kō Tomoko [reading her ethnic name using the Japanese reading system] but then I was told it was Kang Woo-ja [read using the Korean reading system]. They kept calling me that but I wasn't listening. At the end of the school entrance ceremony, they called my name 'Kang Woo-ja', but I didn't realize I was being called. Every single day, teachers kept telling me that it was my name. The teachers who taught me back then, were passionate about that kind of thing, more so than teaching classes.

Still today, the majority of Koreans in Japan use their Japanese names in daily life. This practice originates in the 'sōshi kaimei' (compulsory renaming) decree of 1939 by the colonial authority, which forced Koreans to adopt a Japanese name towards enforced cultural assimilation. After the war, Koreans living in Japan typically continued using their Japanese names in everyday life to avoid racial discrimination. Today, a large proportion of people with South Korean or Chosun nationality still have a Korean 'real name' and a Japanese 'alias'. Of those who have Korean heritage and Japanese nationality, only a small proportion has ethnic names listed on the family register. Even for first-generation Koreans whose ways of speaking and acting clearly reveal that they are from the Korean Peninsula, it is common to use Japanese names. The use of ethnic names in night schools was thus contrary to the generally accepted practice in Japanese society. It is not surprising that it provoked some confusion and resistance.[7] Let us look at Kang Woo-ja's narrative again to see how an education that emphasizes ethnic traits prompted a change in her mindset.

You know, I started to stay with my own people since starting night school. I wonder what my people would say but the biggest achievement at night school is that you get to know about your own ethnic roots. Koreans are Koreans. Japanese are Japanese. Filipinos are Filipinos. Like this, you come to know about your own roots. You discover who you are and also where you are standing and where you are looking. That's all you need to know. Some say the only thing we are missing is the ability to write but it's not just that. We have lived through some incredible times. I am relatively young though...As to why they keep telling us to use our real names, it's because my real name represents the real me. It represents myself. That means my own roots. Our own ethnic background. I find it extraordinary how at these schools the first thing they teach you is who you are. If they wanted to teach that, they must start from 1910 (referring to Japan's annexation of Korea) and earlier...I was surprised that a Japanese [teacher] knew so much about it.

Although the use of Korean names and a curriculum that emphasized Korean culture were implemented out of consideration for the fact that Koreans accounted for the vast majority of students at Chōei Night School, the path to implementing this curriculum was riddled with obstacles. Some students resisted the idea of having to use their Korean names and to study the history of Korea and Koreans in Japan, claiming that they 'did not come to night school to learn about Korea'. Others insisted on using the same textbooks as the full-time junior high schools and felt that their 'intelligence was insulted' when they were given worksheets that were handmade by the teachers. These reactions can be understood as the flip side of the strong desire of women who could not go to school when they were young to go to a 'normal school'. There were also some teachers who believed that the curriculum should conform to the one taught in full-time junior high schools.[8] Hence the school was faced with the question of whether to provide a 'majority' education in accordance with the will of the students or to provide an education from the minority perspective even against the expressed wishes of the students. Overall, the Taiheiji Independence Movement embraced the latter approach.

Oh Bok-deok's comment below implies the gender asymmetry evident in the use of ethnic names.

> When I go to Jeju gatherings [with people from her hometown], I am not addressed by my name. They would just call me '*ajimae*' (aunt or middle aged woman in the Gyeongsang dialects). Because I am a woman, there is no chance to use my name. Even now, I use my Korean name only at night junior high school. It was a good thing that I went to night school and started to use my Korean name. Still now, I use my Japanese name in the neighborhood and parks [even when she is with other Korean women].

Korean women in Japan are identified not as individuals within social relations, but as belonging to a family based on male lineage, and they are hardly ever called by a personal name. When they start using their ethnic names at night school, they begin to recognize themselves as individuals – not as a daughter, a wife, a daughter-in-law or a mother. Being addressed by and identifying themselves with their ethnic name can mark a turning point where the women, who had always been defined in terms of relationship with a man, begins to develop an awareness of 'me and no one else', an individual with her own (ethnic) name. The considerations about the use of ethnic names that have informed the night school policies have focused solely on the reclamation of ethnic identity. However, Oh Bok-deok's narrative indicates that minority women had their names stolen twice – once by colonial rule and once by gender.

Literacy and speaking up

As discussed in the previous chapter, the primary reason that so many Korean women in Japan were illiterate was the gender order. However, because the issue was specific to women, illiteracy went unrecognized as a problem in the androcentric Korean society in Japan. The inconveniences experienced by illiterate women were only addressed as individual problems in the personal domain or through mutual assistance among women.

As Korean women in Japan learned how to read and write in Japanese, their relationship with the society surrounding them changed drastically. As we have seen, literacy not only eliminates various inconveniences in everyday life, but also brings about changes in women's subjectivity. The epitome of this process is the emphasis in night schools on lessons of composition. Composition lessons are not merely about composing sentences in Japanese but have the additional objective of 'creating a personal history', or creating your own life path.

The Korean women who enrolled in night school began by learning how to hold a pencil and then moved on to studying the Japanese alphabets and writing their own names, copying each character slowly and carefully in their notebooks, over and over. The compositions written with the words learned this way are filled with life experiences that have never been told before, including experiences of colonial rule and the war, as well as the racial and gender discrimination experienced in Japanese society and within their families. For example, one woman wrote that she had not been taught how to write despite her father being a teacher of Chinese classics on the grounds that she was female whereas another woman wrote that she was physically assaulted by police when she was working as a shell diver because she could not write her name when questioned during a crackdown.[9] Composition required expressing experiences and thoughts that they had kept to themselves, having been unable to tell anyone, even family members. One woman said, 'Knowing how to write is my happiness as a human being' and that only when she had become able to write her own name, had she 'felt human' for the first time.[10] Learning to write provides the opportunity to put thoughts into words and to reflect on and express their own experiences.[11] The long-suppressed voices of the women finally began to be expressed.

Interestingly, the composition lessons in night schools enabled Korean women to express long repressed feelings and emotions in the Japanese language rather than Korean. This raises an important question about why it could not be their mother tongue that was used. This points to the deep-seated relationship between gender and the discourse production of Koreans in Japan. In the society of Koreans in Japan, the intellectual class has been dominated by men. The nationalist discourses produced to redress the colonial past were presented as if they were gender-neutral, but actually they presented men as the acting subjects and women as non-existent. For example, most of the educational resources used in training schools for adult women run by Chongryun aim at instilling patriotic spirit and loyalty as overseas citizens of the Democratic People's Republic of Korea. In the context of decolonization, mastering the Korean language was directly linked to the internalization of national characteristics and national ideologies. Whenever women were mentioned in textbooks, their roles as a 'wise mother and good wife' to assist Korean men in Japan and protect their family for their country was emphasized. Words related to sexuality, households and reproduction are not taught, leaving women with no means of expressing the central issues that they face. After having learned Hangeul, women were given opportunities to engage in activities outside of the home through participation in Nyeoseongdongmaeng or *omoni* (mothers) meetings at ethnic schools as members of the ethnic community.

However, these activities emphasized women's contributions to the organization, expecting them to take reproductive roles as mothers in the community, and occluded anything that would enable them to express themselves as social subjects in Japan's public space (Ryang 1998). While the organizations of Korean women in Japan, such as Buinhoe and parent associations for ethnic classes in public schools, have in fact made substantial contributions to the development and continuity of ethnic organizations, there was no space in which to publicly criticize the patriarchy which lies at the root of those ethnic organizations.

Meanwhile, women have been actively engaged in oral communication, sharing experiences with one another within a women-only space that was not under the direct control of the patriarchy. However, although '*sinsetaryeong*'[12] and other communicative activities provided outlets for outpourings of emotions, they could never be harnessed to generate the power required to overturn the structures of oppression, if for no other reason than because women had themselves internalized a gender order that positioned themselves as subordinate to men and had generally accepted the hardship that they had endured as simply a matter of '*palja*' (fate). In the androcentric public space of Koreans in Japan, women were, regardless of their participation, constantly 'othered' and marginalized. They were unable to speak in their own voices and no one else spoke on their behalf because there was no audience who would listen.

This state of Korean women in Japan – having been discursively excluded from public space – is fully in accordance with Spivak's (1998) concept of 'subaltern women'.[13] Inability to write makes it exceptionally difficult to produce and disseminate a discourse that would unite the experiences, feelings and thoughts of Korean women, situating themselves as social subjects and fostering a sense of identity as a collective entity. The lack of communication resources was a major factor that made Korean women invisible in the public domain in Japan.[14]

So far I have been examining the political significance of literacy for Korean women in Japan. The problem of illiteracy tends to be overlooked in Japan, where it is assumed that the literacy rate is more or less 100%. Nevertheless, literacy is directly linked to a politics of social transformation as per the earlier discussion of Freire and hooks. Women's liberation is no exception. Bunch (1983), for example, argues that it is necessary to develop fundamental reading and writing skills before studying theories of women's liberation. Her reasoning is that a lack of basic literacy skills not only limits women's analytical and intellectual thinking abilities, but also leads them to consider their own thoughts and experiences as unimportant and prevents them from looking to change the situation in which they find themselves. As a matter of fact, women's critical thinking abilities are often already limited by traditional gender norms. If we assume that the aim of teaching feminist theories is to enable women to think systematically and to empower them to actively engage in the world around them, then the importance of literacy is obvious (Bunch 1983: 256–257). Bunch thus sees literacy as a precondition for any movement for social change. She points out several political aspects of literacy:

1. Literacy provides a means of conveying ideas and information that may not be readily available in the popular media.
2. Reading and writing help to develop an individual's imagination and ability to think, whereas much of mass culture, especially television, pacifies and encourages conformity rather than creativity.
3. An individual's access to a variety of interpretations of reality through reading increases her capacity to think for herself, to go against the norms of the culture, and to conceive of alternatives for society.
4. Reading and writing aid each woman's survival and success in the world, by increasing her ability to function in her chosen endeavors.
5. The written word is still the cheapest and most accessible form of mass communication. This makes it useful for those with limited resources. (Bunch 1983: 257)

hooks (1984; 1994) also points out that the acquisition of literacy enables women to comprehend the world as a structural whole and to develop critical thinking, in turn empowering them to initiate political movements to reform oppressive structures with their own hands. For subaltern Korean women in Japan, learning the Japanese language – the language of their previous colonizer and of the mainstream society in which they live – provided a powerful resource in the Taiheiji Independence Movement. Among other things, during the independence campaign, women made full use of the Japanese language in filing a complaint about racial discrimination in the local community, petitioning and negotiating with the administration and liaising with other civil movements.

Student councils

The student councils of night junior high schools played an important role in turning Korean women into oppositional subjects and developing a movement that challenged oppressive social structures. Student councils are not established to serve the interests of the school administration. Rather, they exist to encourage the growth of students as a collective that can take responsibility for their own interests and deal with various issues themselves. In the student councils, students engage in lively debates and discussions on equal footings about matters of common interest; in this case, the operation of night schools. The student councils are a place of politics where matters are raised, students are consulted, votes are taken and representatives are elected. They are founded on the assumption that all students are equal, regardless of nationality, ethnic affiliations, or differences arising from different places of origin.[15]

Most of the women who most vigorously participated in the Taiheiji Independence Movement had very little experience of organizational activities such as those coordinated by the main Korean ethnic organizations, typically because they had been 'way too busy with things around the house and work' or they 'had not had much interest'. Generally, they considered the ethnic organizations and labor unions to be 'things that are run by men'. Among the fourteen participants in my life story research, only two had 'participated with enthusiasm' in a women's organization affiliated to an ethnic organization. One of them has been a passionate district leader of Nyeomaeng for several decades when she had spare time from work, active in collecting donations, delivering bulletins, and arranging personal visits and meetings.[16]

The other women had some experience participating in mass mobilization events, such as rallies and demonstrations organized by Korean ethnic organizations. Partly owing to the fact that they lived in areas where large numbers of Koreans had settled, they had immediate experience of historical events such as the Hanshin Education Struggle and the fingerprinting refusal movement. They have also participated in New Year's functions and contributed to petition signing, collecting membership fees and organizational fundraising campaigns as part of the mutual support among fellow Koreans. For the most part, however, their participation was of the passive kind; they were not involved in planning and operating the ethnic organization, nor did they attend regular executive meetings.[17]

As for their involvement in Japanese society, all fourteen women were members of neighborhood associations (chōnaikai), attending to rostered duties such as managing community notices and garbage collection. However, none of them had held key positions in the associations. Similarly for local seniors' clubs; they occasionally made appearances at dinner parties or New Year's functions, but only one of them had been a regular participant. 'Koreans do not feel comfortable going' to organizations that are predominantly Japanese. Their interactions with their Japanese neighbors are generally limited to simple greetings. It appears that no close relationships have developed even after almost half a century of living in a neighborhood. There are invisible racial boundaries in local communities, and Korean women are highly conscious of the fact that they are 'outsiders' the moment that they step outside their homes. The Japanese teachers they met at night school were the first '*Ilbon saram*' (Japanese person) with whom they built a relationship that was more than basic greetings, which made their encounters with their teachers all the more significant.

It is therefore quite significant that, although only a few of them had been actively involved in the organizations in their respective local communities or ethnic communities prior to the Taiheiji Independence Movement, seven of the fourteen have served in key positions in the student council and the Night Junior High School Student Council Association. Even when we take into account that there is a bias in my sample, which results from targeting women who were active participants in the movement, the result highlights the effect that attending night school and becoming literate has had on the women's involvement in collective activities.

The first student council meeting that I attended was notable for the energy with which the first-generation women were participating. People raised their hands, one after another. As soon as one woman began to deliver an eloquent speech, another would demand the floor. The audience would either applaud to express their approval or express their disagreement equally as clearly. Each and every one present actively participated in the debate. Teachers provide administrative support but the operation of the student council is overwhelmingly in the hands of the students themselves.

They speak in Japanese fluently, although with distinctive Korean pronunciations. The Japanese language – a foreign language and the language of the 'ruler' – became one of the factors that helped build the solidarity among these Korean women and steered them towards collective action. The Japanese language played an important role in overcoming invisible chasms that result from a variety of differences, including which part of the Korean Peninsula they came from, whether they have South Korean or Chosun nationality and whether they belong to Mindan or Chongryun. It allowed them to focus on what they had in common, rather than their differences, and thus provided a strong foundation for a movement to fight against the structure of domination.

The Taiheiji Independence Movement began when students' dissatisfaction with the extension classrooms erupted at a student council meeting. Appalled by a shortage of teachers and classrooms and by poor facilities, the students decided to take action and protest against the education authority. The student council discussed key matters such as the policy and approach of the campaign. According to several participants in these discussions, occasionally an intense dispute broke out between the students who were keen advocates of the protest action and those who believed that 'the movement gets in the way of studying'. In any event, the student council functioned as a place where students could exchange opinions. It was instrumental in maintaining the movement for eight years and consequently achieving their goal of an independent school.

In this section, I have outlined some of the key factors that helped Korean women to create 'counterpublics', focusing on the education of the oppressed, learning the language of the host society and the student council as a forum for open and frank debate. The women involved had all experienced some ethnic rights and community activities previously, either directly or indirectly. But as discussed in Chapter 1, there was almost no room in the Korean community in Japan for women to be active as political subjects except as directed by men, and the only activities Korean men considered to be acceptable for women were those that confirmed their roles as 'mothers' or 'wives'. Compounding their gender-based exclusion from the public sphere, illiterate Korean women also lacked resources necessary to initiate a movement. They had poor command of Japanese, the language used in the mainstream society, and possessed none of the skills, networks or access to the public authorities necessary to set a campaign in motion on their own. It appears that the major drivers of the Taiheiji Independence Movement were: the night junior high school expansion movement that had been underway since the late 1960s, successful mobilization of minority resources in the Kansai region, and the acquisition of skills at night school that would prove useful for conducting the campaign. Needless to say, the women were not merely passive recipients of an education; they rose in opposition and faced conflicts from time to time, as illustrated in the discussion of the use of ethnic names. Perhaps it is because those other issues had been continuously discussed that they could respond immediately to initiate a campaign against the administrative measure to send Korean students to an extension classroom.

Finally, attention should be paid to the fact that there were no Korean men in night schools. 'We [women] might not have carried out the movement if there were Korean men [present]', Park In-seok said. Had there been even one Korean man present, the initiative may have been left in his hands.

Public night school as a pathway to the public domain

'You may say Japan is big but where else can we find a hundred to hundred-fifty Korean people gathering every single night?'[18] This teacher's remark indicates the crucial role played by the night schools in the process of bringing together first and second-generation Korean women as a collective group in Japan. This raises interesting questions regarding the fact that a type of subaltern counterpublic of Korean women emerged in Japanese public schools.

As previously discussed, there are numerous differences among the population of Korean women in Japan, including nationality, organizational affiliations, place of origin, generation and family structure. These differences flare up at different times and in different contexts. For example, during my participant observation, there was an instance when a woman who associates herself with Chongryun began voicing a favorable opinion about the leader of North Korea, which immediately sparked a bitter war of words. I also observed that because most of the night school students are from Jeju Island – like the resident Koreans in Osaka in general – some of the women who did not come from Jeju Island tended to be more reserved. Leaving aside these differences, the dignified manner in which the women expressed their opinions, laughed loudly and engaged in arguments can be considered to have been made possible by the fact that they were the majority in this particular context.

Public night schools are educational institutions for those who did not complete their education at school age for a variety of reasons. Until its change of policy in 2015, the Ministry of Education had maintained that Japan had achieved almost universal literacy around the beginning of the period of rapid economic growth (late 1950s) by virtue of the postwar education system. Public night schools were seen as redundant on the grounds that they were no longer necessary.

Under these circumstances, a citizens' movement 'from below' highlighted the number of illiterate people who had been rendered invisible. This movement picked up momentum, leading to the establishment of additional night schools from the late 1960s. The public night junior high schools differ from full-time public schools in that their history includes this citizens' movement. Nevertheless, they are still public institutions administered by the boards of education of their respective municipal governments and are part of the public education system. It must have been quite a surprise for both the campaigners' and the administration that Korean women in Japan – middle and older-aged migrant women from the former colony with foreign nationalities – crowded into the educational institutions whose primary responsibility is to provide an education primarily aimed towards promoting loyalty to the nation-state and assimilating people into a single cultural/national identity as 'Japanese'.

The night schools, as we have seen, played a determinant role in the processes through which a collective entity of Korean women developed into a 'subaltern counterpublic' with some degree of autonomy. As discussed in Chapter 2, women's organizations affiliated with ethnic organizations for Koreans in Japan are subordinate to the parent organizations which retain exclusive decision-making authority. Similarly, in the parent associations at ethnic schools and ethnic classes in public schools, although the mothers typically perform the core roles, it is the fathers who act as the representatives. This is also the case with regular parent-teacher associations. The development of a 'subaltern counterpublic' which positions women as social subjects was therefore highly unlikely, even where women constituted a quantitative majority, due to the underlying and deep-seated gender order.

At night schools, Korean women formed a collective group linked by 'common historical experiences'. The Taiheiji Independence Movement provided an opportunity for Korean women who had been invisible until then to emerge into the public domain as instigators of an autonomous movement. In this movement, public schools provided the opening – a 'window' – for Korean women to enter the mainstream Japanese society. It was no 'mere coincidence' that a subaltern counterpublic of Korean women was created in the night schools. Rather, it was because, and only because, these night schools were public institutions that were themselves marginalized, and therefore not completely bound to the rules of the public authority, that they could provide an opportunity for these women to become social actors.

In order for an alienated and marginalized minority to build a counter movement that is more than simply a temporary release of frustration but ensures that the message of the protest is conveyed, there needs to be some sort of access to the public. In this regard, Korean women in Japan were disadvantaged. Like Korean men in Japan, they were excluded from the host society on the grounds of the ethnic- and class order, but the Korean women were further disadvantaged by the gender division of the public domain.

From the 1970s there was a continuous expansion of the areas in which Koreans could participate as citizens. They benefited from a wave of campaigns to abolish discrimination based on ethnicity and nationality, which were sparked by the Hitachi Employment Discrimination Trial. The Nationality Clause was removed from the eligibility criteria for public service officers, including teachers, technical and general administrative officers at the municipal level; then from the requirements for academic staff at national universities and legal apprentices at the national level. The Nationality Clause was also removed from the social security schemes such as public housing, the national pension, national health insurance, child allowance and other social welfare programs. However, because of the gendered division of Korean society, Korean women generally were not direct beneficiaries of these reforms, enjoying only limited benefits through the male head of their households. In contrast, the Taiheiji Independence

Movement was a campaign in which women demanded and achieved administrative policy changes and recognition for themselves as acting subjects.

Korean women reconsidered their relationship to Japanese society upon learning about the structures of oppression in the postcolonial world order. The Taiheiji Independence Movement was an extension of this reconsideration. When the decision to relocate Korean students to an 'extension class' was announced, the women saw this as another act of the racial discrimination that they had experienced all of their lives. Korean women in Japan emerged as political subjects to protest and confront the hierarchical structure that held 'Japanese' and 'Japanese nationals' as superior and 'Koreans' and 'foreign nationals' as inferior. It was a public school, which was supposed to promote national conformity, that provided the opportunity for a collective group of Korean women to be formed, generating a subaltern counterpublic against the mainstream society. It may be paradoxical but public night schools created a pathway for these women – who had henceforth been excluded from the public domain in both the Japanese-host and Korean-ethnic societies – to enter the public domain.

Althusser theorizes the process of subjectification in terms of ideology. Ideology only exists, he argues, by constituting concrete individuals as subjects. All ideology calls out, or interpellates, individuals as subjects with concrete identities. For example, a police officer hails a person: 'hey you'. When the person turns around, he/she identifies him/herself as the interpellated other and is thus transformed into a subject that submits to the authority of the police.[19] It is inside ideological structures that individuals find their position and are interpellated as subjects (1976). Schools are ideological apparatuses of a nation, institutions whose primary function is to interpellate subjects who will submit to the authority of the state.

The Taiheiji Independence Movement can be seen to be a result of the Korean women in public night schools who were interpellated by the nation 'turning around' in an unexpected way. When those women who had been alienated from the mainstream society were called out by Japan for the first time, they turned around as 'Koreans in Japan' who had always been subjects of historical oppression. As foreign nationals inextricably bound up with the language and culture of Korea, these women were too far removed from the 'citizen' category that the Japanese government sought to form through education. They resisted the 'interpellation' by which the state sought to assimilate them into the host society as subordinate beings. Public night schools were themselves the result of a citizens' movement, and as such are places where many conflicting ideologies are intricately interwoven. That is precisely why the new oppositional movement led by Korean women was able to take shape.

Formation of oppositional subjects during the movement

This section will take a closer look at the Taiheiji Independence Movement with an aim to reveal important aspects of these newly created oppositional subjects. It will focus on three parts: mainstream Japanese society, the personal domain and the ethnic community.

Oppositional subjects in defiance of mainstream society

The night school expansion movement spread across the country from the late 1960s. The Taiheiji Independence Movement is particularly remarkable, however, in that it was organized predominantly by the students and alumni, and it was successful in getting an independent school established after eight years of negotiating with the administration. While this movement is significant in a number of respects, one important characteristic that merits mention is its character as a liberation movement – an ethnically motivated liberation movement by Korean women in Japan. Although the movement was directed against the local boards of education, it was the deep-rooted racial discrimination in Japanese society, which manifested symbolically in the decision to send Korean students to an extension class, that the Korean women were in fact protesting. It was because of their experiences in a society where racial discrimination is taken for granted that the women reacted so acutely to such an administrative measure. The independence movement became a catalyst for those women to express their long-accumulated distrust of and anger towards Japanese society. This can be seen in the following quote from the Taiheiji Declaration of Independence issued in April, 2001.

> As we carried out the campaign, we came to the realization that the prejudice against night schools and discrimination against Koreans lies at the root of the problem of independence of Taiheiji Extension Class. We cannot allow discrimination to extend to night schools. We have been shouting out that our pride will not allow it.

The Taiheiji Independence Movement was compared to the Hanshin Education Struggle fought in Osaka half a century earlier, a fierce resistance movement by Koreans in Japan against the state authority which tried to close ethnic schools. Shortly after the onset of the Taiheiji campaign, it was dubbed the 'Second Hanshin Education Struggle'. How did these two movements that are fifty years apart come to be associated with each other? Park Yun-gyeong's recollection of the forced closure of ethnic schools can provide some insight here.

> After the war, several Korean schools opened. There happened to be one that opened just here. My eldest son entered that school. But it was forced to close down straight away. Then another Korean school opened. When that school opened, so many policemen came crushing in. They came almost every day. Such a horrible thing. During class, children had to be prepared to run away or hide under the desk. The school was closed down again. Next was Taiheiji Elementary School. He changed school three times. We kept moving like that. He was six at the time of the liberation [referring to the end of war]. That time, the Korean school was only just opened and no one cared about the age. Anyone would join in. Now they have an ethnic school in Taiheiji but before that, it was an extremely old place, a tin roof building in some open space area. We called that a school and everyone gathered there to study. There was no money. Really, no one had money. Everyone worked together to run the school. People with knowledge would share knowledge and people with money would share money. Everyone chipped in and teachers worked so hard without pay…(Ethnic) organizations didn't matter back then. Later, whether you are *aka* (communist) or *shiro* (capitalist) started to matter though. I just sent my children there, wanting them to learn Hangeul. It was part of the preparation to go home (to Korea).

Immediately after the liberation, self-directed schools for Koreans in Japan were set up in many parts of Japan to teach school children

Korean language and other subjects on the premise that they would be returning to Korea. Park Yun-gyeong's family also sent their children to school not because of political belief but as part of the preparation to return home. Her narrative illustrates how people joined their efforts to build schools to provide ethnic education in anticipation of returning to their home soil against the background of a celebratory mood following the liberation from colonial rule. In 1947, in Osaka, there were eighty-one elementary schools and two junior high schools for Koreans in Japan. There were more than 10,000 students in Osaka (Yang Young-hoo 1994: 77). However, as the cold war between the United States and the Soviet Union unfolded, GHQ began increasingly pressuring ethnic schools under Choryun (predecessor of Chongryun). Police officers stormed into school premises and interrupted classes. Then, in 1948, the Ordinance for ethnic school closure was issued by the Ministry of Education. Koreans objected and this developed into a large-scale resistance movement that later came to be known as the Hanshin Education Struggle. Park Yun-gyeong joined the demonstration and marched, hand-in-hand with her comrades, singing *Urinara Kkot* (Flowers of Our Nation), a song of hope for independence that was sung in Korea under colonial rule.

> At that time, to protect Korean schools, Koreans from the entire Kinki region came to the Osaka Prefectural Government. There were buses after buses, non-stop. You know, an incredible number of demonstrators' buses arrived at the park in front of the government building, the Osaka Castle Park. They came from all over the Kinki region. Everyone wore a headband. We walked on the street endlessly. We did that so many times. But they would come to crush us down in the end so we thought it was no use and decided to enter the government building. The day they entered the government building, I was home because my husband went. A boy that lived across from here was shot with a gun and killed. Seventeen-year-old boy. He was shot and died.

In January 1948, the Ministry of Education issued a circular entitled 'Regarding handling of the establishment of Korean schools' which ordered Korean school-age children to attend public schools regulated under the School Education Act. This meant, in essence, Korean language education was no longer an option. As a consequence, a fierce clash took place between the police force which tried to force the closure of Korean schools and Koreans who tried to stop the suppression. In Osaka, on the 28th of April 1948, over 15,000 Korean school-age children and their parents gathered at a park in front of the prefectural government building and staged a demonstration; and amid the turmoil, a young Korean man died from a gunshot by the police force (Yang 1994: 79–88; Higuchi 2002: 160–163). Park Yun-gyeong said, the 'boy', Kim Tae-il, lived in her neighborhood.

While the struggle spread to all corners of the country, Osaka was the site of the most violent collision between protesters and the police force. Despite failing to stop the clampdown on ethnic schools, the Hanshin Education Struggle became a significant part of collective memory and was later recognized as the beginning of the ethnic rights movement by Koreans in Osaka. Forty-five years later, the Hanshin Education Struggle became associated with the Taiheiji Independence Movement.

– How did the night junior high school independence movement start?
There was no vice principal or a school nurse in Taiheiji [extension class]. You know, the organizers [of the independence movement] were the students. Because students did it, teachers could support us. Even if teachers wanted to do something, they wouldn't be able to without us standing up for ourselves, considering their position. At first, there were over 400 students in Chōei. That means there were more students at night (class) than daytime (class). There were nine classes. Then, the parents association of the daytime students filed a complaint, saying it was inconvenient for their kids. You see, we had a campaign going on for more teachers [referring to a campaign to call for an increased number of teaching staff at night school; even before the surge in the number of students became a problem among the daytime school]. We were asking them to build more schools. Then, all of a sudden, they said we were going to Taiheiji and that was shocking. There was nothing there. The blackboard was more like a sheet of veneer. You try to write and wipe. It doesn't write or come off. In a place like that, there were four classes at that time. Downstairs was empty but we were placed up on the third floor where it was unbearably hot but there was not even a curtain. So, we brought old curtains ourselves and put newspapers on the windows. There was no clock and we couldn't tell time so teachers

would come to check. There was simply nothing there. Of course, there is not a single painting in rooms like that. It was such an awful condition. Sports grounds had no electricity. The auditorium, too. We had physical education classes in the dark. If we tried to enter the school through the field, we would step into a puddle. It couldn't be more miserable than that…So, that was our education. We were talking about doing the Hanshin Education Struggle one more time. Let's go and do a sit-in. We actually put that in action and did a sit-in at the board of education for four days. Our teacher's beard was growing out of control and with his messy hair and the beard like that, he was sitting at the entrance of the board of education on a sheet of newspaper. He looked no different to a homeless man…A lot of people rallied around us on the third and fourth day. It was just us doing a sit-in but those people who came to support us would spread out mats and eat on them so that made it difficult for the people of the board of education to go in and out. It started raining and everyone held an umbrella. So many newspaper companies came and it was made into such a big deal. We were dumbfounded. Then we went to the prefectural government office, many times. We entered many different rooms and I saw many lawmakers.

– What was on your mind?

We were talking about entering the building if things didn't work. It wouldn't help if we kept going like that forever. We were saying since we started it, we had to see it through to the end. We wouldn't have started it if we were going to give up halfway. We put our lives on the line.

The women were sensing the unwelcoming atmosphere of the local community toward the night school every day – they were despised as 'Chōsen grannies coming together at night'. When the parent-teacher association and educational administration took a string of actions in response to a newspaper article about the growing number of students, the women saw it as a 'sign of discrimination'. The student council immediately decided that they were going to demand the establishment of an independent school. As the movement gained momentum, people began to realize that it was on a continuum with the Hanshin Education Struggle which had occurred almost half a century ago. The focus started to shift to the 'ethnic' problem. Park Yun-gyeong describe these beginnings in a composition.

Formation of Oppositional Subjects

> For the past number of years, there was not a single day that I did not think about the independence of Taiheiji Extension Class. We students have been leading the movement to establish a night junior high school in Taiheiji, with the resolution to create *'urihakgyo'*[20] with our own hands. When I think about the frustration of not having been able to go to school as a child and the unspeakable hardship I have gone through since coming to Japan, that made me even more determined that Korean people must come together to create our school at any cost. I was also certain that if we came together, we could definitely make it happen. When someone told me 'A decision has been made to make Taiheiji an independent school', I went to the school straight away. I wanted to check if the name plate at the school gate had been changed to Taiheiji Night Junior High School. It had not. From that day, I went to check every single day. Without the replacement of the name plate, I could not be convinced of the independence. The name plate is not just a piece of wood. It means a lot for us to have a name plate – for us to study with pride that this is our school.

Park Yun-gyeong considered the name plate that read 'Taiheiji Junior High School Night Class' as the formal acknowledgement of the voice of Korean women in Japan. This implies that the Taiheiji Independence Movement was indeed a political action by Korean women to demand recognition of their identity.

The women expressed their anger toward the racial discrimination which they suffered for all of their lives through the Taiheiji Independence Movement. The following is Park In-seok's account of it.

> When I came to Japan, I was discriminated against. I was sad. I got into debt, too. I was caught by the police and thrown into a juvenile classification home for nine days alone when I was seventeen or eighteen (for carrying rice from a black market during the postwar chaos). I was taken to the police station. They got me a state-appointed lawyer and I ended up in a court. There were young Korean girls in the prison. Discrimination was shocking. We were given leftovers, food scraps that would otherwise end up in the bin in the ration. Even children would know they were discriminated against. Of course I was not going to fight back. That was the way things were back then. When I won a bloomer from a raffle, too, the Japanese people nagged at me 'Why you'. I can't forget it, that look on the Japanese people.

Photo 5.1: Name plate at the time of independence

Source: Provided by Taiheiji Night Junior High School

Park In-seok felt angry at the administrative decision to move students from Chōei Night Junior High School to the extension class with no regard for the students' situation.

> We were suddenly told in February [of 1993] to go to the extension class but we couldn't accept that. We said to our teachers: 'That's impossible!' 'Don't be silly!' I actually live closer to Tennōji Night Junior High School (another public night junior high school in Osaka City) but my work was on this side of the town. Even people coming from Ikuno wouldn't want to leave a familiar place…Extension class means we would have to go to Chōei for events like a graduation ceremony. Extension class is a temporary shelter. We used the back gate of the building as an entrance. Extension class meant discrimination against Koreans. The board of education didn't want

to do things that cost them and they were pressured by the PTA, too. The parents of the daytime students complained it was a bad image for the school to have many Koreans. The tax spent on Koreans is a waste. We Koreans were treated like a nuisance [by the Japanese parents], making it look like it was for their children. The PTA and the board of education are birds of a feather. Discrimination is such a terrible thing. The root problem was discrimination against Koreans. The extension classrooms ordeal wouldn't have happened if [the students of the night school had been] Japanese...It [the issue of increasing number of students in Choei] was featured in the newspaper and the parents of the daytime protested in the parent-teacher association. Then we were thrown into a bin just like rubbish.

Park In-seok later took her deep distrust and animosity against Japanese society out through the independence movement. The four-day sit-in staged in October 1993 became widely known in the local community through newspapers and television. Some of the Japanese residing around the night school, who had had no interaction with the school until then, began showing support. At the same time, the president of the student council, who was highly exposed in the mass media, became victim of a hate campaign, including ambush, anonymous letters delivered to her home and silent phone calls.[21] As we can see, the local community's reaction was mixed and the eight long years of the movement placed substantial stress on the participants. One way or another, the movement provided an opportunity for Korean women who had been living inconspicuously in the community for decades to begin claiming their own 'voice'. It was a significant change when they expressed anger about discrimination and demanded the recognition of an identity that had been unjustly distorted. While demanding that the extension classrooms become an independent school, they protested against the injustice of their oppression in a variety of ways, and in doing so, gradually created an oppositional Korean identity.

Here is another quote from the Taiheiji Declaration of Independence,[22]

> From April 2001, our school got to start as Taiheiji Night Junior High School. For 8 years [of our movement], there were many difficulties. We thought every day why Taiheiji Extension Class could not be

an independent school. It may be that we are wrong to demand independence. It may be that our voice calling for independence is too small. Or perhaps the administration is at fault after all...We came to realize in the course of our campaign that the underlying cause of this Taiheiji extension class independence movement was the prejudice against night junior high schools and discrimination against Koreans...We won independence. We will pride ourselves on winning this movement and endeavor to study at Taiheiji Night Junior High School with our heads held high.

Oppositional subjects in the private sphere

The Taiheiji Independence Movement helped Korean women in Japan to become political subjects in the public sphere. At first glance, though, it appears to have no connection with the private sphere. Women's activities in the public sphere, however, were closely related to their positioning in the private sphere. Kang Woo-ja's case helps us to see how this public sphere activity led to the formation of a new subject within the family domain. Kang Woo-ja was the president of the student council and a leading figure in the movement. Her eloquent speeches at negotiations and meetings with the administrative authority were often broadcast on television and featured in newspapers. Kang Woo-ja is a second-generation Korean who speaks Japanese as her mother tongue. She decided to enter night junior high school because she had not gone to school when she was a child. She lost her father when she was young and grew up in a rural village in prewar Western Japan with no connection to the Korean community in Japan. She came to learn about the Korean community for the first time when she moved to Ikaino upon marriage.

> It was only after I got married that I became conscious of my Korean identity. And that was not because of my teacher. It was an old Korean woman who lived in the neighborhood. My husband was also poor and the youngest in the family. It was common to rent a room back then and [the owner of the house] happened to be a person from the village [where her husband's family came from in Korea]. On top of that, the person was a relative of my mother-in-law. I was thrown into that kind of environment. I grew up eating Japanese pickles in rural Japan, you see. Then, I got married and all of a sudden, I was

Formation of Oppositional Subjects

> so-called *banjjokbari*,[23] not Japanese but not Korean either. She said she had to teach me the way. The word *banjjokbari* is a very insulting term. I was called that by my mother-in-law, too. I felt hurt. Ikaino is a unique place. There are a lot of Koreans. It's very far from the station and inconvenient for transportation. It worked out well that I came from the countryside [and therefore was malleable]. I didn't feel it was annoying [when given unwanted interference]. That's because I didn't know anything. Apparently a girl without a father is not so appreciated. So, they thought they had to train me. They even taught me how to do laundry. Slap and rinse, slap and rinse. Those old women who lived close by who claimed to be my relatives. I didn't feel it was hard but I was just doing all I could. I was taught all about *jesa* by those aunties, too. The year after I got married, I started performing *jesa*. The aunties were all excited. I can say with pride now that I know everything about it, regardless of whether I can perform it properly or not. I was looked after really well. Because of them I can now identify myself as Korean.

When she moved to Ikaino upon marriage, Kang Woo-ja joined a group of fellow Korean women in which the hierarchical order based on age and generation was even stricter than the Japanese society in which she had grown up. Since all she had known was the Japanese society until then, she was thoroughly trained on Korean culture and customs, cooking and language from her mother-in-law and other older women. She committed herself to fit in as the wife of a Korean man. Meanwhile, however, the issue of 'race' was causing a tension between her and her husband.

> I didn't mind learning things [from older women] but there was one thing I did mind. My husband. You know, actually, I wanted to be Japanese [when living in the countryside before marriage]. My husband was a quiet man but had a strong sense of national consciousness. He used to tell me different stories when there was no TV or radio. Stories like his grandpa did such and such long time ago. Stories from the past. But I know what he would say next. He would tell you how women should behave. I hated it and couldn't stand it. We are Korean and stay Korean. We will never become Japanese. We can't think the same way as Japanese. My heart broke every time he said those things. All I knew was Japan. I could only speak Japanese. I could understand Jeju language when the aunties talked to me but

I couldn't speak it. I was taught a lot of things but still I couldn't say 'I'm happy to be Korean'; I didn't want to say it. When my husband said Koreans were superior to Japanese, I got upset. I have given that topic a lot of thought. Until I got married, I had only seen myself at the bottom. I wanted to be accepted in the rural village. But we were not considered humans. We couldn't say anything. The reason we had to feel this way is because of the [foreigners'] registration. If not for this, we could be part of them [referring to Japanese]. Until I got married, I was thinking how I could become Japanese and how I could be the same as them. It's not that I didn't want to marry a Korean but I married without knowing what it was like. I cried for three days but three days only. After that, I gave up. However, my husband kept telling me the story of the river in Korea and I hated it so much. I wonder what this feeling of strong admiration for Japanese people was about. Such a terrible pity. I want to take it back. My mother says such was the times but I wish I were a little more right-minded. I was like that until I entered night junior high school. It all changed after I entered night school.

Kang Woo-ja's first-generation-Korean husband treated her harshly because she was born in Japan. Denigrated by the person who is supposed to be the closest to her over her 'ethnicity', she grew increasingly resentful of the patriarchy that subordinates women to men. After moving to Ikaino, she, on the one hand, gained an understanding of Korean ethnic culture, while on the other hand, developed a deep inner conflict against sexism that is ingrained into the 'ethnic consciousness'. As described in the previous chapter, her husband opposed her entering night school for two years until she finally enrolled at the age of fifty-three.

Until I entered night junior high school, I had trouble with my husband for two years. After all these years...When I started going to school, he was completely closed off. When I would come home and tell him that, he would just be like 'humph'. He was pleased that I was developing ethnic consciousness. He understood that kind of thing... My husband I don't think is proud of his wife 'studying'. It would be a big problem if he found out I was raising my voice and speaking in public everywhere [during the independence movement]. Oh yes. But he never told me not to go to that sort of place. He used to bug me about going out. He knows my work hours so would be checking if

I'm home by a certain time. You know, you sometimes go on a trip. He would quiz me 'What trip you women need to make'. He never opens his mouth without saying 'you women'. Still, if I think about how my husband's brother is, my husband was relatively open. He considered men as more important but he also used the word gender equality. He would say women should act like women but also said that men had to get their act together for women to act like women…I didn't bother to argue how he made me look like the wronged one. He would get angry when things were looking bad for him. He was afraid of losing an argument with a woman. Then he would bring up the women thing. I hated that. It was frustrating.

After she finally entered night school, her mindset changed significantly and it began affecting the politics between her and her husband. She says she regained her 'own voice' at the night school and reconsidered her relationship with her husband.

What I can say about the time is, I was letting my voice out when I went to school. Because we couldn't speak at home, we were told to let our voice out at school. The teacher told us to let our voice out, and with the voice, let ourselves out. I couldn't say anything at first. After about half a year, I was finally able to say 'Kang Woo-ja' when answering phone calls…My husband would tell me to 'go' when we see people campaigning. We would go to negotiations [with the educational administration]. He had no idea I was leading the negotiations. So, I couldn't show him the documents, those that mentioned president of the student council. I couldn't show him if the name (Kang Woo-ja's) was written on it. He looked at other documents. He would tell me 'You must attend this' or 'Take a day off work and go to this'.

Although her husband was against her enrolling in night junior high school, he did appreciate her starting to use her ethnic name, as a positive step to foster an ethnic consciousness. After entering night school, she slowly started to voice her opinions even in front of her husband. She broke her silence and began expressing her own 'voice' – expressing her thoughts as a Korean and as a woman. Her husband actively supported her participation during the night junior high school independence movement provided that she would not 'stand at the forefront' so as not to deviate from the gender norm. The truth, however, was she was the president of the student council.

My children knew [that she was involved in the campaign]. I kept quiet about it though. If you ask me why, it's because my grandchildren went to school. That is Kang Woo-ja's grandchild, they say. You see, I was told not to take the newspapers [that reported the campaign]. When I happened to receive it, I had to hide it. That was a lot of trouble. My husband would be in a bad mood whenever there was a phone call asking for Kang Woo-ja. The interviews were done at school. My husband may have known about half of what was going on but he didn't know I was leading the campaign. He was aware that I was participating in the campaign, though. 'You must help the campaign.' 'Go if they need more people.' It was like that when we did the sit-in. When I was sacked from work [for taking too many days off for the campaign], my husband said that it didn't matter. When I told him I wouldn't be able to prepare lunch for him for a certain day because I would be away during the lunch time, he would ask me what it was this time. I would tell him this time there would be some event at the prefectural government building, he would tell me that I must go. He cared about the movement a great deal. It's just his wife should not put herself forward too much because she is a woman.

Most of the women who led the movement reported that they rarely talked to their family about affairs at school and the movement. The reason for this appears to be their awareness of departing from the traditional gender norm. Hardly any effort to be accepted or have a discussion to alter the views of the family members was observed from the women. Instead, they secured their freedom to study at night school in exchange for impeccably managing 'their' household chores and work as a 'wife' and 'mother'. To that extent, the night school independence movement did not bring about a fundamental change in the gender structure in which these women were confined. Nevertheless, the movement provided them with a pretext for contributing to the ethnic society, allowing them a greater freedom to engage in political life outside of the private sphere.

The night junior high school independence movement denounced the racial inequality within the local communities but it never recognized the asymmetrical gender relationship as a problem. The Taiheiji Independence Movement was directly linked to the interests of Korean women and contributed to their advancement. But the fact that lack of schooling and illiteracy is a gender specific issue was hardly acknowledged.

While collecting the life stories of the women who had actively participated in the movement, I was often confronted by the fact that the women had internalized the view that men are masters and women are servants. Although the gender issue is sometimes raised within the context of human rights education at night schools, students seem to have almost no perspective that would help them to radically reframe the gender structure as an issue relevant to Korean women in Japan. According to an interview with a male Japanese teacher, when he explored discrimination against women in a class on International Women's Day, he received a lukewarm response from the students. One student even commented that 'hens must not crow'.[24] By the time Korean women in Japan enter night school, they would have already fulfilled their roles as 'daughter-in-law', 'wife' and 'mother'. Many of them have achieved the relatively strong position of 'mother-in-law'. This may dampen any motivation to explore the problems of gender discrimination in night school classes.

So it appears that, while the issue of gender discrimination was not highlighted either in the night school classes or in the independence movement, the women's participation in the movement had an impact on gender politics within the private sphere, as evident in Kang Woo-ja's case.

Oppositional subjects in the ethnic community

Let us now examine how the independence movement by Korean women promoted the formation of an oppositional subject in the community of Koreans in Japan. Korean ethnic organizations are part of everyday life for Koreans living in Korean town in Osaka, in sending children to ethnic schools, attending organizational events, subscribing to organizational newspapers, having family members as staff, and so on. While those women who went to night school were members of either Mindan or Chonryun, they were generally uninterested in playing active roles in the ethnic organizations. After all, the act of going to school, especially a Japanese school, was a deviation from the norm for married, mature-aged Korean women.

This situation changed, however, when the Taiheiji Independence Movement emerged. It attracted support from the local younger-generation Koreans who were moved by the desperate appeal of these '*omoni*' (mothers) and '*halmoni*' (grandmothers) to 'Please open a night junior high school for us'. On the occasion of the sit-in in front of the Higashi-Osaka City Board of Education in October 1993, ethnic teachers and members of Minsokukyō[25] based in Higashi-Osaka City came to cheer and helped by handing out flyers and supporting the campaigners with chants of '*igyeora*' (win) and a soup-run. An ethnic teacher came to cheer with the children from her ethnic class,[26] considering it to be part of their ethnic education. Local Korean restaurants brought food. Ethnic newspapers featured stories on the movement.[27] In short, many generations of Koreans became involved in the Taiheiji Independence Movement.

The movement led by elderly Korean women drew support from a broad range of people as it echoed all of the postcolonial campaigns by Koreans in Japan to protest against discrimination by the public authorities. While exhibiting the characteristics of an ethnic movement, this campaign also prompted women to constitute themselves as oppositional subjects which countered the patriarchy within the ethnic community. I will explore this from the perspective of the gender order within the ethnic community based on the narrative of a later-generation Korean woman.

Chung Kwi-mi (third-generation, born in the 1950s) was born and raised in Ikaino and established a career as a medical specialist, both in a private hospital and with a municipal health provider. She has been an activist since her late teens and has been continuously involved in ethnic emancipation and feminist campaigns in the local community through organizations such as Hancheong and Yeoseonghoe. The Taiheiji Independence Movement began when she was working as a teacher for an ethnic class in a public school in Higashi-Osaka City. She later became an instructor at Uri Seodang, a self-directed learning center for Korean women in Japan who were obliged to graduate from night school due to an administrative decree to stringently enforce a maximum time limit of study in March 1994 (see the discussion in Chapter 3). This provided an opportunity for her to become involved with the older Korean women in the community. Her underlying motivation was the gender discrimination that she had encountered while working as an ethnic instructor.

> There were occasions when I clashed with Korean male instructors in regards to education goals. To give you a specific example, there

is a Korean children's song. There is a song called '*Gaeguri*', which means 'frog'. How I understand it is that it is probably a song from a father's perspective, sung by a father. *Gaeguri* croaking ribbit, ribbit, the song goes. It goes *adeul* (son), *sonja* (grandchild) and *myeoneuri* (daughter-in-law), '*da moyeoseo*' (everyone come together). So, it's singing about a family. It's about a family lineage, you see. It mentions a daughter-in-law, a grandchild and a son. I wondered why *omoni* (mother) is not mentioned. Why daughter is not mentioned. I never sing this song because I hate this expression. I didn't realize it when I was younger but I noticed it when I was campaigning for Yeoseonghoe and then decided to never sing this song again. When I told this story to some male ethnic instructor colleagues, they said I was too obsessed. I tried to tell them no issue would be sorted out if I don't obsess about things, giving them all sorts of different examples but they say all those were too trivial. It was very hard to make them understand so we had no choice but to break away from men.

Chung Kwi-mi has always placed importance on education 'at the field level' and was therefore critical of the androcentrism of the Korean community in Japan. This lead to her being somewhat isolated at times. With traditional Korean education, it was difficult to achieve both ethnic liberation and women's emancipation. As she was struggling with this dilemma, she met the group of Korean women who were studying at night schools.

> They had no way to hide it, particularly the first-generation women, in this Japanese society. Especially our *halmoni* couldn't even go to school because they are women. Men went to school. Our *halmoni* just supported their family and siblings without going to school. They just lived every day but that in itself was a huge contribution to the Korean community in Japan. Compared to that, we, as second- and third-generation Koreans, I think, made hardly any contribution to the Korean community. To me, the reason is because we haven't been looking at how the first-generation Koreans lived, especially the women, our *halmoni*. We must understand how they have been protecting their children and family in this Japanese society while they looked Korean in every way and couldn't speak Japanese well, let alone write it. They overcame all that and that's why they are steadfast, caring and strong. Of course, I don't mean we must live like that but

we must know who has been protecting our livelihood in Japan and how they have been doing so.

Her approach to the night school independence movement displays a feminist perspective in addition to an ethnic liberation perspective. That is, she recognizes the senior Korean women in Japan, who had been rendered invisible, and reconsidering their experiences, which are different from men's, and considering their role as the bearers and transmitters of Korean ethnic cultural resources. It may be important for subsequent-generation Koreans to not only learn the Korean language and culture as abstract knowledge, but to directly communicate and interact with the first-generation women. It seems, after all, that the women who were born in Korea have been ignored simply because they were 'women', ignoring the fact that they had strong ethnic knowledge and extensive historical experience. As we have seen throughout these chapters, in most Korean ethnic organizations, men held exclusive decision-making power. In both the official and informal history of Koreans in Japan, women are invisible. It may be, however, that the Korean community in Japan is what it is now because of the selfless contributions of first- and older second-generation women.

Through her interaction with elderly women who were studying at night schools, Chung Kwi-mi began to absorb and inherit the words, culture and history that they embodied. Her determination grew and matured while she served as a volunteer instructor at Uri Seodang. She then put that determination into practice through being involved as medical staff in the founding and management of the day care home and service center Sarangbang.

Uri Seodang and Sarangbang are by-products of the night school independence movement. They became activity centers for local Korean women after the social movement lost its *raison d'etre* with the opening of the independent night school. Both organizations receive financial assistance from government under the respective life-long education program by the Ministry of Education and Elderly Care Insurance System. Uri Seodang and Sarangbang have created an opportunity to forge transgenerational solidarity and provide the foundation for maintaining the subaltern counterpublics created by those women. These organizations will be discussed in detail in the next chapter.

Local multiculturalism and *halmoni*

The first generations of Korean women in Japan were segregated, rendered invisible and objectified in mainstream Japanese society. However, during the Taiheiji Independence Movement, they raised their profile in the local community through campaigning and came to be recognized as subjects with a particular identity. These subjects who emerged in the public space differed from both of two extreme views of Korean women in Japan – one being powerless, passive women victimized by male chauvinism and the other being resourceful 'great *omoni*' devoted to their family. These social actors were not dependent on any men, nor was their identity reducible to being someone's mother or wife. Rather, they appeared as oppositional subjects who directly confronted the public authority and demanded their own rights with conviction. The Korean women who emerged in the local public space through the movement are now affectionately referred to as *'omoni'* (mother) or *'halmoni'* (grandmother), which have now acquired new significations under the principle of multiculturalism.

Yamawaki, Kashiwazaki and Kondo define multiculturalism as 'a process by which people belonging to heterogeneous groups build equal relationships whilst respecting each other's cultural differences' (2003: 140). Multiculturalism seeks to find ways for residents whose ancestry stems from different countries to live in harmony while entailing contradictory notions of 'diversity' and 'equality'.[28] The word 'multiculturalism' has become an important concept in policy-making in those municipalities with large populations of foreigners. In the Taiheiji Independence Movement, Nikkan Shimin no Kai, a civil organization, stood by the students and provided powerful support in their negotiations with the boards of education and other processes. In Higashi-Osaka, Nikkan Shimin no Kai is one of the most active lobbying organizations concerned with the policies directed at the city's foreign residents.[29]

The population of Higashi-Osaka City is approximately 500,000, of which around three percent are foreign nationals. South Korean and Chosun combined are the largest group of foreign nationalities, accounting for around 13,000 out of the total of 17,000 foreign nationals.[30] Multiculturalism developed as Higashi-Osaka City policy as follows. First, in 1982, the Basic Guidelines for the Protection of

Photo 5.2: Women from Uri Seodang participating in the international festival

Source: Taken by the author

the Human Rights of the Korean and Other Foreign Residents of Higashi-Osaka City were drafted. The aim of these guidelines was to:

> represent our commitment to guaranteeing fundamental human rights for all citizens including foreign residents, in pursuit of our basic goal of eliminating all forms of discrimination and successfully dealing with various issues facing our society today, in compliance with the Japanese Constitution and international covenants on human rights, and with an accurate understanding of the historical backgrounds of the Korean people living in Japan and their current social situation.

In the 1990s, the number of so-called 'newcomer' foreigners who came to Japan for work and study skyrocketed. Hence, the 'internationalization of the community' became an issue for the local government. In 1992, the Higashi-Osaka City Internationalization Policy (renamed the Higashi-Osaka City Internationalization Promotion Policy in 2008) was adopted. Then, in response to further changes in the environment, the city created the Council to Review the Basic Guidelines for the Protection of Human Rights of the Korean and Other Foreign Residents of Higashi-Osaka City and the Council of Advisors to Discuss Policy Measures for Foreign Residents of Higashi-Osaka City in 2001. The Basic Guidelines for Support Measures for the Foreign Residents of Higashi-Osaka City: Developing a Community Friendly to People of All National Origins was formulated based on proposals from those two councils. The Basic Guidelines outlines three basic objectives: 'to comply with the principle of equality between foreign and Japanese nationals', 'to realize a multicultural, multi-ethnic society' and 'to encourage foreign nationals' participation in local activities'. The specific actions to be taken include: enhancing administrative services such as welfare for the elderly; enhancing educational and cultural services including support for ethnic schools and multi-ethnic, multicultural education; and internationalizing administrative services such as increasing the participation of foreign residents in municipal administration (Higashi-Osaka City 2003).

The Korean women who studied at night schools did not necessarily directly benefit from this series of multicultural measures. Uri Seodang, however, a self-directed school for Korean women, receives a subsidy from the government as a social education program and Sarangbang receives a subsidy as an elderly care insurance program. Uri Seodang has also been granted NPO status. They participate in multicultural events in Higashi-Osaka City, seeking opportunities to gain exposure to the public. Through both of these organizations, the Korean women who study at night schools are involved in the city's multiculturalism as *halmoni,* a symbolic figure of Korean women.

Multiculturalism in Higashi-Osaka City is promoted at the grassroots level, with mutual interactions among different groups of foreign residents and campaigns that support them increasing each year. These groups include the two major ethnic organizations for Koreans in Japan, Mindan and Chongryun, as well as Uri Seodang, Higashi-Osaka Minzoku Kōshikai (Higashi-Osaka Association of Ethnic Instructors), Nikkan Shimin no Kai, Higashi-Osaka Dōhō Hogosha no Kai (Higashi-Osaka Association of Parents of Korean Students), Chūgoku Kikokusha Kyōkai (Society of Returnees from China), Higashi-Osakashi Kyōshokuin Kumiai (Higashi-Osaka City Teachers Union) and JICHIRO (All-Japan Prefectural and Municipal Workers Union).

Since 1996, these organizations have jointly hosted the Higashi-Osaka International Festival every year, with sponsorship by Higashi-Osaka City. Under the slogan 'My city is a city of Asia. My city is a city of the world', the event features twenty-five participating organizations including organizations of Koreans in Japan such as ethnic schools and Korean youth organizations, Japanese emigrants and their descendants from Vietnam and South America, Chinese people and people from Okinawa. It typically draws a crowd of about 6,000.[31] Night school graduates participate as one of the main organizers of the festival. At the stand with a banner that reads 'Night Junior High School', a group of high-spirited *halmoni* in traditional Korean costume sell Korean food and rice wine. For the grand finale of the festival, *halmoni* take the stage to perform traditional Korean singing and dancing.

An international festival is a place in which minority groups and cultural resources tend to be 'displayed'. It often emphasizes a hypostasized ethnic culture. However, the women from Uri Seodang take advantage of the festival as active civic subjects rather than being passively 'displayed'. During my participant observation at the International Festival (2002), I observed women handing out leaflets calling for guarantees of ethnic education and condemning the injustice of an assault against students of Chongryun-affiliated ethnic schools.[32] This illustrates how the women took advantage of the festival as a place to express their opinions.

As shown above, the active subjects that emerged from the night schools can be characterized as active 'citizens' at the local level. It corresponds to the 'citizenship' proposed by feminist sociologists, defined by active participation and practice as well as identity (Lister 1997; Siim 2000),[33] rather than merely a legal status with equal rights and duties as defined by Marshal and Bottomore (1992). The campaign for an independent school demanded both redistribution and recognition by the municipal government. Having no suffrage in Japan, the Korean women utilized a public institution – night school – as a foothold and adopted a non-institutional means – social campaigns – to access local politics, in an effort to achieve equal membership at the local level. Yes, this self-directing subject/citizen is embedded in internationalization and multiculturalism at the community level, but its formation is not attributable to these external factors alone; it would not have occurred without the performativity of the campaign itself. The public expression of the historical experiences and ethnic traits that are performatively etched in their bodies constitutes a civic subject with an ethnic culture in the local community.

The word '*halmoni*', which has now become almost assimilated into the Japanese language of the social movement sector, refers to an identity that is characterized by its Korean language and cultural origins as well as specific historical experiences. Notwithstanding the difference between Korean language and culture ingrained in their lives and that of the modern South Korean society, the Korean women in Japan have used this identity strategically to create positions for themselves in the local community.

Uri Seodang, which operates on the campuses of Chōei Night Junior High School and Taiheiji Night Junior High School, is currently constituted as an NPO. It acts as a hub for initiatives and activities of local Korean women as a whole, not only the alumni of the night schools. Uri Seodang was begun in 1994 as a self-directing school created for about forty women who were forced to graduate from night school following an administrative decision to restrict the length of enrolments. Uri Seodang is an independent school that differs in nature from both public night schools and *omoni hakkyo* (literally 'mothers' school', literacy classes for Korean mothers in Japan). It is different in that it is run with a strong awareness of its role as an activity hub and as an organization that represents Korean women in the local community. Uri Seodang is a place for Korean women to uphold the true value of studying at night schools – not only to learn how to read and write, but rather to learn their own history and social position and to nurture a passion for living as a Korean person – even after graduation. Studying at a night school for a certain period of time and acquiring literacy skills alone is not sufficient to empower Korean women to get by in Japanese society as 'Koreans'. The alumni studying in Uri Seodang put their heart and soul into the Taiheiji Independence Movement even though they were no longer permitted to study there. This commitment signified their determination to redefine their relationship with the society in which they found themselves, building a new relationship through practices as 'Koreans' which they came to understand through their studies at night school.[34]

Uri Seodang's activities are not limited to teaching night classes. It has also been proactive in promoting an understanding of the history and social status of the first generations of Korean women in Japan, representing them in the local community and in South Korean society. Its management staff comprise later-generation Korean women who were inspired by the independence movement to meet and learn from their *halmoni*; hence the name 'Uri Seodang, a place to learn from learners'. While young Koreans and Japanese volunteers teach classes, Uri Seodang also provides opportunities for *halmoni* to pass on the language and culture as well as knowledge about the Korean Peninsula and Koreans in Japan. Their public events draw large crowds of local Japanese and young Koreans who want to hear the personal histories of older Korean women in Japan. Furthermore, women from Uri Seodang sometimes visit local public schools to give talks. When I conducted a participant observation at a history-themed 'relay talk', an event in which four *halmoni* gave speeches in turn (March 2002), I was impressed by a group of junior high school students listening intently to their stories. On a different occasion, a group of local high school students came to the Sarangbang day care home to meet *halmoni*. The youngsters appeared nervous at first to meet *halmoni* with whom they rarely had a chance to communicate in a real sense despite living in the same local community. However, as their interactions progressed, they deepened into a communication that transcends generation, race and age.

The *halmoni* share stories of colonial rule, war and postwar racial discrimination in the context of fragments of their daily lives, all of it centered on their family. In this context, the anti-discriminatory and pacifist views they share are obviously shaped by their accumulated life experience, rather than dogmatic assertions of specific beliefs or ideologies. Obviously their perspective is heavily colored by the fraught historical relationship between the Korean Peninsula and Japan, but it is clearly rooted in their 'firsthand' everyday life experience, rather than the abstract and impersonal ideology promoted by the state. The specific topics can be quite distressing, but their straightforward narratives are told with constant humor and laughter. One of the young students commented, 'The *halmoni* were so much more vibrant than us and

Photo 5.3: Rally with former comfort women for the Japanese military in front of the Embassy of Japan in Seoul'

Source: Provided by Anyang Civil University

very welcoming even though they have gone through hard times. I enjoyed talking and eating with them'.[35]

Uri Seodang's members have also develop strong ties with South Korea's civil society. In July 2002, some women from Uri Seodang visited Anyang Civil University, a literacy education institution located in Anyang City in South Korea, with a group of students from Moriguchi Night Junior High School and Chōei Night Junior High School. The exchange program was facilitated by Takano Masao, who was campaigning to increase the number of night junior high schools in Tokyo. Anyang Civil University is operated by campaigners who promote literacy education (called *munhae*) in South Korea. It caters to 450 female students ranging in age from their forties to seventies.[36] The program was designed to develop a sense of solidarity and an awareness that the illiteracy of Korean women in Japan and adult women in Korea share common factors. These include: sociopolitical upheaval from colonial rule, the Pacific War and the Korean War; poverty; and discrimination against women.

In October 2007, the women from Uri Seodang organized a rally supporting 'military comfort women' held in front of the Embassy of Japan in Seoul. They demanded an apology and compensation from the Japanese government with former comfort women (Photo 5.3). In 2008, they sent some members to participate in the sixtieth memorial service for the Jeju April 3 Uprising. They have also spoken as witnesses about their historical experiences in regards to the Jeju April 3 Uprising and the Hanshin Education Struggle in interviews for television programs by Korea's KBS as well as Japan's NHK.[37]

Uri Seodang bases itself in the social space of Korean women in Japan that has been created within public institutions, specifically night junior high schools. At the same time, it is a subaltern counterpublic of Korean women in Japan formed outside the framework of the night schools in response to the segregation of students into the extension classrooms. Uri Seodang is a civil social space that gives rise to discourses that position the women who lived through colonial and postcolonial times burdened with poverty and illiteracy as subjects. It is shaped by the interaction of people who try to listen to and understand their voices and experiences. It enabled these women to communicate directly with the local community and government administration as autonomous subjects rather than individuals who are patronized by the ethnic community or the patriarch of their family. The scope of activities of the Korean women in Japan who unite in Uri Seodang has now expanded beyond the boundaries of the ethnic groups and national borders. The subaltern counterpublics of Korean women in Japan is gradually building connections with different publics created by other minorities such as social campaigns by illiterate adult women in South Korea. In the process it is becoming a part of a transnational subaltern counterpublic.

6 Intergenerational solidarity and the reconstruction of ethnicity

The Taiheiji Night Junior High School Independence Movement, which started in 1993 in Higashi-Osaka City, came to an end eight years later, when the extension class was designated a formal night junior high school in 2001. During the movement, while the campaigners were negotiating with the Board of Education to improve the night school situation, they also founded Uri Seodang, a self-directed learning space, and Sarangbang, a place for aging women to stay during the day. Both of these are still operating today. Since 2009, Uri Seodang has been based in two places: Chōei Night Junior High School and Taiheiji Night Junior High School. Similarly, Sarangbang now operates a day care service center. While both Uri Seodang and Sarangbang are places for women who have studied at night school, they are different types of organizations than public schools. Uri Seodang operates within the Lifelong Learning Promotion Plan by Higashi-Osaka City, and Sarangbang operates under the Long-term Care Insurance System by the Ministry of Health.

The development of these organizations indicates the extent to which the Taiheiji Independence Movement has transformed the activities of Korean women in Japan within local communities. These organizations have been approached by people and organizations that seek to interact with the Korean women who are studying or have studied at night junior high school, including later-generation Koreans, new Korean migrants, night school teachers, Japanese residents and citizens' groups concerned with literacy and human rights. They also have ongoing exchanges with citizens' literacy groups in South Korea and with Korean migrants in other countries. Perhaps the most significant achievement of the Taiheiji Independence Movement was bringing together people of different nationalities, ethnic backgrounds, generations, classes and genders and creating social spaces in which these people can freely congregate, discuss their concerns, criticize the power structures that marginalize them, and create counter discourses to change society. The newly formed ties between older and younger generations of Korean women in Japan is particularly noteworthy. Despite sharing the characteristic of being 'Korean women in Japan', there are significant differences both linguistically and culturally, based on different socio-historical experiences and lifestyles between those who were born in the Korean Peninsula and migrated to Japan in the colonial period and those who were born and raised in Japan. Despite these differences, in both Uri Seodang and Sarangbang, young and elderly, migrants and locally born, long-term residents and newly arrived women of Korean heritage have built relationships of mutual respect, tapping into each other's linguistic and cultural resources for mutual learning. This social space for Korean women in Japan is also notable for the fact that the patriarchy, which is deeply ingrained in the Korean family and ethnic rights organizations, has very limited influence in these organization, although they otherwise retain strong ethnic characteristics.

Uri Seodang and Sarangbang lie in between the Korean ethnic families and communities and the Japanese public sphere, providing bridges between them. It has become apparent that it was actually the gender order of the Korean as well as Japanese culture rather than the racism of Japanese society that had kept Korean women confined to the private sphere and ethnic community. Institutions such as Uri Seodang and Sarangbang are now providing social spaces that foster a new Korean woman-subject in the public sphere. This can be observed in a multitude of activities that have been organized around Uri Seodang. Specifically, both the first-generation women and later-generation women are emerging as active subjects in the local society – the former as the bearers of Korean language and culture as well as historical experiences and the latter as helpers mediating the first-generation women with the host society.

This chapter will examine the relationship between intergenerational interaction and subject formation in the public sphere, focusing on the connections and interactions that occur daily between multiple generations of women in the context of the activities that developed out of night schools.

First, I will introduce the concept of 'socio-cultural mediation' as it has been used to analyze the associative activities of female immigrants in France. This analytical concept helps to reveal the mutual support between first-generation women, who possess the language and culture of their society of origin, and subsequent-generation women who embody the language and culture of the host society. Next, I will outline how this concept helps us to better understand the relationships between the elderly Korean women in Japan and the voluntary organizations that are becoming increasingly active in the areas of concentrated Korean settlement in Osaka. Then I will move on to an analysis of the interactions between elderly Korean women and the younger-generation women who work in the day care home Sarangbang based on participant observation. Finally, I will discuss the ways in which the intergenerational solidarity of women is contributing to women's subject formation in the public sphere.

Socio-cultural mediation by immigrant women

Let us now look at the case of African women from former colonies who settled in France,[1] in relation to solidarity and voluntary activities of female immigrants in a host society. In France, since the 1980s, there has been steady growth in associative activities that encourage mutual support among immigrant women. As part of these activities, the migrant women who arrived first, settling and becoming familiar with the local language and social system, provide assistance to women who have recently migrated from the same place of origin. This assistance takes a variety of forms, including providing information about public residential services and childcare, helping them to meet the requirements for receiving those services and providing advice on family issues. Women migrants encounter different challenges than men when they begin life in the host society. Whereas the first-generation migrant men are positioned at the bottom of the labor market as low-paid manual laborers, the first-generation migrant women assume total responsibilities for the family domain, including housework, child-rearing and nursing care. They tend to be alienated from opportunities for language education and occupational training. Without work opportunities, women must rely on men to meet the economic and legal requirements for life in France, which makes their post-immigration lives more difficult (Freedman 2000).

In recognition of this situation, associative activities have been designed to address the problems of women who are not only subject to racial and gender discrimination in French society but who are also subordinate to men in their private sphere. Quiminal points out the mediatory character of these mutual aid associations – while they conduct wide-ranging activities, they also serve as a socio-cultural bridge between the private sphere in which African women were 'confined' and France's public sphere. These associations help immigrant women who suffer from multiple forms of oppression to develop a deeper understanding of French society, thus enhancing social integration (Quiminal 2000: 39).

Those who perform this 'socio-cultural mediation' are mainly migrant women who are already well-established in France and second-generation women. This type of mediatory activity is not unique to late 20th-century France, but has been carried out in an informal fashion in other migrant societies as well. However, one important characteristic of the associative activities of immigrant women in France is that the role of 'socio-cultural mediation' has been somewhat institutionalized as a result of immigrant integration policies adopted at the local level. At the same time, the socio-cultural mediation role specific to African women is attracting a lot of attention in France as it is at variance with the predominant French integration model, which does not, in principle, make allowance for any individual attributes, such as gender (Ito 1999, 2000).

As discussed in previous chapters, Korean women in Japan were similarly responsible for family care as well as all other aspects of the private sphere. A significant proportion of first-generation women are illiterate and have limited competence in the Japanese language. The language barrier makes it more difficult for them to access the services and resources of Japanese society. Therefore, the women of subsequent generations, who were born and raised in Japan and are familiar with the Japanese language and culture – mostly daughters or daughters-in-law – have been called upon to provide support for their first-generation mothers and mothers-in-law on a wide range of matters that require engagement with Japanese society. However, Korean women in Japan differ from the socio-cultural mediators in France in that there is no state policy to promote social integration of immigrants in Japan, so the socio-cultural mediation activities of subsequent-generation women have no institutional support.

Despite these differences, though, the concept of 'socio-cultural mediation' offers valuable insight into the intergenerational mutual assistance among Korean women in Japan. Importantly, however, as soon as we start down this path we note significant differences between the French and Japanese cases. First, Quiminal assumes that the mediators are the women who have been in the host country the longest, providing support to new migrants. 'Mediation' from this perspective appears to be one-way. In contrast, my participant observation at the Sarangbang day care home revealed that the first-generation women were transmitting Korean culture, language, customs and regional dispositions to the subsequent-generation women along with their historical experiences. The subsequent-generation women were embracing the cultural knowledge and experiences of the first-generation women even while providing 'mediation' support to help the older women get by in their everyday life in Japan. In other words, the study found that this socio-cultural mediation goes both ways. Furthermore, we find that in learning the culture and experiences of the first-generation women, the subsequent-generation women enhanced their identities as 'Korean women in Japan', demanding recognition in mainstream Japanese society and constructing themselves as active subjects.

Prior to the establishment of Sarangbang, the socio-cultural mediation performed by younger Korean women for their elders was generally conducted within households and thus, like the women themselves, was rendered invisible. The intergenerational, bidirectional socio-cultural mediation in the day care home, however, affected the construction of more positive ethnic identity and transformed the subjectivity of all generations of Korean women in the public sphere in Japan. This may be attributable to the fact that the actions moved out of the household and into the social space of the day care home, which is incorporated within the public policy framework.

Mirroring the aging of the Japanese population as a whole, a graph of the age and sex characteristics of the population with South Korean or Chosun nationality gently curves up to a peak at around forty years of age and then slowly declines. Although the total population of South Korean and Chosun residents has been gradually falling in recent years, the elderly population (aged 65 and over) has been increasing while the child population (aged 14 and under) has been decreasing. The elderly population overtook the child population in 1999, reaching 15.1% at the end of 2005.[2] Women comprise the majority due to differences in average life expectancy. In fact, in a survey of the elderly residents in Ikuno Ward in Osaka Prefecture, home to a sizeable population of Korean residents (Zainichi Kōreisha Chōsa I'inkai 2004), a staggering 74% of the 300 valid respondents were female. The aging population of Koreans in Japan is also a women's issue.

Figure 6.1: Shift in total population, child population and elderly population with South Korean or Chosun nationality

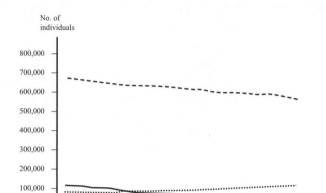

Source: Created by author based on *Statistics on the Foreigners Registered in Japan* of the respective years by the Ministry of Justice Immigration Bureau.

In the society of Koreans in Japan, the aging of the Korean population, and in particular the passing of the first-generation women, tends to be seen as a threat to the community, leading to the erosion of the Korean language and culture. However, as we have seen, the aging of the population has prompted new forms of interaction among Koreans of different generations, including increasing voluntary activities to support the elderly. This has resulted in a wide-spread restructuring of the Korean ethnic community (Kawano 2007). Hence, rather than an 'erosion of ethnicity', it seems that what is actually occurring might more accurately be called a 'revitalization', in which the language and culture of the first-generation women are being appreciated and transmitted to subsequent-generation women.

When the Long-term Care Insurance System was introduced in 2000, it did not contain the Nationality Clause. It thus acted as a catalyst for the inclusion into the Japanese social welfare framework of seniors with South Korean and Chosun nationality, who had been excluded from the National Pension Scheme.[3] The Long-term Care

Insurance System also facilitated a variety of new support services targeting elderly Koreans. As the first-generation Koreans aged, the shortage of services to meet their needs became a serious problem. Existing elderly support services were mainly intended to serve Japanese people. Services that took the food, clothing, housing, customs and language needs of elderly Koreans into account were almost non-existent.[4]

In part, this might have been attributable to the Korean tradition that confined nursing care work to the private sphere, to be performed by wives, daughters and daughters-in-law within the family. However, as more support services specifically catering for elderly Koreans have been established, the care work has become progressively externalized. This has had a profound effect on the patriarchal family structures, and the androcentric ethnic society more generally. Long-term care services are operated by a number of organizations including the existing Korean ethnic organizations Chongryun and Mindan, religious organizations, and civil groups promoting multicultural symbiosis. The types of support provided are diverse, spanning from day care homes which encourage social participation, home-visit care, day care services and residential care facilities. Many of the businesses have been given Korean names[5] and are staffed with young Koreans who are qualified home-helpers, nurses and care workers. In these facilities, the elderly can communicate in Korean, eat either Korean or Japanese meals and perform Korean songs and dances in their recreation programs. Most of the users of these facilities are women, as are almost all of the care providers.

Multidimensional interaction at the day care home

Day care home as an activity hub

The day care home Sarangbang, founded in October 2001, operates under the Machikado-Day-House scheme of Higashi-Osaka City. It aims to 'provide day care services for elderly people who live independently in their own home but require assistance'. With the aging of the Taiheiji Independence Movement participants who had established the self-directed school Uri Seodang, a need arose for a place for them to stay during the day as well as the night. Creating the day care home provided an activity hub for Korean women outside of the night schools which is more open to the local community because the activities are offered in the daytime. In 2007, Sarangbang also started a day care service center which offers nursing care services including assistance with bathing. Combined, the day care center and the day care home service an average of more than twenty users per day. There are around twenty day care homes in Higashi-Osaka. Three of them are predominantly for Koreans. Sarangbang is especially tailored to cater for Korean women and alumni of night schools account for a majority of its users. All of the staff are Korean women. The full-time manager and founder of the operation is a third-generation woman with a nursing qualification who began interacting with first-generation women when she was helping the night school independence movement in Higashi-Osaka City. Similar to the management of Uri Seodang, the steering committee of Sarangbang draws on the network of supporters of the Taiheiji Independence Movement, consisting of ethnic instructors who are subsequent-generation Koreans, members of the Higashi-Osaka Teachers Union and people involved in human rights movements.

Sarangbang was set up in a rented double story private house. The house is furnished like the living room of an ordinary Korean house, decorated with folk art and furniture that the women donated from their own homes. Women gather here on foot or on bicycle in the late morning, have lunch together and spend the afternoons as they please. At lunch time, all users and staff share a Korean meal together, each taking food from many different dishes served on the table while enjoying a lively chat. Lunch is followed by a study session, Korean singing and dancing, an exercise session, or a game of cards. Crafting and calligraphy lessons are organized from time to time. Medical checks are provided by a Korean doctor once a month. Picnics and daytrips are organized occasionally. The Uri Seodang Public Lectures and other seasonal events are accessible for anyone living in the local area. They are regularly attended by children from nearby schools. With literacy campaigners visiting from overseas, researchers, religionists and refugees also attending these events, Sarangbang is a place where people from all walks of life interact with one another.

Korean women who met at night schools typically have to part ways after graduation. The establishment of Sarangbang, however, created opportunities for them to continue learning and socializing beyond the night school, and to engage in a broader array of activities. Let us investigate how the women users perceive this place.

I look forward to coming here because there are a lot of people. When you get old, you get in the way of people. If I go to young people, I just create trouble for them. I feel comfortable here. I can relax. It's close to my house, too.

Day care home A (day care home run by an ethnic organization) is full of men. I attend New Year's event but that place is for men. I only go there when I have some business I must attend.

There is another day care home operated by Mindan's regional chapter in close proximity, but the users are all male. When I visited, they were enjoying board games. Owing to the custom that 'males and females should be distinguished' inherited from the Korean society, it has been taken for granted that all activities, whether it is to do with family, work or entertainment, are separated for men and women, especially of the first generations. The presence of even a single man can make older women feel uneasy, even when women are the majority. Some occasionally drop in at local Japanese seniors' clubs, but they are the exception. It is not easy to blend in with the local Japanese society no matter how many decades they have been living in the same place. Hence there was a strong need for a social space in which Korean women could play the pivotal role.

Subsequent-generation women involved in the day care home

Next, let us move our focus to the younger Korean women who operate the day care home. The staff who come in contact with first-generation women everyday perform many different duties. These include preparing meals, cleaning, shopping, instructing recreational activities, giving advice, handling administrative procedures and coordinating with the government and other relevant institutions.

First, Chung Kwi-mi plays a central role in the operation. She is the representative of Saranbang and Uri Seodang who is a qualified nurse and social worker. She has extensive experience in visiting care in the local area and works as an advisor at a consultation service for Koreans provided by Osaka City. The day care home is a product of her vision, developed from her interactions with first-generation women. She envisaged creating a place that is freely accessible to the older women, allowing them to be 'Korean' all day long in their local area.

She is a third-generation Korean in her fifties from Ikaino, an area of concentrated Korean settlement, but has almost no experience of living with first-generation Koreans. She learned the Korean language and history through the youth group of an ethnic organization and worked on human rights campaigns for local Koreans for many years under her ethnic name. She also served as an instructor in an ethnic class at a public school while also working in home medical care in the area. Even though she had been actively engaged in improving the status of Koreans in the area from an early age, her encounter with the '*halmoni* who were studying at night schools' was a 'complete eye-opener'. She says that she had not taken any notice of those women who could neither write Hangeul nor speak Japanese very well until then; however, from her first encounter she realized and understood that these were the women who had supported and protected the children and families of Koreans in Japan.

> We say 'Uri Seodang is a place to learn from learners'. This is because originally *halmoni* were learners at night junior high schools. But they are not just learners; they also have a lot of knowledge. Especially in terms of ethnic matters. So the idea was to learn from that and that's how we have been operating Uri Seodang…Because I grew up in a family with no one from the first-generation, when I came to Higashi-Osaka and discovered about night junior high schools, how can I put it, it helped me finally really understand. Spending time with first-generation Koreans opened my eyes. Until then, it was all about what sounded right, believing being able to speak the language and acting like Korean, what you call culture and history and things like that, would be enough. Then, I met first-generation Koreans, who had been living completely as who they are, as Koreans. I thought these people were the real resources for learning and then I became involved deeper and deeper…I was actually born and raised in Ikaino. Naturally there were Koreans around but, despite being born and growing up in Ikaino, there was really no one who would teach me to be aware of the fact that I was Korean. If anything, I pretended I had nothing to do with them whenever I saw first-generation Koreans. I would walk as far away as possible from them.

Hyun Yumi (second-generation, in her thirties) grew up in Tokyo. She has also been involved in an ethnic organization since her late teens and devoted herself to campaigning in her spare time. She moved to Ikuno Ward in Osaka City when she married a Korean man from Ikaino. She supported her family by working as an insurance agent and administrator but she was discontented that her work kept her away from the ethnic rights movement. When she was offered a job as staff at Sarangbang, she immediately took the opportunity, thinking it would allow her to contribute to her fellow Koreans. Although she had lived with her first-generation grandparents before marriage, she says, 'Family interaction alone does not readily reveal the real image of first-generation Koreans'. Even when first-generation Koreans live together with their children or grandchildren's generations, talking about their deeply troubled experiences inflicts emotional pain. She claims that, in order to uncover the real image of first-generation Korean women as fellow countrywomen, we must look from outside the family. In this sense, Sarangbang enables building relationships that are different from 'family' and provides an opportunity to listen to life stories as 'fellow countrywomen'.

> Although [work at Sarangbang] is different to the kind of ethnic movement I have been involved in for a long time, I think it is still part of the ethnic movement. It is somewhat related to rights and interests of Koreans in Japan. It's not completely unrelated to it. I am hoping that my presence here could help second and third-generation women know more about how they live, about their *omoni* and first-generation women and broaden their choices. This place is for first-generation women but also a place for all of our fellow Korean women in Japan. There is a lot we can gain from here.

Another staff member (in her forties, second-generation) is from Ikaino but had no involvement in the ethnic rights movement at all. She barely had any connection with the Korean community except for her family; nor did she have any particular interest. When her child started to attend an ethnic class, she slowly began making contact with the ethnic community.

> For me, although I may be labeled Korean in Japan, I had no connection with Korean people. One reason is because I went to Japanese school. Even when you live here (a Korean neighborhood in Osaka), you wouldn't have a connection unless you choose to. I only found out there was a world like this when I came to Sarangbang.

Meeting with first-generation women at the day care home has various implications for subsequent-generation women. First, engaging with first-generation women from outside the family offers a multidimensional understanding of women who had been living within the Korean ethnic community who had little contact with Japanese society. Second, daily contact with first-generation women provides access to first-hand knowledge of the culture and language of Korea. For Korean women who were born and raised in Japan, first-generation women are literally a 'living learning resource'. The words spoken by first-generation women are the real-life Korean language, which cannot be learned from textbooks. Furthermore, much ethnic culture and insight can be acquired from observing subconscious body languages and habits. Third, Sarangbang provides opportunities to listen to *women*'s experiences as opposed to the traditional andro-centric history of Koreans in Japan. Incidents and worries of everyday lives told by women have been dismissed as being 'trivial' simply because they are women. At Sarangbang, the narratives of women that have previously been brushed aside as 'old stories' or 'complaints' are reconsidered in relation to the multi-layered oppressions of colonialism, racism and sexism. Fourth, Sarangbang provides valuable work opportunities for young Korean women who tend to be alienated from the Japanese labor market. In addition to providing them with an income, more importantly, working at the day care home enables women, who might otherwise be forced to withdraw from the public sphere after marriage – to serve as a daughter-in-law, wife and mother – to continue to be actively involved in the ethnic society.

Intergenerational solidarity of women and ethnic resources

As discussed, Korean society is strongly influenced by Confucianism, in which the hierarchy of sex, age and generation is of major importance. Within families and organizations that are defined patrilineally, young women are in inferior positions. Women within a family have close contact with one another, for instance between mother and daughter or daughter-in-law. Nevertheless, there is often a conflict of interests between them as their lives center on their husband/father and son. Despite the strong links between women, their relationships are determined by the patrilineage as long as families are patriarchal.

Moreover, women in Korean neighborhoods in Japan generally work for family-operated businesses, which are largely controlled by the men in the family. As women find it very hard to enter the labor market due to the ethnic and gender order, it is difficult for them to achieve economic and psychological independence, even more so than Japanese women. Hence, women continue to be dependent on patriarchal households.

Let us now look at the kinds of interactions Sarangbang facilitated among women. The staff call the elderly users *'omoni'* (mother) or *'halmoni'* (grandmother). Using family titles metaphorically helps to bridge various generational gaps and encourages the development of intimate relationships among people who are not related. In some cases the relationship between staff and users is likened to the daughter-in-law/mother-in-law relationship.[6] It is safe to say that there is no direct patriarchal influence as there is within households. This means that, unlike family and typical ethnic organizations, the social space of Sarangbang allows for developing relationships between women largely free of patriarchal intervention. In the process, intergenerational solidarity is created beyond the superficial relationships typical of caregivers and clients, with the category 'fellow countrywomen' as an intermediate.

Among a variety of interactions, I will focus on the exchange of ethnic resources between the generations. First, first-generation women continue to still be heavily influenced by the language and culture, value, behavioral pattern and way of thinking of the Korean society in which they were born and raised, despite having lived in Japan for more than half a century. They subconsciously put these Korean ways of living into everyday practice. In contrast, the language and culture of the subsequent-generation women are more strongly affected by the Japanese society in which they were born and raised. They have absorbed Japanese ways of thinking, values and behavioral patterns through the mass media, educational institutions and friends. In short, first and subsequent-generation women differ significantly in their ethnicities, which has been a significant cause of generational gaps. At the same time, life factors that are specific to women, including cooking, sewing, knowledge about child-rearing and wisdom for everyday life, have been undervalued due to the male-dominant value system. First-generation women have been deemed 'pre-modern' and 'outdated' – especially because of their illiteracy.

At the same time, for subsequent-generation Korean women, it is a 'given' that they have learned Japanese cultural and linguistic skills. From one perspective, their acceptance of Japanese language and culture is assimilation of their former colonial master's culture, and they are to be looked down upon as '*banjjokbari*'. Hence the Korean women who would assume the role of nurturing the next generation were denigrated for not being familiar with the language and customs of their ancestors. In contrast, those Korean women who are well acquainted with Korean food and *jesa* were appreciated as 'good daughters-in-law'.

In Sarangbang, the female staff assistance includes accompanying to and interpreting at government welfare service desks, gathering information about elderly care, consulting on various issues and liaising with relevant institutions, helping with or handling procedures, negotiating with local education providers and campaigners. 'We are managers of *omoni*', one staff member said. The Japanese language, culture and insight into the Japanese society that subsequent-generation women have are absolutely indispensable for first-generation women to access public services and deepen their exchanges with the local community. Subsequent-generation female staff support women who are highly disadvantaged linguistically and culturally, thus contributing to improving the lives of first-generation women.

Meanwhile, first-generation women transmit Korean language, culture and customs to subsequent generations through their everyday interactions at Sarangbang. First-generation women provide feedback on the Korean food served for lunch, take the lead in traditional Korean singing and dancing and teach Korean language, folk stories and proverbs. First-generation women tell their life experiences from time to time. By listening to these stories, subsequent-generation women reinforce their identities as Koreans in Japan and strengthen their connections with their ethnic heritage. Korean women in Japan who have 'traditional Korean' ethnicity are received positively and expected to perform a variety of roles in activities to promote multicultural symbiosis at the local level. In this way, subsequent-generation women inherit ethnic cultural resources from first- and second-generation women and utilize them as they emerge as active subjects in mainstream society. Women are enabled to serve as bridges between and contribute to both the

Korean community in Japan and the public sphere once they have acquired both Japanese and Korean language and culture.

As discussed, first-generation and subsequent-generation women are engaged in 'socio-cultural mediation' across the board, by sharing their respective cultural knowledge with one another. Casual solidarity is formed among women based on mutual assistance freed from the patriarchal domination found in families and ethnic organizations. The mutually complementary intergenerational women's solidarity is positively effecting the formation of new forms of women's subjectivity in the public sphere.

Reconstructing the gender and racial order

This chapter has thus far revealed how Korean-born and subsequent-generation women are leveraging the respective Korean and Japanese linguistic and cultural attributes they possess to help one another and in the process forming new types of subjectivity in the public sphere through their activities at the Sarangbang day care home. The cultural attributes exchanged between the different generations serve as critical resources for transforming Korean women into active subjects within their host society. The bidirectional 'socio-cultural mediation' observed in the daily interactions at Sarangbang is invaluable for Korean women in the minority position in Japanese society, providing a sufficient reason for increased intergenerational solidarity.

One point that needs to be highlighted is that a new form of relationship became available in the day care home, a complementary relationship in which women positively recognize mutual differences and assist one another by taking advantage of these differences. This stands in stark contrast to the adversarial relationship between mothers-in-law and daughters-in-law that is commonly found within the patriarchal family framework.

While the externalization of nursing care facilitated by the Long-term Care Insurance System has alleviated the burden of care work from women within families, the gender structure that imposes caring duties on women is less-easily transformed. As evident at Sarangbang, where all of the staff are women, the gender structure of the culture in which women are responsible for all reproductive labor has not changed. However, as at Sarangbang, the intervention by the Japanese administration in the aged care sector through the

Long-term Care Insurance System, responsibilities which had long been borne by the female members of households were brought into the public sphere, with positive implications for the subjectivity of minority women in mainstream society.

The subaltern counterpublics created by Korean women at night schools did not merely involve elderly women but helped subsequent-generation Korean women who became involved with it to form a new oppositional subjectivity in mainstream society. The interconnectedness created between the women of different generations in the counterpublics may bring about sweeping changes in the years to come, with effects on families and ethnic organizations, gender and even the culture of Koreans in Japan.

An interesting point from the perspective of subject formation is that, in the social space of the day care home, conversations both affirming and criticizing the ethnic and gender orders in mainstream society occur daily even as many of the interactions within the home amount to reversals of the order. For example, according to mainstream social norms, teachers and students, Japanese and Koreans, men and women, elderly and youth are binary pairs in which the former is hierarchically positioned as superior to the latter. However, in the counterpublic space created around the night schools, this hierarchy has been disrupted as oppositional subjects who dispute the established order have formed through interactions between people across these categories. This can be seen in the reproduction of the Korean celebration of '*charye*' at the day care home for Lunar New Year.

Charye is a Confucian ceremony conducted at home for New Years. It is performed to honor paternal ancestors. The men of the lineage perform a series of ritual acts: specifically lighting incense, bowing in honor, offering wine and reciting a prayer. Then all participants have a banquet together. Women do not participate in the ceremony but are responsible for its preparation. For Koreans in Japan, family events such as *charye* have assumed additional importance for their role in maintaining Korean traditions and marking the ethnic boundaries distinguishing Koreans from Japanese.

Charye was celebrated at Sarangbang following the suggestion of staff members. Ceremonial goods, offerings and food were prepared by the younger women, who worked in teams for several days. At the *charye* ceremony itself, three men – an adult Korean man, a Korean

Photo 6.1: Charye *at the day care home*

Source: Taken by the author

boy and a Japanese teacher at a night school – performed the ritual with nervous looks on their faces as a dozen first and subsequent-generation women watched (Photo 6.1). When they finished the prayer, the Japanese man received a round of applause. Someone said to him 'You may as well become Korean'. It would appear from this event that respecting the gender norm is a higher priority than the ethnic boundaries, however, the picture of a Japanese man subjected to the 'gaze' and judgment of Korean women signifies the reversal of the ethnic order between Korean and Japanese, and the gender order between men and women.

Preparation for ceremonies, including cooking, is designated women's work; moreover, women positioned as 'daughters-in-law' are judged on the quality of their food. Hence, this particular ceremony has been criticized both in South Korea and in the Korean community in Japan as a typical example of discrimination against women.[7] The second-generation women who worked in the day care home wanted to replicate the ritual as part of learning the culture from the first-generation women despite being aware of the criticism. They hoped to continue the traditional Korean culture in the face of severe discrimination and pressure for assimilation. They also hoped that the women, whose participation is traditionally restricted to performing the ancillary work, would become the bearers of the traditional culture by reproducing the event themselves. The *charye* that was held at the day care home was performed to celebrate the Lunar New Year, welcoming both men and women, rather than honoring paternal ancestors (Chung Kwi-mi 2003). This mirrors the intention of the women to keep the 'traditional culture' alive by deconstructing it, rather than simply abandoning it because of gender discrimination.

It also appears to have been a way to indirectly raise the problem of the gender order in the public space of the day care home. The existence of this alternative public space – created with first-generation women's autonomous movement as the starting point – played a substantial role in the success of the subsequent-generation women's initiative. This space is a place where first- and subsequent-generation women, as well as Koreans and Japanese, can recognize differences in one another's background and face one another as individuals to some extent, rather than 'daughter-in-law' and 'mother-in-law' or '*Ilbon saram*' (Japanese person) and '*Chosun saram*' (Korean person). The reproduction of *charye* in this context was an act of defiance to create a new public value in the ethnic society and families, made possible by the existence of the 'subaltern counterpublics' created by Korean women in Japan.

To sum up, the movement that developed around night junior high schools is a multidimensional 'open' space for organic engagement of not only elderly Korean women, but also people from a variety of backgrounds for whom assumptions about ethnicity, gender, generation and age are being challenged, and new subjects are emerging.

7 Korean women in Japan and subaltern counterpublics

I have discussed the struggle over the nature of public night junior high schools that took place in Higashi-Osaka in the 1990s, focusing on the Korean women who were the primary actors of the movement. I have also examined the process through which they created relatively autonomous social movements, based on the concept of a 'subaltern counterpublic'. One of the reasons I began this research was that their goal, its significance and the originality of their social activism have rarely been properly evaluated despite the fact that Korean women have conducted a range of socially transformative movements in postwar Japan. While many factors may have contributed to this, the most significant one is that Korean women in Japan have generally been considered to be subordinates within the androcentric Korean community and families owing to the patriarchal ideology, a perception that went unchallenged because the affected women had themselves internalized this ideology. The night junior high school independence movement in Higashi-Osaka is a remarkable case in that it was a social movement in which women fought for their own rights independently of the existing ethnic rights organizations. Although it is a rare case as far as movements are concerned, it had universal implications, for it reflected the social situation in which Korean women generally found themselves. This study was intended to explore the situation of Korean women in Japan who are living, simultaneously, different temporalities – the postcolonial time at the nation level, the life course at the individual women's level and the generation at the ethnic society level – as well as different spaces – the transnational life space, the local social movement sphere in Kansai and the areas of concentrated settlement of Koreans in Osaka – by focusing on the Taiheiji Night Junior High School Movement.

In this chapter, I will review the findings of each chapter and then discuss some key points.

In Chapter 2, I outlined social theories relevant to the autonomy of women's movements and the roles given to women within a nation or an ethnic group, to provide an analytical perspective for understanding various social movements conducted by Korean women in Japan in relation to gender structures. Then, I examined postwar social movements that were led predominantly by Korean women in Japan through an analytical framework, which is designed by combining two elements: autonomy as a movement organization and autonomy from family gender roles. Korean people's ethnic rights movements in Japan are influenced by the politics of the Korean Peninsula, racial discrimination in postcolonial Japanese society and ethnocentric policies governing foreigners. On top of this, women's rights movements are also inseparable from the gender norms that exclude women from public sphere politics and forces their dependency on men. I used the following categories to classify the women's movements: ethnic rights movements under the 'wise mother and good wife' ideology, gender equal ethnic movements, maternal citizens' movements and postcolonial redress movements. It must be noted, however, that no particular movement can be characterized by only one of these categories; every one exhibits different characteristics to varying degrees. On the surface, many Korean women's movements in Japan were heading in the opposite direction from the women's liberation movement. Holistically, however, in a context in which their activities tended to be confined to the private sphere, they deliberately chose courses of action that enabled participation in politics in order to improve, if only slightly, the situation in which they found themselves. Since the 1990s, they began to be active in relatively more autonomous movements. The Taiheiji Independence Movement arises in this context.

In Chapter 3, I focused on local minority movements in Kansai and citizens movements demanding the expansion of night junior high schools, which set the scene for the Taiheiji Independence Movement. I was able to confirm that the subaltern counterpublics formed by Korean women in Japan, through interactions with many different minority movements, came into existence as an open social space. The board of education framing the large number of students in night schools as a problem, setting-up the extension class with inadequate resources and facilities, and segregating the students were infused with the historical experience of racial discrimination. The Korean women who constituted a majority of the students reacted to this latest act of discrimination by forming the Taiheiji Independence Movement. The women who had long been perceived as being unable to represent themselves and therefore rendered invisible have arisen as social actors, joining forces with other social activists through the night school independence movement.

In Chapter 4, using their life stories, I analyzed the processes through which the women who participated in the Taiheiji Independence Movement came to enter night school in their later life, against the concept of life course. The issue of illiteracy and lack of schooling specific to Korean women in Japan is the result of complex interactions of ethnicity, economics and gender – being 'Korean', in poverty and women (Kim Pu-ja 2005; Kim Mi-seon 2008). This chapter illustrated that the life course of Korean women in Japan was largely determined by gendered family roles, with the women typically having internalized the patriarchal ideology that confined them to these roles. Despite that, we found that the women have been making the best possible choices within the given circumstances. Enrolling in night school was one of the choices that they made. Attending night school and learning to read and write implies participation in the host society beyond the ethnic boundary. In some cases, enrolling in night school meant confronting a husband who objected to deviating from the norms of both Koreans and women. Standing up against the conventions that prohibited women from being educated and engaging in extra-domestic activities, the research participants employed an array of strategies for 'bargaining with the patriarchy'. I argued that attending night school was itself a practice of resistance for Korean women in Japan.

In Chapter 5, I discussed the acquisition of the host society's language, education as a counter to oppression and debate within the student council as the underlying factors for the emergence of the subaltern counterpublics at public night schools. These factors were presented through the life stories of the research participants in conjunction with the participant observation at night schools and Uri Seodang. It is incredibly rare for Korean women in Japan to build a collective and organizational platform because of divisions according to nationality, ethnic affiliations, places of origin, religion and age cohort, as well as generally being confined to private sphere activities. As we have seen, Korean women comprised the majority of the students, had shared experiences of illiteracy, lack of schooling and a passion for study. As part of the public education system, the night schools provided a forum for these women to shape a collective identity based on their relation to mainstream Japanese society. The public night schools, in effect, mediated between the mainstream society and the private sphere. The individual women, who had until then been almost completely excluded from mainstream society, were interpellated by the public authority at night school, and in the process became active subjects. By learning to communicate in the Japanese language and in writing, they joined the mainstream society and developed negotiating skills. The social space that developed out of the night school became a local activity hub for Korean women when they created Uri Seodang – which would later become an NPO – a self-directed learning institution formed during the Taiheiji Independence Movement. The life stories of my research participants reveal that, although the collective was formed primarily in protest against the racial discrimination of the mainstream society, it also wrought changes to the traditional gender structures of both the private sphere and the ethnic community. After Taiheiji Night Junior High School achieved independence, the oppositional subjectivity of Korean women became collective goods. They are now positively identified as *halmoni* or *omoni* who possess cultural resources derived from Korea as well as from sharing their experiences of colonialism, wars and postcolonial Japan. Through continuing engagement in these roles, the women are maintaining their position as oppositional subjects and actively building relationships with the host society.

In Chapter 6, I discussed the development of a new form of solidarity between first-generation and subsequent-generation women in the aged care operations in Uri Seodang and Sarangbang, which became activity hubs for Korean women after the end of the Taiheiji Independence Movement. Using participant observations from these two venues I explored the usefulness of the notion of socio-cultural mediation to understand this new solidarity. The core activity of Uri Seodang and Sarangbang is to provide support for elderly Korean women in Japan. At the day care homes and service centers, the women who receive support come into regular contact with the subsequent-generation women employed as staff to provide this support. Relationships between the two groups is not a fixed provider-recipient relationship; instead, both groups take advantage of the opportunities offered by the other party, exchanging Korean and Japanese language and culture respectively. In this process they perform a mutual sort of socio-cultural mediation to mainstream society. The language and culture learned through mutual exchange becomes, within mainstream society, a useful ethnic resource that facilitates the formation of a positive ethnic identity for both groups of women. At the same time, a new intergenerational solidarity also provides a driving force for transforming the gender structure in the Korean community and the racial order in the host society.

Emergence of Korean women as social actors

Chapter 2 analyzed the formation and organizational structure of Korean women's social movements in postwar Japan. It also analyzed the characteristics of the campaigning subjects in terms of prevailing gender structures and offered a perspective from which to relativize Korean women's social movements and the women's liberation movement in Japan. The situation in which individual Korean woman in Japan are placed varies, depending on nationality (Japan, Chosun or South Korea), ethnic organization affiliation (Chongryun, Mindan or other), place of origin or place where they grew up (Korea or Japan, Korean neighborhoods in Japan, or other), marital status (married, single, separated, divorced, or widowed), the presence or absence of children, age, generation, educational background (ethnic school or Japanese school) and occupation. The implications of women's liberation varies depending on an individual woman's circumstances. I have highlighted the diversity of the social movements conducted by Korean women in Japan while also revealing the factors inhibiting their political participation; i.e., the gender order prevalent in both Korean and Japanese society. Although the social movements of Korean women in Japan did not conform to either the ethnic rights movements of Koreans in Japan or to the Japanese women's liberation movement, I established, based on primary sources and interviews with activists, that the movements gave rise to a type of agent of liberation within the social context in which the individual women were positioned. This book was an attempt to redefine Korean women, who have typically been portrayed as passive objects, as the primary actors and uncover the process through which active subjectivity was formed.

This book has provided an in-depth analysis of the course of events that allowed first-generation Korean women to overcome a lifetime of isolation and deprivation and stand up to demand their rights and recognition. Accommodating people who have been socially alienated, public night schools have enabled discrete and disconnected minorities to build face-to-face relationships and form collective bodies, providing a critical perspective on the mainstream Japanese society. For Korean women in Japan, public night schools provided their first school experience. The Taiheiji Independence Movement has been called the 'Second Hanshin Education Struggle' because it developed on the continuum of the Korean people's ethnic rights movements in collectively demanding the rights of those who migrated from former colonies to receive an education. However, this movement differed from the traditional movements in that it was initiated by Korean women independently of men, and it generated a multiplicity of subaltern counterpublics through its interactions with a variety of organizations representing the interests of people from diverse ethnicities, genders and nationalities.

I have also described the views and positions produced by the social situation in which Korean women find themselves. In the words of Kang Woo-ja.

> Night junior high schools for adults should not exist. At the same time, they must exist. Night junior high schools should not allow discrimination and prejudice. We foreigners living in Japan lived through discrimination in the prewar, wartime, and postwar periods. We longed to be able to read and write and entered school, thinking we can finally reclaim the literacy that is our *han*[1] (long lasting profound sorrow or regret).[2]

There are people who would have completed primary education as children under normal circumstances but were denied the opportunity for a variety of reasons. Every individual has the right to receive an education. The significance of the public night schools is that they guarantee this right. Because public night school is a place where a certain class of people who have been excluded from the mainstream society come together, it must be free from discrimination and prejudice, and it must extend its efforts to combat discrimination and prejudice beyond the school grounds. Among the students of night schools, Koreans have a unique perspective on the history of the colonial era, through the war and into the postcolonial era. Learning to read and write will not only enable them to enjoy improved conveniences in everyday life, but will also provide tools for participating in the mainstream society and transforming it for the better. As Freire observed, literacy paves the way not only for social participation but also for social transformation from the perspective of the oppressed.

The identity of the Korean women who came together in night schools is based in a history of the violence of colonial domination and war, racial discrimination and the division of their motherland, all remembered along with the small events of daily lives. It is different from the abstract national identity based on history. It is based on deep-seated concrete memories of everyday life.

From a macro-level perspective, this movement that took form in the 1990s gave rise to a new subjectivity for Korean women in Japan, one that is not bounded by the nation in the new post-Cold War context. Although the Korean Peninsula remains divided, the ideological clash has eased since the collapse of the East-West structure. Hence, the things that divide the Korean community in Japan have shifted from the politics of the motherland to a wide range of factors such as gender and generation. Despite its apparent separation from this political condition, the night school independence movement, which happened to develop in the 1990s, made the axiom of the identity of Koreans in Japan, which had traditionally been dictated by nationality and ethnic organization, less relevant and presented in its place an identity defined by gender, such as '*omoni*' and '*halmoni*'. First-generation and prewar-born second-generation women have long provided the backbone of the ethnic community and families in Japanese society, which has oppressed Koreans. The terms '*omoni*' and '*halmoni*' in the new social movement identity do not mean the mother or grandmother of a specific person; rather, they refer to women who know and speak the language that originated in Korea. *Omoni* and *halmoni* provide historical testimonies as part of school education programs and cheerfully perform Korean traditional dance and music at festivals. Through such activities, they break the racial order that holds Japanese to be superior as well as the gender order that confines women to the private sphere, enhancing their position as members of the local society who contribute to the multicultural symbiosis.

This book has depicted Korean women in Japan as agents of social transformation. It is quite a different image from the passive and othered one traditionally attributed to first-generation and prewar-born second-generation Korean women in Japan. The subaltern counterpublics that they created are building horizontal relationships between different minority groups and between the different generations of Korean women in Japan, opening pathways for restructuring the traditionally asymmetric ethnic and gender regimes. The signs of social change remain limited today; nonetheless, if a social movement plays the role of 'vanguard', if it serves as a 'mirror of society' and a 'prophet' (Touraine 1980), this movement can be regarded as a herald of changes in Japanese society as well as the Korean community in Japan. It is significant that Korean women are driving this transformation. Much of its transformative potential lies in its aim to form pluralistic solidarity with the grassroots women at the core, beyond the framework of nations, while remaining locally based.

Implications for the subaltern counterpublics

I will move on to theoretical implications for the subaltern counterpublics that can be drawn from analysis of the Taiheiji Independence Movement. The research aimed to shed light on the events underlying the formation of the subaltern counterpublics that transformed Korean women in Japan who had been excluded from or marginalized in the mainstream society into active social agents (subjects). Fraser's (1992) metaphysical argument looks at interrelationships between various subaltern counterpublics in an attempt to revitalize the public sphere model based on plurality, presenting the public sphere as a space where multiple discourses overlap. Her 'subaltern counterpublic' theory did not, however, reflect the full reality of minority women who were excluded from or marginalized because of the gender and racial/ethnic order and who significantly lacked the resources necessary to communicate effectively in the language of the dominant population. By using the case study of the night school independence movement, I was able to show in concrete terms how those women – who are a minority within a minority group – created subaltern counterpublics.

After achieving its original objective, the Taiheiji Independence Movement continued its activities at Uri Seodang. Uri Seodang became an operational center for Korean women, who formed ties with and interacted with a wide variety of associations, including those of (other) night school students, literacy campaigners, subsequent-generation Korean women and local residents, as well as citizen's movements in South Korea. They are trying to create new social values by challenging and promoting solidarity across many boundaries and divisions between: public/private sphere; Japanese, South Korean and Chosun nationals; men and women; and different generations. The dynamics that are evolving around the existing ethnic, gender and class orders can be seen as part of the 'diverse multilayered public spheres' that span the local and global levels (Kurihara, Morris-Suzuki and Yoshimi 2000: 112). According to Kurihara et al. (2000), diverse multilayered public spheres should replace a single public sphere. These new public spheres are envisaged as having structures in which multiple factors intersect and interact with each other as they divide and aggregate. In other words, rather than 'merely' plural as Fraser envisaged it, the public sphere is developing multiple layers at both the micro and macro levels.

The movements that occurred in Higashi-Osaka empowered women who had been oppressed by the patriarchal order within their families, the ethnic community and the nation-state to be able to express narratives with their own voices, questioning the patriarchy from the inside. The subaltern counterpublics created by Korean women in Higashi-Osaka did not destroy the existing hierarchies and structures. However, the creation of an alternative public space based on horizontal relationships among women and independent of patriarchal controls has had tremendous transformative significance.

The reproduction of the *charye* (a Confucian ritual to honor the ancestors) at the day care home, discussed in Chapter 6, is a clear example of an attempt to dispute and reconstitute the 'ethnic culture' in a non-essentialized fashion. As an embodiment of the patriarchal ideology, such Confucian rituals have been criticized as sexist. Rather than simply abandoning the practice on that basis, in the independent public space at the day care home, the memorial service to honor ancestors and symbolize family unity was transformed by the women into an ethnic cultural event to pray for the happiness of all. The ceremony that was performed recast the dominant–subordinate relationship typical of both the male–female and Japanese–Korean relationships in mainstream Japan. More specifically, in the *'charye'* performed as Lunar New Year event at the day care home, three men (a Korean man, a Japanese man, and a Korean boy) performed the ritual, in accordance with the tradition, while several dozen Korean women watched. While the traditional division of gender roles was closely followed – men perform the ritual; women prepare the altar and watch the ceremony – the gaze that the women cast on the men as they performed the prayer clearly indicated that the women were the 'watching subjects' whereas the men were the 'objects being watched'. This is a reversal of the gender order, which treats men as dominant subjects and women as subordinate objects, as well as the racial order, which places Japanese as superior and Koreans as inferior. The reinterpretation of the 'traditional culture' in this example, coupled with the subversion of the gender and racial orders, were only possible because of where it occurred – the day care home run by Korean women in Japan. Subaltern counterpublics encourage women's activities that bring about changes to the existing racial and gender structure.

It has been pointed out in recent feminist political theory that, within the framework of multiculturalism, defending the cultural rights of minorities often means also continuing the oppression of women within the minority culture (Okin 1999, 2005). However, as can be seen in the reproduction of *charye*, minority women can also become active subjects who reconfigure their ethnic culture. There is, however, a necessary precondition for that to happen; subaltern counterpublics for women must have been created and sustained.

As observed in the Higashi-Osaka case, the new public sphere constituted by Korean women in Japan is maintaining an active local base in Kansai, engaging with the *munhae* (literacy) movements in South Korea, and redefining itself as a minority. At the same time, it is expanding its network of cooperation by identifying common traits such as illiteracy or being women. The movements carried out by Korean women in Japan are playing a part in the ongoing formation of transnational subaltern counterpublics in today's globalized world, a process that may shake the constituent boundaries of nations to their core. In what ways pluralist, cross-domain public spheres interact with the mainstream public sphere and transform it by introducing counter-discourses that create a new political arena needs to be further researched.

Finally, I must highlight the particular importance of the acquisition of language resources in the formation of subaltern counterpublics. In proposing a 'multiplicity of publics' model, Fraser labels the spaces in which minorities create self-affirmative discourses 'subaltern counterpublics' and positions them as alternatives to the mainstream public sphere. By definition, a public sphere centers on communication. In order to form subjects through the acts of listening, writing, and speaking – in short, through the practice of discourse – a certain competence in linguistic communication is a minimum requirement. Those with greater communication skills have a privileged status in discourse production. It is no exaggeration to say that in the night school movement, the acquisition of literacy skills played a major role. Submitting requests, collecting signatures, speaking in meetings, creating flyers, liaising with other activist groups and of course negotiating with the authorities all require fairly advanced communication skills. The older Korean women in Japan at night schools who achieved such language competency are what I term an elite class of those women, leaving the appropriateness of the expression open to review.[3] Subaltern counterpublics are not intrinsically open to everyone; ultimately, only those who have the necessary language skills can partake in discussion and otherwise participate. As long as a public sphere is defined as a social space where relationships are developed through discussion, there will need to be consideration of how to ensure the public sphere participation of minorities who lack language skills.

The subject in this book was limited to the collective actions of Korean women in Japan. Needless to say, subject formation of Korean women in Japan also takes place at the individual level; especially in local societies, different kinds of subjects are formed as women provide guest lectures at schools and participate in international exchanges. This book does not cover the various activities conducted by individuals and, thus disregards many emerging social actors. For example, a large proportion of the volunteer instructors who teach the historical background, culture and identity of Koreans in Japan in public schools are women, as are most of the hosts of social clubs and the owners and operators of businesses providing Korean food, clothing and culture. These often involve international connections, but are usually small operations carried out in ways that are relevant to the everyday lives of women. How these activities and the female subjects who are involved in them relate to the participation in and formation of civil public spheres need to be explored in future research.

Notes

Chapter 1

1 Koreans in Japan (*Zainichi Chōsenjin*) in this book refers to Korean people who migrated to Japan during or immediately after the period of Japanese colonial rule in Korea (1910–1945) and their descendants. It includes all Koreans living in Japan regardless of their nationality: South Korean, North Korean or Chosun, Japanese or other. The term Chosun derives from *Chōsen*, a Japanese word meaning Korea. When Alien Registration started in 1947, before the Korean peninsula was divided into two states, the nationality of Koreans in Japan was described as Chosun on Alien Registration Card. The term Chosun referred to a geographical area, rather than a nationality. Later the Koreans in Japan who identified with a South Korean nationality was changed to *Kankoku*, meaning the Republic of Korea. Chosun came to mean the Democratic People's Republic of Korea, or North Korean, with which Japan has not established diplomatic relationships. Koreans registered as Chosun were to be treated as North Korean nationals in Japan.

Furthermore, South Koreans who migrated to Japan since the 1970s are called 'new comers', while those Koreans in Japan who migrated earlier are classified as 'old comers'. While there are several terms to refer to them including '*Zainichi Kankoku Chōsenjin*', '*Zainichi Korian*' and '*Zainichi Chōsenjin*', each expressing different political positions, I will use '*Zainichi Chōsenjin*' (=Koreans in Japan) as it was the expression used by the participants in the social movements that are the topic of this study. I will use the term 'Korea' when referring to the entire Korean Peninsula as a region and describe the language and culture originating there as 'Korean language' and 'Korean culture' or similar. I will use the conventional short forms 'South Korea' and 'North Korea' for the Republic of Korea and Democratic People's Republic of Korea, respectively.

In this English translation of the original work, for simplicity, I will frequently shorten 'Koreans in Japan' to 'Koreans'.

2 Ministry of Justice Immigration Bureau Statistical Survey of Registered Foreigners 'Kokuseki chiiki betsu zairyū shikaku (zairyū mokuteki) betsu zairyū gaikokujin (The number of foreign nationals by status of residence (purpose of residence) by nationality (place of origin) as of the end of 2015.' http://www.moj.go.jp/housei/toukei/toukei_ichiran_touroku.html (Download on July 2 2016).

3 Ministry of Justice Civil Affairs Bureau 'Kikakyoka shinseishasū, kikakyokashasū oyobi kikafukyokashasū no suii' (Shift in the number of applicants, the number of the permitted and not permitted for

naturalization in the period from 1952 to 2015. http://www.moj.go.jp/MINJI/toukei_t_minj0.html (Downloaded July 2, 2016).

4 The buraku are a social minority group, ethnically and linguistically indistinguishable from other Japanese people. They face discrimination in Japan because of an association with work once considered impure, such as butchering animals or tanning leather. In particular, they often have trouble finding marriage partners or employment. Website of IMADR (The International Movement Against All Forms of Discrimination and Racism). http://www.imadr.org/sayama/buraku.html (Downloaded December 13, 2016)

5 For Korean female night junior high school students in general, see: Iwai (1989), Inatomi (1988, 1990), Munekage (2005) and Seishun Gakkō Jimukyoku (2004). Films *Gakkō* (School) (directed by Yamada Yōji, 1993) and *Konbanwa* (Good evening) (directed by Mori Yasuyuki, 2003) are also available. Academic research on the topic is scarce. Kim Mi-seon (2008) presented discussion on the illiteracy issue of Korean women in Japan and roles of night junior high school from the linguistic point of view. The present study is the first attempt to study Korean women students of night junior high schools from a social movement perspective.

6 The Ministry of Justice Immigration Bureau Statistical Survey of Registered Foreigners by nationality and municipal of residence (2016).

7 Feminist political sociology argues that modern civil society is based on the political separation of family from the public domain and that this public/private dichotomy is gendered, with the public associated with males and the private associated with females. Pateman argues that the association of females with the private domain itself is not the problem; the problem lies in that men's civil participation in the public domain assumes a patriarchy in the private domain which asserts men as the heads of household; and this male domination is structured into the public domain (Pateman 1988).

8 Drawing on the work of Ryan, Fraser points out that during the 19th century, North America saw the rise of diverse ways of accessing public life devised by women of different classes and races who had been excluded from the official public sphere. Some of these took the forms of charitable organizations and protest campaigns. It is striking how these women made creative use of the gender order to gain access to public life. Elite bourgeois women imitated men's associations even while taking advantage of norms such as motherliness and homeliness in their public activities. Meanwhile, the women of non-privileged classes slowly shortened the distance to public life through supporting androcentric working class movements (Fraser 1992).

9 While Fraser proposes 'subaltern counterpublics' as a democratic model, she notes that 'subaltern counterpublics' do not necessarily embody democratic or egalitarian intentions and they do not intrinsically overcome the problems of exclusion and marginalization (Fraser 1992: 124).

10 For instance, the problems confronting white middle-class housewives who were not fulfilled by the life of housework and child rearing, and therefore aspired to the right to work in pursuit of self-actualization as depicted in Betty Friedan's *The Feminine Mystique* is considerably different from the situation confronted by African-American women. African-American

women had no choice but to work, as African-American men were situated at the bottom of the labor market due to racial discrimination and were typically unable to sustain a family on their meagre wages.
11 According to *Shakaigaku shōjiten* (Hamashima Akira et al. eds. 1997), the term 'patriarchy' means: 1) a system in which a male who is the head of the family rules its members with powerful authority and 2) rule, suppression and discrimination by males against females. It is generally the latter meaning that is employed in feminist movements and studies. Kandiyoti (1988) noted that the term 'patriarchy' has typically been regarded as a fixed concept at the abstract level and called attention to the fact that patriarchy takes various forms and that women have adopted a variety of strategies as appropriate for their class, caste or race to resist oppression, which she referred to as 'bargaining with patriarchy'.
12 Examples include Pak Il-bun 'Nisei josei ōini kataru' (Second-generation women speak out), *Tong il pyong ron*, Vol. 147 (1977) and 'Zadankai: Josei ni totteno zainichi dōhō shakai' (Discussion meeting: What Korean brethren society means to women), *Mintō*, Vol. 4 (1988).
13 Choi Seon-hee 'Chōsen josei toshite ikiru michi: Minzoku no hokori o mune ni' (The way of living as Korean women: Living with national pride), *Tong il pyong ron*, Vol. 182, 1980.
14 The following quote from Park Hwa-mee (1993) illustrates a view that a Korean woman in Japan developed from life experiences in Western culture:
> I had always had an ambivalent feeling of fondness and irritation toward my mother who submitted to being an 'enduring mother' in our Confucian/patriarchal household of Koreans in Japan. It was only after I 'ran away from home' to the United States for the third time that I was finally able to figuratively commit 'parricide (matricide)' and 'destruction of the family'.
> (Park Hwa-mee 1993: 63)
15 For example, a media channel for Koreans in Japan *Horumon bunka* 4 (1993) ran a feature on the changing image of the Korean family in Japan which discussed the second-generation women's objection to the prevailing gender order.
16 There were several hundred Korean international students and workers in Japan prior to Japan's annexation of Korea in 1910 (Komatsu, Kim and Yamawaki 1994). There was also a dramatic increase in the number of people who moved from Japan to Korea following Japan's annexation of Korea. There were approximately 170,000 Japanese people in Korea at the time of annexation and around 710,000 in 1944 (Tanaka 1995: 59–60).
17 The transfer from Korean family registry to Japanese one or vice versa was not permitted unless for acts affecting personal status such as marriage and adoption. Residential transfer across the Sea of Genkai between Interior Territory and Korean Peninsula thus entail no transfer in family registry. Similar treatment of family registration was applied to Taiwan under Japanese colonialism.
18 Male citizens who lived in the interior territories, technically including Korean men, had previously been granted both suffrage and eligibility for election since gender had a more prominent influence than race (Tachi 1995).
19 The Alien Registration Ordinance was abolished and replaced by the Alien Registration Act when the San Francisco Peace Treaty took effect

in 1952. The Alien Registration Act was abolished in July 2012 when the foreigners with mid to long term resident status under the Immigration Control Act were subject to Basic Resident Registration Act.

20 An extensive campaign to refuse fingerprinting was conducted by Koreans and other foreign nationals in Japan in the 1980s. The law was revised in 1986, introducing the 'one-time-only fingerprinting' rule. In 1991, fingerprinting was abolished for permanent residents and was completely abolished in 1999. Japanese government restored the requirement of fingerprinting foreigners for anti-terror reasons in 2007, from which special permanent residents of Korean and Chinese origin are exempt.

21 Statistics from 1953 show that 19% of the Korean population in Japan received assistance from the Ministry of Welfare. The Japanese government's project to repatriate Koreans to North Korea in the 1950s was driven by a desire to reduce welfare costs, as well as public security concerns (Higuchi 2002: 176–186).

22 Data obtained from Sōmusho Tōkeikyoku *Heisei 17-nen kokusei chōsa jinkō gaikan sirīzu 6: Rōdo jōtai, sangyō, shokugyō betsu jinkō* (2005 population census of Japan overview series 6: Population by labour force status, industry and occupation) (2005) Table 5 (222–223).

23 Calculated based on the data from Sōmusho Tōkeikyoku *Heisei 17-nen kokusei chōsa hōkoku dai-7-kan: Gaikokujin ni kansuru tokubetsu shūkei kekka* (2005 population census of Japan No. 7: Results of special tabulation on foreigners) (2005) Table 6 (166–167).

24 Interview with a member of Mearihoe (November 2001).

25 In 1970, a man with South Korean nationality passed the employment examination during Hitachi Software's hiring process and was offered a position. But when he told the company that he is Korean national and thus could not submit a copy of the Japanese family registry, a common necessary documentation to commence employment, the company withdrew the offer of employment. In 1974, the Yokohama District Court ruled in his favor and ordered that he be paid compensations and damages. In a similar case, in 1976, the high school teacher's union joined forces with the Nippon Telegraph and Telephone Public Corporation worker's union to combat racial discrimination in Kansai in the wake of an incident in which the Nippon Telegraph and Telephone Public Corporation had barred a student from Nishinomiya Nishi High School from sitting the employment exam on racial grounds.

26 Among other things, successful applicants were instructed to use Japanese names after naturalization. In the late 1980s, there was a movement among naturalized Koreans in Japan and people who were granted Japanese nationality for having a Japanese parent to identify themselves as 'Koreans with Japanese nationality' and to have Korean-style names listed on the family register. Consequently, the use of Korean names was legally approved and the naturalization administration ceased to instruct successful applicants to use Japanese names. Refer to Minzokumei o Torimodosu Kai (1990) for more information on Koreans with Japanese nationality.

27 The initial pro-socialist Korean organization formed in Japan was Choryun, which was forcibly dismissed by Japanese authority under GHQ control in 1949 and was succeeded by Chongryun in 1955.

28 *Jesa* and the genealogy book have been denounced by Korean women in Japan since the 1990s as symbolizing the patriarchal characteristics of Korean society in Japan. Refer to Park Hwa-mee (1993) and Jung Yeong-hae (1993).
29 Interview with Chongryun-affiliated second-generation and third-generation Korean women in Japan. December 2001.
30 The expression 'distinction between sexes' means that men's behavior and areas of activities should be distinguished from that of women. The idea that 'women obey three masters' means that a woman obeys her father before she is married, her husband after marriage and her son after her husband's death. The phrase 'once married, no longer part of the family' means married daughters are the same as strangers. The 'seven valid causes for divorce' lists the grounds upon which men could unilaterally divorce their wives: disobedience towards parents-in-laws, infertility (inability to bear a son), talkativeness, theft, malignant disease, jealousy and adultery. The principle 'separation between the inside and the outside' means that men stay outside and women stay inside plus men do not talk about inside matters and women do not talk about outside matters.
31 These include Park Kyoung-Sik (1989) and Kajimura (1993). Yang Young-hoo (1994) is a study of Korean people's movements in Osaka. Zainichi Chōsenjin Undōshi Kenkyū Kai has been publishing *Chōsenjin shi kenkyū* (Research on the History of Koreans in Japan) since 1977.
32 For pre-war movements, which emerged from the political situation in colonial times, Lee Soon-ae (1977, 1978) describes in detail women's liberation campaigns initiated by Korean female students in Japan.
33 These include Fukuoka and Tsujiyama (1991), Fukuoka (1993), Fukuoka and Kim (1997) and Kim Tae-young (1999). As opposed to the essentialist perspective on ethnicity and monolithic interpretation of identity presented in the resistance discourses produced by first- and second-generation Koreans, these studies address various aspects of increasingly diverse identities by analyzing the process of identity formation of more recent generations.

Chapter 2

1 Refer to Chapter 4 of Seo (2006) for details on interaction between women's movements of Japanese women and Korean women in Japan.
2 In this chapter I will not examine the National Christian Women's Association listed in Table 1.1 since it requires a different research approach, incorporating religious factors in addition to gender and ethnic factors.
3 Whereas there were Korean women in Japan involved in the anti-colonial independence movement prior to World War II, they were mostly so-called elite women of colonial Korea, such as Christian students who had been sent overseas to study. These movements were almost completely detached from the majority of Korean women in Japan at the time.
4 A pro-North Korea national organization of Koreans living in Japan. It was established in 1955 under the current name after its predecessor League

of Koreans in Japan (*Choryun*), which was founded in 1945, was forced to dissolve by the GHQ and the Japanese government. It positions itself as an organization for 'overseas nationals' of the Democratic People's Republic of Korea.
5 A pro-South Korea national organization of Koreans living in Japan. It was established under the name *Zainippon Chōsenjin Kyoryū Mindan* in 1946. It was renamed *Zainippon Daikanminkoku Kyoryū Mindan* following the founding of South Korea in 1948. In 1994, the word '*Kyoryū*' (temporary stay) was eliminated from the name, forming the current name *Zainippon Daikanminkoku Mindan* (Korean Residents Union in Japan).
6 Mindan did not formally object to the display of the nationality 'Chōsen' (Korea) in the Alien Registration Ordinance. Dissatisfied by this inaction, Oh Ki-moon concluded that she 'could not rely on men' and allegedly sought to negotiate with GHQ on her own as a 'representative of Buinhoe' to have Chōsen changed to 'Kankoku (Republic of Korea)'. This led to the establishment of Buinhoe's Tokyo headquarters. Oh Ki-moon became the first Director of Buinhoe and served seven terms of office (Kim and Kim 1993: 16).
7 Quoted from 'Zadankai ima kikitai omoni ga ayunda michi' (Round-table discussion: Now is the time we hear about the path mothers took), *Mindan Shimbun* (1 January 2006).
8 Official website of Nyeoseongdongmaeng. Downloaded on 15 August 2011. http://www.nyomengcafe.com/
9 In recent years, there has been a push to encourage joint participation by men and women in Chongryun. The Women's Affairs Division was set up in 2003 as a specialized division of the Central Committee, which is committed 'to improvement of women's position and roles through guiding Nyeomaeng and supporting advancement of fellow countrywomen into a variety of fields' (*Choson Sinbo*, 10 May 2003). The Countrywomen's Council tasked to study issues faced by women within the society of Chongryun was inaugurated in September 2004 and soon made recommendations to improve the treatment of female officials and teaching staff (*Choson Sinbo*, 24 November 2005).
10 Ōnuma Yasuaki mentioned the role of Buinhoe in his discussion of the impact that the movement to refuse fingerprinting had on Japanese society. 'At that time, Bae Soon-hee, a woman with exceptional leadership qualities, was the chair of Buinhoe. She confidently led Buinhoe and stood at the vanguard of the movement while executives of Mindan were all over the place looking restless and flustered.' (Ōnuma and Suh 2005: 215)
11 In addition to Buinhoe, Zainichi Kankoku Minshu Joseikai (Korean Women's Society in Japan for Democracy) and individual women joined the Korean Women's International Network.
12 Interview with an officer of Nyeomaeng in Tokyo. May 2002.
13 A social gathering of Japanese women who are married to Chongryun-based men is organized at a chapter of Chongryun (*Choson Sinbo*, 26 June 2002).
14 This is evident in the following narrative by a woman who was committed to Nyeomaeng's activities:
   How happy [the inauguration of Nyeomaeng] made us. The news that our motherland was liberated and the Law of Equal Rights for Men and Women was promulgated shook our hearts and led us to realize women

are also the main characters of society. The establishment of Nyeomaeng was the first step to a whole new path that will give women the power to determine their own destinies. (Pak Il-bun 2002: 128)
15 Within the Chongryun community, married couples who commit themselves together in patriotic movements are glorified, but women are expected to support their husbands' engagement with organizational activities behind the scenes while at the same time actively participating in Nyeomaeng. To this end, husbands and wives are expected to work separately, under Chongryun and Nyeomaeng respectively. Wives often support their families economically by running their own businesses, so that their husbands can devote themselves to Chongryun activism (Interview with a Nyeomaeng activist in Osaka, March 2002).
16 Women's suffrage was granted in Japan in December 1945. Around this time, a series of women's associations were established by leading pre-war activists, including the New Japan Women's League chaired by Ichikawa Fusae and the Women's Democratic Club. In 1948, the Trade Unions Women's Committee and several regional women's organizations came together to form the Japan Council of Democratic Women. In response to these democratic women's organizations, GHQ instigated the creation of organizations of housewives, resulting in the establishment of the National Federation of Regional Women's Organizations in 1952. Independently of both of those movements, the Japan Housewives' Association developed as a consumer interest group in 1948, out of a protest about defective matches. The Japanese Society for the Defense of Children was set up in 1952. The first Japan Mothers Congress was held in Tokyo in 1955, with 2,000 participating women speaking about the difficulties in their lives. This congress, which drew women from a wide array of backgrounds, is considered to be a landmark event for mass women's movements as it resulted from the initiative of women themselves (Fujiwara 1998: 15–23).
17 A detailed testimony on this matter is given by Yang Young-jee, who was the chair of Mindan Buinhoe's Tokyo headquarters at the time (Yang Young-jee 1997).
18 From Zainichi Kankoku Minshu Tōitsu Rengō (Federation of South Koreans in Japan for Democracy and Unification) website. http://chuo.korea-htr.org/membership-org.shtml downloaded on 5 January 2011.
19 Interview with a member of Tokyo Yeoseonghoe, October 2001. There have been changes in recent years, with more women joining chapter-level executive roles in Hantongryun.
20 More specifically, this refers to its participation in the Korean Women's International Network, founded in Seoul in 2001. The Network was sponsored by the Ministry of Gender Equality and Maeil Business Newspaper and included around 400 female leaders at home and abroad. Its goals were to expand contacts between women and facilitate the exchange of information between Korean communities inside and outside the country, discover talent and promote global networking, in order to enhance international competitiveness (*Tōitsu Nippō* August 2001).
21 The Apuro Josei Jittai Chōsa Purojekuto (Appeuro Women Survey Project) was launched mainly by Osaka Yeoseonghoe members. This research project facilitated cooperation with Ainu women and women of the *buraku*

(outcast) communities as other 'minority women'. Refer to Hokkaidō Utari Kyōkai Sapporo Shibu et al. (2007) for details.
22 Nabi means butterfly in Korean. It is a symbol of hope in the movement seeking redress for comfort women in South Korea. Café Nabi is a loose network of Korean women in Osaka, holding seminar events and publishing a newsletter. Women in Café Nabi took a central role in the Apuro project in 2016, which conducted a social survey of over 1000 Korean women in Japan.
23 These new social movements included the National Joint-Struggle Student Movement, consumer movements, peace movements and anti-pollution movements.
24 For Kawasaki Omoni no Kai, refer to Song Pu-ja (2007) and Kawasaki Kodomo o Mimamoru Omoni no Kai (1995).
25 Other associations of Korean parents who send their children to public schools have emerged in many other areas of concentrated Korean settlement and are actively engaged with school management and boards of education. Despite the title 'parent association', it is usually women who take the central role in these organizations. However, it is not uncommon for men, or fathers, to be representatives of these organizations, even though the mothers are responsible for most of the day-to-day operations. This characteristic can also be found in predominantly Japanese PTAs. I have elected to describe here Mearihoe as an example of a Korean parent association initiated by women.
26 Adapted from 'Kodomo no Kenri Jōyaku: shimin, NGO hōkokusho: Kiso hōkoku' (Citizens and NGO study on the Convention on the Rights of the Child: Basic report) appended to the twentieth issue of Mearihoe newsletter (1997).
27 Interview with Kang Yeong-ja, at Higashikujō Madang in November 2001. Also Kang Yeong-ja (1995, 2008).
28 Interview with Kang Yeong-ja, at Higashikujō Madang in November 2001.
29 Kyoto City website. http://www.city.kyoto.lg.jp/sogo/page/0000025139. html downloaded 20 November 2011.
30 Interview with Yang Ching-ja, a former Dokushokai member. April 2004.
31 Another movement organization focusing on the issue of military comfort women Chōsenjin Jūgun Ianfu Mondai o Kangaeru Kai (Korean Military Comfort Women Issue Study Group) was formed in Kansai around the same time, but they will not be discussed here.
32 For details on the activities of Yeoseong Net, refer to Seo (2005, forthcoming). Kim Pu-ja (2009) is a detailed overview on Yeoseong Net activism by a former member.
33 Shin Min-ja, 'Anata wa nani iro desuka (Which color is yours?)', *Allim* vol. 1, p. 3. *Saekdong* is symbolic of the Korean people, a stripe pattern composed of five colors which is found in traditional Korean clothes, dishes, and decorations.
34 Jūgun Ianfu Mondai o Kangaeru Zainichi Dōhō Josei no Kai (1991: 1).
35 Needless to say, there is a substantial difference in the nature and scale of abuse experienced by Korean women in Japan and military comfort women. In one of the interviews that I conducted with former members of Yeoseong Net, Yang Ching-ja said that she became increasingly aware

of the dissimilarities as she interacted more with military comfort women in South Korea. Refer to Seo (2005; forthcoming).

Chapter 3

1 The residential areas of these marginalized people are scattered along an arc running from the eastern to the southwestern region of Osaka along the Osaka Loop Line. Mizuuchi likened the elongated curved area connecting these regions to the *banlieue rouge* (red suburbs, traditionally communist-dominated area) in Paris and named it 'the crescent moon area of the minorities' (Mizuuchi 2005a: 33).
2 More specifically, when the Osaka League of the Okinawa Prefectural Association took action to prevent the distribution of a social integration reader because it drew parallels between discrimination against Okinawans and discrimination against buraku – a parallel which they deemed offensive – younger Okinawans, especially second-generation Okinawans, became highly critical of the association, accepting the parallels as quite valid, and taking sides with the buraku, rather than the discriminatory mainstream (Mizuuchi 2005a: 49).
3 The address Ikaino was changed to Ikuno in the 1970s. Since then Ikaino has been used as the name of a place that does not exist in address system.
4 As discussed in Chapter 1, the ethnic rights movements of Koreans in Japan was split between Mindan and Chongryun, which supported South Korea and North Korea respectively. Chongryun especially had little interest in the questions of suffrage or eligibility for public office since they identified themselves as foreign-based North Korean citizens and refused to participate in Japanese domestic politics.
5 It is important to recognize, however, that interactions between minorities are not always positive. Sometimes members of marginalized minorities discriminate against each other, as can be seen in the incident described below. In the early 1970s, Hyogo Prefectural Minatogawa High School, which was then 'leading the liberation education' movement, added the subject 'Korean language' to the regular curriculum. This was the first time in the history of Japan's public high schools that Korean was taught in the regular curriculum. At the welcome ceremony for new teacher, the teacher in charge of the subject, Kim Si-jong, was told to 'go back to Korea' by students with a buraku background (Kim Si-jong 2001). It is important to recognize that discrimination cannot be reduced to a single axis such as 'race' or 'class' and that it is necessary to pay attention to not only the relationship between discriminators and discriminated but also to relationships among the discriminated.
6 The Ministry of Justice Immigration Bureau website. Statistical Survey of Registered Foreigners (2010). http://www.moj.go.jp/housei/toukei/toukei_ichiran_touroku.html.
7 In late 2010, the population of Ikuno Ward was approximately 130,000, including about 28,000 with South Korean or Chosun nationality.
8 The Ministry of Justice Immigration Bureau website. Statistical Survey of Registered Foreigners (2010).

9 The inter-city commuting from Ikuno Ward to Higashi-Osaka City continued until the opening of the night class at Osaka City Higashiikuno Junior High School in Shin-imazato, Ikuno Ward, Osaka City in 1997.
10 The Ikuno Minzoku Bunkasai (Ikuno Ethnic Culture Festival) was an annual festival initiated by a group of like-minded Japanese-born Koreans in 1983. It was intended to project the cultural identity of Koreans living in Ikaino to the wider community. The ethnic cultural network was reinforced by young Koreans practicing traditional theater, dance and musical instruments. The festival came to an end in 2004, on the occasion of its 20th anniversary, having been followed by a number of other Korean festivals that were initiated during its brief lifetime.
11 According to the Korea NGO Center website, accessed 1 December 2011. http://korea-ngo.org/kyoiku/kyoiku03.html.
12 Night junior high schools are also called 'night classes'; in fact, the Ministry of Education, and the boards of education refer to them as 'xx Junior High School Night Class', treating it as a class in a school. However, in the context of the night junior high school expansion movements, they are generally referred to as 'night junior high schools' to connote that they are separate, independent schools rather than auxiliary facilities of daytime junior high schools.
13 The only legal basis for the operation of the public night junior high schools is the provision on 'Providing Lessons under the Two-shift System' in Article 25 of the Enforcement Ordinance of the School Education Law, which states that the municipal board of education must notify the prefectural board of education about such programs.
14 Refer to 'Yakan chūgakkō seitosū no sui'i' (The shift in number of night junior high school students) (*Dai-50-kai Zenkoku Yakan Chūgakkō Kenkyū Taikai kinenshi* [The 50th National Night Junior High School Study Conference commemorative publication] p. 117).
15 The literacy survey conducted by the Ministry of Education in 1955 targeted 2,000 people between the ages of 15 and 24 in Kanto and Tohoku. Despite the fact that 10 to 15% responded that they had difficulty reading and writing, the Ministry concluded that 'the literacy issue has been resolved', neglecting the people who had missed out on an education (Yakan Chūgaku Zōsetsu Undō Zenkoku Kōryūshūkai 1997: 9).
16 The recommendation for abolishing night junior high schools was submitted to the Ministry of Education by the Administrative Management Agency and the Administrative Inspection Bureau under the title *Nenshō rōdōsha ni kansuru gyōsei kansatsu* (Administrative inspection regarding child labor) in 1966.
17 Refer to 'Yakan chūgakkō setsuritsu haishi nenpyō' (Timeline of establishment and closure of night junior high schools) (*Dai-50-kai Zenkoku Yakan Chūgakkō Kenkyū Taikai kinenshi* [The 50th National Night Junior High School Study Conference commemorative publication]) pp. 115–116).
18 The website of *Zenkoku Yakan Chūgakkō Kenkyūkai* (National Night Junior High School Study Society). http://www.zenyachu.sakura.ne.jp/public_html/jishuyachu.html.

19 Refer to *Dai-54-kai Zenkoku Yakan Chūgakkō Kenkyū Taikai: Taikai shiryō* (The 54th National Night Junior High School Study Conference: References), 2008, pp. 58–60.
20 Okinawa Sangosha Sukōre Night Junior High School located in Naha City, Okinawa Prefecture, is an example of the latter case. Founded in 2004, it has a little over 30 students with the average age of 72 as of 2010. *2011-nendo dai-57-kai Zenkoku Yakan Chūgakkō Kenkyū Taikai: Taikai shiryō* (The 57th National Night Junior High School Study Conference 2011: References). p. 75.
21 Adapted from Shirai Zengo 'Yakan Chūgaku Sonohi Sonohi (78)' (Night school, from one day to the next [78]) (21 August 2008). http://www.journalist-net.com/shirai/2009/08/post-3.html.
22 *Heisei 27-nendo Monbu Kagaku Hakusho* (White Paper on Education, Culture, Sport, Science and Technology, 2015), p.155.
23 *Dai-23-kai Zenkoku Yakan Chūgakkō Kenkyū Taikai: Taikai kiroku*, (The 23rd National Night Junior High School Study Conference: Proceedings) 1997, pp. 55–57. *Dai-50-kai Zenkoku Yakan Chūgakkō Kenkyū Taikai kinenshi* (The 50th National Night Junior High School Study Conference commemorative publication) 2004.
24 Article 26 of the Constitution of Japan describes the rights to an education. The rights to education are also outlined under Article 3 and 10 of the Basic Act on Education, Article 13 and 14 of the International Covenant on Economic, Social and Cultural Rights (ICESCR) set forth in United Nations' covenants on human rights as well as UNESCO's Declaration of the Right to Learn.
25 'Many problems remain unresolved regarding matters including education due to the inadequate postwar resolution associated with the invasion and colonial rule' (*2002-nendo dai-48-kai Zenkoku Yakan Chūgakkō Kenkyū Taikai: Taikai shiryō* [The 48th National Night Junior High School Study Conference 2002: References] p.64).
26 In a survey of women from buraku communities in 2004–2005 (1,405 respondents), 86% responded that they 'have no problems reading newspapers' whereas only 79.1% answered that they 'have no problems writing' (Hokkaidō Utari Kyōkai Sapporo Shibu et al. 2007). Lack of schooling and illiteracy are pervasive problems for people from buraku communities, and as with Koreans in Japan, these problems are more acute among women. A national survey of buraku conditions in 1984 revealed that 6.1% did not attend school (against the national figure of 0.3%), and more than 60% of them were female. In fact, 7.9% of the buraku women surveyed did not attend school (Yakan Chūgaku Zōsetsu Undō Zenkoku Kōryūshūkai ed. 1986: 58).
27 Takano reports having been especially moved by the words 'previous movements, though seemingly motivated by compassion, actually corrupted many of our brothers' and 'the time has come when we can be proud of being *Eta*' (highly derogatory term, meaning full of filth, long used to refer to the buraku people). He was convinced that being a night junior high school student is something to be proud of, not ashamed of, and committed himself to fighting against the very nature of discrimination

that takes away independence from those discriminated against (Takano 1993: 66–69).

28 In Nara Prefecture, Nara ni Yakan Chūgaku o Tsukuru Kai (Association to Create Night Junior High Schools in Nara) was founded in 1975, after the Osaka Prefectural Board of Education restricted non-Osaka prefectural residents from enrolling in night junior high schools. A private night school run by citizens was opened in 1976. The movement found success when the private school was converted to a public school in 1978. This school was nicknamed 'Noodle School' as it served noodles for a late-evening meal (Kawase 1978).

29 Chōei Chūgakkō Yakan Gakkyū, *Otona no chūgakusei* (Adult junior high school students) (1989) pp.114–128. Chōei Yakan Chūgakkō, *Higashiosakashiritsu Yakan Chūgakkō 30-nen no ayumi* (The 30-year history of Higashiosaka City's night junior high schools) (2002) pp. 4–5.

30 At the Higashi-Osaka City Council Second Regular Meeting on 16 June 1992, lawmaker Kakehashi Nobukatsu mentioned the *Sankei Shimbun* article. He claimed that the nighttime students outnumbering the daytime students and the construction of a new separate building for Chōei Night Junior High School were pressing issues. He inquired to the Higashi-Osaka City Superintendent of Schools about a plan to erect a separate campus in the southwestern part of the city. Likewise, at the Third Regular Meeting (17 September), another lawmaker, Kataoka Tatsuya, identified a number of problems including that most of the students at the night school lived outside of the city; and observed that the surging student numbers was affecting the daytime classes and facilities. He requested the Higashi-Osaka City Board of Education to take steps to ensure 'adequate operation'. (Adapted from the minutes of the Higashi-Osaka City Council Second Regular Meeting 1992 and the Third Regular Meeting)

31 When told that 'Some people claim that [this measure] is discrimination against Korean people', the Higashi-Osaka City Board of Education's response was, 'We have never heard of such a claim. We created an extension class because there was already one school in Higashi-Osaka City'. The reason given for the erection of an independent school in 2001 was that it was a 'high-level decision from the top'. Interview with Higashi-Osaka City Board of Education in May 2004.

32 Hayashi Jirō and Higashimura Yukiko (1994), Chōei Yakan Chūgakkō (2002) and Uri Seodang (2009).

33 'Kyōshitsu to sensei o fuyashite yakan chūgaku no harumonira suwarikomu' ('We need more teachers', Elderly Korean women from night junior high schools stage sit-in), *Tōitsu Nippō*, 9 October 1993. 'Seitotachi ga suwarikomi Higashiōsaka Taiheijichū zōsetsu motome Shikyōi mae' (Student sit-in staged at municipal board of education for expansion of Higashi-Osaka Taiheiji Junior High), *Asahi Shimbun*, 8 October 1993. 'Kyōshitu, kyōin fuyashite yakangakkyūsei 40-nin suwarikomi' ('We need more classrooms and teachers', 40 night class students stage sit-in), *Mainichi Shimbun*, 5 October 1993. 'Dokuritsukōka o fu ni yōbō' (Request for independence forwarded to the prefecture), *Asahi Shimbun*, 9 October 1993.

34 'Yakan chūgaku ni motto rikai o Higashi-Osaka no harumonira fesuta de uttae' (Elderly Korean women appeal for more understanding of night schools at festival), *Tōitsu Nippō*, 20 November 1993.
35 A letter of Protest by Taiheiji and Chōei Student Councils to the superintendent of Higashi-Osaka board of education, dated December 14, 1997.
36 In this incident, in December 1994, a staff member of the Osaka Municipal Transportation Bureau told a student of Uri Seodang to 'Go back to Korea' during a conversation in which the officer was asking to see the student's travel pass. The Higashi-Osakashi Kyōshokuin Kumiai (Higashi-Osaka City Teachers Union) and Minsokukyō which organized Uri Seodang confirmed the fact and then engaged in negotiations with the Municipal Transportation Bureau. The outcome was that the bureau agreed to provide training to prevent future incidents and to create a workplace environment in which Korean staff could work under their real names.
37 Taiheiji Night Junior High School renamed Fuse Night Junior High School when it moved to Fuse Junior High School campus in April 2016.
38 Interview with a night junior high school teacher. January 2005.
39 Anyang Civil University is not a formal university, but a non-profit organization operating in Anyang.
40 Anyang Civil University has an active involvement in the local society through literacy education, from recycling campaigns to provide support for the elderly and unemployed (Zenkoku Yakan Chūgakkō Kenkyūkai Dai-51-kai Taikai Jikkō I'inkai, 2005: 147–155).
41 According to the data on foreign students in Japan (of which a significant portion is assumed to be Korean) in the 1981 edition of *Zenkoku Yakan Chūgakkō Kenkyū Taikai: Taikai shiryō* (National Night Junior High School Study Conference: References), there were 53 men out of 1449 foreign students, or four percent. At Chōei Junior High School Night, of the non-Japanese students, there were three men and 226 women.
42 The performative female subjectivity of this movement can be observed from the name of its spin-off self-directed learning institution: 'Uri Seodang' (our village school). Typically, literacy institutions for Korean women across Japan are called *omoni hakkyo* (mothers' school). The adoption of the gender-neutral word *uri* ('our', also 'Korean'), rather than *omoni* ('mother'), which is descriptive of the family role, indicates that the women are seen as subjects who learn.

Chapter 4

1 The study also shows the following: the combined figure for male and female: proportions of those who 'can read Japanese passages', 'can read *hiragana* and *katakana*', 'cannot read Japanese but can read Korean characters (Hangeul)' and 'can read neither Japanese nor Hangeul' were 44%, 21.2%, 5.8% and 29.3% respectively (Mainichi Shimbun, December 19, 2004).
2 Following liberation, the Korean Peninsula became a proxy for the confrontation between the United States and the Soviet Union. In 1948,

an armed uprising broke out on Jeju Island under the guidance of the Workers' Party of South Korea against the separate election in South Korea backed by the United States. The Korean Constabulary was sent in to suppress the turmoil. Approximately 80,000 islanders were massacred during the conflict, which lasted a little over seven years. There were thousands of stowaways on ships to Japan, especially Osaka, to escape from the conflict.

3   *Seodang* is a village school from the Chosun period that provided introductory education for elementary students similar to *terakoya* in Japan. The learning objectives included reciting Chinese classics and calligraphy.
4   Oh Bok-deok's narrative is reconstructed based on the author's notes; therefore, the quote here is only an approximation of her actual storytelling.
5   Park In-seok's narrative is reconstructed based on the author's notes.
6   '*Darōyomi*' literally translates to 'guess-read'. she is referring to the act of reading by roughly guessing the meaning when one does not understand the meaning.
7   The television program Park In-seok saw was *Konnichiwa, Okusan* (Hello, Mrs. Housewife), which was broadcast shortly after the establishment of Tennōji Night Junior High School. This program was highly influential; there were more than a few who enrolled in Tennōji Night Junior High School after watching this program by chance.
8   Shin Yun-jeong's narrative is reconstructed based on the author's notes.
9   *Yangbang* is one of the social statuses in Korean society. It originated from the aristocrat class whose members were eligible to become government officials in the Goryeo Dynasty and Yi Dynasty but it gradually came to refer to a privileged status.
10 Patriarchy has been defined as: 1) a system in which a male who is the head of the family rules its members with powerful authority and 2) rule, suppression and discrimination by male against female. It is generally the latter meaning that is employed in feminist movements and studies (Hamashima et al. 1997).
11 Im Yong-gil's narrative is reconstructed based on the author's notes.
12 *Gye* is a traditional mutual aid organization in Korea. It is an optional financial system which resembles *tanomoshi* in Japan.
13 This narrative is reconstructed based on the author' notes.
14 People, mostly first-generation Koreans in Japan, who are not eligible to receive the basic pension for the elderly under the national pension program due to Japanese nationality requirement until 1982 receive an allowance of 10,000 yen per month from the city government.
15 '*Matome*' refers to the finishing tasks such as button sewing and hemming. Matome is a typical piecework in which Korean women in Osaka are engaged to support their family.
16 Jin Soon-nam's narrative is reconstructed based on the author's notes.
17 This is an old Korean saying which means that one's education and skill cannot be taken away by others, while money or fortune can be.
18 Lee Geo-ryeon's life story is reconstructed based on the author's notes.
19 Jeju Island was not only a successful farming community, but also a successful producer of seafood, which made it possible for women to secure some degree of economic independence working as a diver.

However, women's engagement in the public realm was considered to be an 'odd custom' by the bureaucrats and intellectuals on the mainland, where the Confucian order was more pervasive. This factor contributed to prejudices against the society and culture of Jeju Island that is still apparent today as evident in the characterization of it as 'full of three things' (abundance of rocks, wind and women).

Chapter 5

1 For example in Tatsumi park at the heart of a Korean neighborhood, in the early morning, up to ten Korean women come together to have a chat or exercise. In the afternoon, dozens of Korean men come together to play Japanese board games.
2 See *Shōwa 52-nendo dai-23-kai Zenkoku Yakan Chūgakkō Kenkyū Taikai: Taikai kiroku* (The 23rd National Night Junior High School Study Conference 1997: Proceedings), 1997.
3 Freire delivered a lecture during the International Literacy Year commemorative campaign in Osaka (in 1989) and engaged in an exchange with people who were working on literacy issues in Osaka, including those involved in night junior high schools and the buraku liberation movement (Kokusai Shikijinen Suishin Higashiosaka Renrakukai 1990).
4 hooks praises Freire's observations about the dignity of subjects who had been silenced as well as the subjectivity of the oppressed but is critical of his insensitivity to the fact that oppression and exploitation manifest differently for women than for men (hooks 1994).
5 Interview with a teacher of Chōei Night Junior High School (November 2001, January 2005) and interview with the Vice Principal of Taiheiji Night Junior High School (March 2003).
6 This is a reference to the Alien Registration Certificate that was used for official identity checks. Foreign nationals residing in Japan normally used a Certificate of Registered Items in the Foreign Resident Registry as an official identity document. Since the abolition of the Alien Registration Act and revision of the Immigration Control Act in 2012, 'Special permanent resident certificates' are issued to 'special permanent residents': Koreans and Taiwanese who migrated to Japan under colonial rule and their descendants, instead of the former Alien registration certificate. Together with mid and long term foreign residents, special permanent residents are registered in the Basic Resident Registration system in the same way as Japanese nationals,
7 Korean students in Japan have been encouraged to use ethnic names as part of ethnic education since the 1970s. Some argue that this practice is problematic in that it entails an asymmetrical power relation between the Japanese teachers who enforce it and the students who are forced to accept it.
8 Interview with a teacher of Chōei Night Junior High School, January 2005.
9 *Otona no chūgakusei 7* (Adult junior high school students vol. 7), 1994, pp. 86–88.

10 *Otona no chūgakusei: Sōritsu sanjū-shūnen kinen bunshū*) (Adult junior high school students: Collection of essays in commemoration of the thirtieth anniversary of the founding), 2002, pp. 6–11.
11 Some women oppose this practice. They argue that: 'It is unnecessary; I just came to study how to write', 'I want to do the same things as the daytime students' and 'Even if I write my life history, what does a Japanese teacher know about us?' The strong resentment against written language and the emotional scars carried by those who could not go to school – something that is taken for granted in Japanese society – is believed to underlie such reactions. Interview with the Vice Principal of Taiheiji Night Junior High School, March 2003.
12 Korean women in Japan have expressed themselves in the form of '*sinsetaryeong*', a special kind of first-person storytelling ritual, even while they were barred from speaking up. Nevertheless, *sinsetaryeong* is principally performed as a personal narration within a personal space, allowing only temporary alleviation of frustration.
13 According to *The Routledge Critical Dictionary of Postmodern Thought*, the term subaltern means subordinate. It is a notion associated with marginality. Subaltern subjects are those marginalized by the authority of 'the center' owing to either race, class or gender (Sim 1999: 366). For the definition of 'subaltern woman' used here, refer to Chapter 1.
14 According to a night school teacher, some of the people involved in Korean ethnic organizations have criticized the Korean women who study at night schools and learn Japanese language for adopting 'the language of the ruler' which 'leads to assimilation'. This criticism is at its root the same criticism levelled against Korean children of subsequent generations who are educated in mainstream Japanese schools rather than in ethnic schools. However, the case of women who are learning to read and write late in life is rather different than that of subsequent-generation Korean children who were born and raised in Japan in that the former were also excluded from literacy in Korean society prior to their migration because they were women.
15 In the areas of concentrated Korean settlement in Osaka, many come from Jeju Island, which sometimes triggers emotional conflicts between '*Jeju saram*' and '*yukji saram*' (*yukji* refers to the mainland Korean Peninsula) among students. There are also divisions between students associated with Chongryun and those associated with Mindan. However, those frictions tend to be superficial in the context of night school student councils. During the Taiheiji Independence Movement, disagreements over substantial movement policy reportedly caused more serious conflict than hostilities between the Japanese and Koreans or disputes between students from different hometowns.
16 She explained her eagerness to be involved in these organizational activities in terms of the separation of her family that resulted from the division of Korea. This woman had fled from Jeju to Japan at the age of twenty-two to escape from the massacre that followed the Jeju April 3 Uprising (1948). In Japan she met a Korean man who shared her ideology and they started living together. They had a child together, but when the wife he had left in Korea migrated to Japan, their relationship ended. She brought up the child on her own for a while, but decided to send the child

to live with its father when he and his family 'returned' to North Korea in the 1960s, believing that living in the motherland where there was no racial discrimination would give the child a better future. She could not go to North Korea as an accompanying family member as she was not legally a 'wife'. She was therefore left in Japan by herself. She said that the reason she so enthusiastically participated in Chongryun's local activities in Japan was simply that she hoped that her contributions to the organization would make it easier for her to visit her child in North Korea.

17 There were some who said that they had made donations to both Chongryun and Mindan. It tends to be assumed that Koreans only support either the ethnic organization for the Republic of Korea or the one for the Democratic People's Republic of Korea, but this is not necessarily the case. In Korean neighborhoods, supporting ethnic organizations is also a way of socializing.

18 Interview with Hiyashi Jirō, Chair of the Higashi-Osakashi Kyōshokuin Kumiai (Higashi-Osaka City Teachers Union), January 2005.

19 The discussion of Althusser's theory of subjectivity here owes much to the advice of Prof. Emeritus Ishizuka Michiko.

20 '*Urihakgyo*' is a Korean word meaning 'our school'. The term *urihakgyo* is often used to refer to ethnic schools as opposed to Japanese schools; however, Park Yun-gyeong is most likely to have literally meant 'the school where we (Korean women in Japan) study'.

21 The antagonism was not only by local Japanese; some Koreans also expressed antipathy toward the night school independence movement. One participant was told by a Korean female acquaintance, 'You are disgraceful. All you have to do is study. You are coaxed into it by your teacher.'

22 Taiheiji Yakan Chūgakkō Seitokai, Chōei Yakan Chūgakkō Seitokai, Chōei and Taiheiji Yakan Chūgakkō Dōsōkai, 2001, *Taiheiji Yakan Chūgakkō no dokuritsu o iwau kai* (Meeting to celebrate the independence of Taiheiji Night School), p. 57.

23 The Korean term *jjokbari* means 'pig's feet'. It came to be used by Koreans as a derogatory term for Japanese in reference to the Japanese *tabi* socks which separated the big toe from the others. When '*ban*' (meaning half) is added at the beginning, it means 'half-Japanese' used as a derogatory term for Koreans in Japan, particularly of second- and subsequent-generations.

24 This comment is a derivation of the Korean proverb: 'It goes ill with the house where the hen sings and the cock is silent'. Interview with the Vice President of Taiheiji Night Junior High School, February 2003.

25 Minsokukyo is an abbreviation of Minzoku Kyōiku Sokushin Kyōgikai (Convention for Ethnic Education Promotion), an organization of ethnic heritage class teachers in public schools in Osaka prefecture.

26 Ethnic classes refer to extracurricular classes set up in public schools for children of Korean heritage to learn the Korean language and culture.

27 Major Japanese newspapers such as Asahi, Mainichi, Yomiuri, Sankei, and ethnic newspaper Tōitsu Nippō also covered the movement.

28 In her evaluation of 'internationalization' as a principle of municipal governments' policy toward foreign residents, Kashiwazaki points out its limitation as a dichotomous approach. While this notion driven by the relationship between 'Japanese' and 'foreigners' may have been more acceptable in times when Koreans represented most of the foreign

residents in Japan, the concept of 'multiculturalism' which views residents as consisting of 'people with diverse origins and cultures' is a better alternative principle for foreign resident policy (2002a).
29 Interview with Mr. Gōda Satoru, President of Nikkan Shimin no Kai (at the time of the interview) (March 2002) and website of the same organization. http://www.e-sora.net/shimin/
30 The Ministry of Justice Immigration Bureau website: http://www.e-stat.go.jp/SG1/estat/List.do?lid=000001074828 downloaded 1 December 2011.
31 Flyer 'Dai nana-kai Higashiosaka Kokusai Kōryū Fesutibaru' (The 7th Higashi-Osaka International Festival) and Nikkan Shimin no Kai website http://www.e-sora.net/shimin/index.html.
32 Students of Chonryun affiliated ethnic schools, especially girls in their school uniforms which were designed according to Korean traditional styles, have been assaulted on the way to and from school, especially at the time when the political relationships between Japan and North Korea are strained due to missile launches, the returns of Japanese abductees from North Korea, and so on.
33 Siim (2000) defines citizenship as a status, a practice and an identity and suggests two dimensions of citizenship – a vertical dimension designating the relationship of rights and duties between the state and individuals and a horizontal dimension designating citizens' attitude and their initiatives to form organizations and social campaigns. The social movement by Korean women in Japan conforms to the horizontal dimension, forming a citizenship through practice and identity.
34 Interviews with Nishio Yoshiaki, a teacher of Chōei Night Junior High School and a teacher of Uri Seodang, conducted in November 2001 and January 2005.
35 A field trip for local junior high school students in March 2003 (at Ikuno Ward KCC Hall) and participant observation of a group of local high school students visiting Sarangbang day care home.
36 'Manabu emi Nikkan issyo Osaka no yakan gakkyū ga shikiji kyōshitsu hōmon' (Learning bringing a smile in Japan and South Korea: Osaka's night class pupils visit literacy class), *Asahi Shimbun* dated 27 July 2002.
37 NHK 'ETV Tokushū: Higeki no shima Saishu: 'Yon-san Jiken' zainichi Korian no kioku' (ETV Special: Tragic island of Jeju: Memories of Koreans in Japan of the 'Jeju April 3 Uprising') broadcast on 3 January 2009 and NHK 'NHK Supesharu: Shirīzu Nihon to Chōsen Hantō 4: Kaihō to bundan: Zainichi Korian no sengo (NHK Special: Series Japan and the Korean Peninsula 4: Liberation and division: Postwar Koreans in Japan)' broadcast on 25 July 2010.

Chapter 6

1 In the 20th century, France experienced a labor shortage caused by the demands of industrialization. It therefore accepted a huge number of immigrants, especially from their former colonies. As a result, immigrants from the former African colonies have come to constitute

a significant proportion of the French population. The aggressive migration program was wound up in response to the economic stagnation following the oil crises of the 1970s, but the families of those who had already migrated to France were permitted entry on humanitarian grounds. Hence, many women migrated to France as family members of men who had migrated earlier. Those women not only brought about significant changes to the composition of the immigrant community, but have also made a substantial contribution to the family formation and development of the immigrant society.
2 According to the 2005 Population Census of Japan, the elderly comprised 20.1% of the total population.
3 Koreans had lost their Japanese nationality upon conclusion of the San Francisco Peace Treaty in 1952. They were thus institutionally excluded from the National Pension for not being Japanese nationals when the collection of pension contributions began in 1961 pursuant to the National Pension Act of 1959, as the pension eligibility specified 'Japanese citizens aged 20 to 60 years who reside in Japan' under the Nationality Clause. In 1982, following the Japanese government's ratification of the Convention relating to the Status of Refugees, the Nationality Clause was abolished in accordance with the principle of equality of treatment between nationals and foreigners. However, even after the removal of the Nationality Clause, foreign residents in Japan aged 60 and over remained unable to join the pension scheme. Furthermore, even those who were aged under 60 at the time, unless they were aged under 35, could not satisfy the eligibility criteria that required a minimum length of participation of 25 years before reaching 60 years of age and therefore remained effectively excluded from the National Pension Scheme.
4 For example, some Koreans in Japan do not understand instructions during X-ray examination such as 'lying face-up' and 'deep breath' even though they have no problem with daily conversations. Others pretend to understand the words they do not know because they feel strongly from their past experiences of discrimination that they do not want to be 'made a fool of' by Japanese. Refer to 'Fukushi genba kara mita zainichi Korian kōreisha fukushi no genjō to korekara (Current and future state of welfare for elderly Koreans in Japan as seen in welfare institutions)' in *Kikan Sai*, Vol. 29 (1998). It has also been reported that a person was given a lower nursing care level than needed based on the assessment of care requirements as the person did not understand Japanese and answered 'Yes' to all questions. Refer to 'Kōreisha ni taisuru jinken ishiki o takamete hoshī (Calling for better awareness of human rights for elderlies)' in *Sai*, Vol. 35 (2000).
5 Examples include Sarangbang (guest room), Anbang (women's lounge), Bada (sea), Urijip (our house), Kōrai Kurabu (Goryeo Club), Eruhwa (a cheer of encouragement chanted while someone sings), Sanboram (purpose in life), Doraji (Bellflower, a Korean folk song).
6 For instance, one staff member remarked about some of the clients that 'it would have been hard if she had been my mother-in-law'. Despite that, because their relationship is not too close yet not too far, she explains, she can take it as 'another representation of the ingrained attitude' of first- and second-generation women who survived through tough times.

7 An article titled 'Zainichi dōhō ni totteno chesa: Sosen uyamau kokoro o gishiki ni kazoku daikaigō no ichidai ibento (What Jesa means to Koreans in Japan: A major event that unites family together for ancestor honoring ceremony)' provides a good reference on the significance for Koreans in Japan of ceremonies that honor the ancestors (*jesa* is a similar ceremony to *charye*, performed on different occasions):

> In the society of Koreans in Japan, *jesa* has undergone a fair bit of streamlining with generational change and the growth of nuclear families. However, no matter how much its format changes, it seems that our respect for our ancestors has been duly passed on across generations. It is not just a sense of obligation that Koreans of second and later generations are feeling. It is a place where they confirm the cultural lineage that has been inherited across space and time. (Mindan Shimbun, 10 February 1999)

According to the article, a video created by a group of Koreans in Japan 'Chesa: Minzoku no inori (Jesa: Prayers of the Koreans)' (directed by Oh Deok-soo, 1989, produced by Zainichi Bunka o Kiroku Suru Kai) sold more than 1,000 copies. Sai Takanori (2001) described the dilemma he faced of *jesa* in the community of Korean residents from the perspective of a Korean man in Japan, as it is considered as a piece of the ethnic minority culture but at the same time labeled as male chauvinism.

Chapter 7

1 *Han* in the Korean language is an expression of a deep, complex and mixed emotion which is said to be unique to Koreans.
2 Kang Woo-ja, 2001, 'Iwau kai ni yosete (For the celebratory meeting)', *Taiheiji Yakan Chūgakkō no dokuritsu o iwau kai* (Meeting to celebrate the independence of Taiheiji Night Junior High School), p.8.
3 I heard the expression 'elite grannies' used to refer to middle aged or older Korean women in Japan who study at night school. It suggests how extraordinary it was for middle aged and older Korean women to learn to read and write.

Bibliography

Ajia no Onnatachi no Kai (Asian Women's Association), 1977–1992, *Ajia to josei kaihō* (Asia and Women's Liberation), Inaugural preparatory issue–Vol. 21.

Althusser, Louis, 1976, 'Idéologie et appareils idéologiques d'Etat (Notes pour une recherche)', *Positions* (1964–1975), Paris: Les Editions Sociales, pp.67–125.

Anderson, Benedict, 1991, *Imagined Communities: Reflections on the Origin and Spread of Nationalism*, London, New York: Verso.

———, 1992, 'The New World Disorder', *New Left Review* 193: 3–13.

Asakawa, Akihiro, 2003, *Zainichi gaikokujin to kika seido* (Foreign residents in Japan and naturalization system). Tokyo: Shinkansha.

Basch, Linda, N. G. Schiller, and C. S. Blanc, 1994, *Nations Unbound: Transnational Projects, Postcolonial Predicaments, and Deterritorialized Nation-states*, Longhorne, PA: Gordon and Breach.

Bhattacharjee, Anannya, 1997, 'The Public/Private Mirage: Mapping Homes and Undomesticating Violence Work in the South Asian Immigrant Community', J. Alexander and C. T. Mohanty eds., *Feminist Genealogies, Colonial Legacies, Democratic Futures*, New York: Routledge.

Brah, Avtar, 1996, *Cartographies of Diaspora: Contesting Identities*, London and New York: Routledge.

Bunch, Charlotte, 1983, 'Not By Degrees: Feminist Theory and Education', C. Bunch and S. Pollack eds., *Learning Our Way: Essays in Feminist Education*, New York: The Crossing Press.

Butler, Judith, 1990, *Gender Trouble: Feminism and the Subversion of Identity*, New York: Routledge.

Cho, Hae-joang, 2002, 'Kankoku no kafuchōsei ni kansuru kaiseki teki bunseki: Seikatsu sekai o chūshin ni' (Analysis on South Korea's patriarchy: Focusing on the everyday world), Haruki Ikumi tr., *Kankoku shakai to jendā* (Korean society and gender), Tokyo: Hōsei University Press.

Chōei Chūgakkō Yakan Gakkyū (Chōei Junior High School Night Class), 1987–2002, *Otona no chūgakusei* (Adult junior high school students), Inaugural issue, Vol. 16.

Chōei Yakan Chūgakkō (Chōei Night Junior High School), 2002, *Higashiosakashi-ritsu Yakan Chūgakkō 30-nen no ayumi* (The 30-year journey of Higashi-Osaka City's night junior high schools).

Choi, Seon-hee 1980, 'Chōsen josei toshite ikiru michi: Minzoku no hokori o mune ni' (The way of living as Korean women: Living with national pride), *Tong il pyong ron* (Unification review), Vol. 182.

Chōsenjin Jūgun Ianfu Mondai o Kangaeru Kai (Korean Military Comfort

Women Issue Study Group), 1991, *Chōsenjin jūgun ianfu mondai shiryō shū* (Collection of materials on the issue of Korean military comfort women).

———, 1992, *Chōsenjin jūgun ianfu mondai shiryō shū* 2 (Collection of materials on the issue of Korean military comfort women 2).

Chow, Esther Ngan-Ling, D. Wilkinson, and M. B. Zinn, 1996, *Race, Class & Gender: Common Bonds, Different Voices*, Thousand Oaks, London, New Delhi: Sage Publications.

Chung Kwi-mi, 2003, 'Chare (Chesa) no saigen' (Reproduction of charye [ritual]), *Porappi* (Purple), Vol. 170.

Chung, Jang-yeon, 1995, '"Pakkusu ekonomika" jidai no tōrai to zainichi shakai' (The arrival of the 'pax economica' era and the society of Koreans in Japan), *Seikyu* (Blue hills), 24: 62–69.

Coll, Kathleen M., 2010, *Remaking Citizenship; Latina Immigrants and New American Politics*, Stanford: Stanford University Press.

Crenshaw, Kimberley Williams, 1989, 'Demarginalizing the Intersection of Race and Sex: A Black Feminist Critique of Antidiscrimination Doctrine, Feminist Theory and Antiracist Politics', *The University of Chicago Legal Forum* 139: 139–67.

———, 1994, 'Mapping the Margins: Intersectionality, Identity Politics, and Violence against Women of Color', M. A. Fineman, R. Mykitiuk eds., *The Public Nature of Private Violence*, New York: Routledge, 93–118.

Dai-50-kai Zenkoku Yakan Chūgakkō Kenkyūkai Jikkō I'inkai (The 50th National Night Junior High School Study Conference Executive Committee), 2004, *Dai-50-kai Zenkoku Yakan Chūgakkō Kenkyū Taikai Kinenshi* (The 50th National Night Junior High School Study Conference Commemorative Publication).

Daikan Minkoku Joseibu (Republic of Korea Ministry of Women's Affairs), 2001, *Korean women's international network participation list*.

Eley, Geoff, 1992, 'Nations, Publics, and Political Cultures: Placing Habermas in the Nineteenth Century', Craig Calhoun (ed.), *Habermas and the Public Sphere*. Cambridge: MIT Press, 289–339.

Enloe, Cynthia, 1989, *Bananas, Beaches and Bases: Making Feminist Sense of International Politics*, Berkeley and Los Angeles: University of California Press.

Fraser, Nancy, 1992, 'Rethinking the Public Sphere: A Contribution to the Critique of Actually Existing Democracy', Craig Calhoun (ed.), *Habermas and the Public Sphere*. Cambridge: MIT Press, 109–42.

Freedman, Jane, 2000, 'Women and Immigration: Nationality and Citizenship,' Freedman and Carrie Tarr, eds., *Women, Immigration and Identities in France*, Oxford and New York: Berg, 13–28.

Freire, Paolo, 1970, *Pedagogia do Oprimido* (Pedagogy of the Oppressed), Mexico City: Siglo XXI Editores.

Fujiwara, Chika, 1998, *Jirei ni miru josei no shimin katsudō to seikatsu* (Women's civil actions and daily lives: Case studies), Tokyo: Kōgaku Shuppan.

Fukuoka, Yasunori, 1993, *Zainichi Kankoku Chōsenjin: Wakai sedai no aidentitī* (Koreans in Japan: Identity of recent generations), Tokyo: Chūkō Shinsho.

Fukuoka, Yasunori and Kim Myung-soo, 1997, *Zainichi Kankokujin seinen no seikatsu to ishiki* (The life and consciousness of young South Koreans in Japan), Tokyo: Tōkyō Daigaku Shuppankai.

Fukuoka, Yasunori and Tsujiyama Yukiko, 1991, *Hontō no watashi o motomete: 'Zainichi' nisei sansei no joseitachi* (In search of my real self: Second- and third-generation Korean women in Japan), Tokyo: Shinkansha.

Gilroy, Paul, 1993, *The Black Atlantic: Modernity and Double Consciousness*, Cambridge: Harvard University Press.

Glazer, Nathan and Daniel Moynihan, 1964, *Beyond the Melting Pot: The Negroes, Puerto Ricans, Jews, Italians, and Irish of New York City*, Cambridge: MIT Press.

Grewal, Inderpal, and Caren Kaplan, 1994, 'Introduction: Transnational Feminist Practices and Questions of Postmodernity', Grewal and Kaplan eds., *Scattered Hegemonies: Postmodernity and Transnational Feminist Practice*, Minneapolis: University of Minnesota Press, 1–33.

Guha, Ranajit, 1998, '"Sabarutan kenkyū" dai-1-kan eno jobun' (Preface to 'Subaltern Studies' I), *Sabarutan no rekishi* (Subaltern History), Takenaka Chiharu tr., Tokyo: Iwanami Shoten.

Gurūpu Jamae (Sisters' Group), 1997, *Zainichi Korian josei no tameno empawāmento wākushoppu hōkokusho* (Report on empowerment workshop for Korean women in Japan).

Habermas, Jürgen, 1989, *The Structural Transformation of the Public Sphere: An Inquiry into a Category of Bourgeois Society*, Thomas Burger with Frederick Lawrence tr., Cambridge: MIT Press.

————, 1992, 'Further Reflections on the Public Sphere', Thomas Burger tr., in Craig Calhoun ed., *Habermas and the Public Sphere*, Cambridge: MIT Press, 421–61.

Hall, Stuart, 1990, 'Cultural Identity and Diaspora', Jonathan Rutherford ed., *Identity: Community, Culture, Difference*, Lawrence and Wishart; London, 222–37.

————, 1996, 'Introduction: Who Needs 'Identity'?', S. Hall and P. du Gay eds., *Questions of Cultural Identity*, London: Sage, 1–17.

Hamashima, Akira, Takeuchi Ikuo and Ishikawa Akihiro, 1997, *Shakaigaku shōjiten shinpan* (The compact dictionary of sociology new edition), Tokyo: Yūhikaku.

Han, Tong-hyon, 2006, *Chima chogori seifuku no minzokushi: Sono tanjō to chōsen gakkō no joseitachi* (Ethnography of Hanbok school uniform: Its origin and women in Korean schools), Tokyo: Sōfūsha.

Hanada, Tatsurō, 1996, *Kōkyōken toiu nano shakai kūkan: Kōkyōken, media, shimin shakai* (Social space called public sphere: Social space, media and civil society), Tokyo: Bokutakusha.

Haramura, Masaki (director), 2004, *Ama no Ryang-san* (Ryang the diving woman).

Hashimoto, Miyuki, 2010, *Zainichi Kankoku Chōsenjin no shinmitsuken: Haigūsha sentaku no sutōrī kara yomu "minzoku" no genzai* (The intimate sphere of Koreans in Japan: The current situation of the "nation" drawing from the stories of spouse selection), Tokyo: Shakai Hyōronsha.

Hayashi, Jirō and Higashimura Yukiko, 1994, 'Osaka no yakan chūgaku zōsetsu undō no uneri' (The surge of night school expansion movement in Osaka), *Kyōiku hyōron* (Education Review), February 1994: 48–53.

Heitlinger, Alena, 1999, 'Émigré Feminism: An Introduction', Alena Heitlinger ed., *Émigré Feminism: Transnational Perspectives*, Toronto, Buffalo and London: University of Toronto Press, 3–16.

Higashiosaka City, 2003, *Higashiosakashi gaikokuseki jūmin shisaku kihon shishin: Tomoni kuraseru machizukuri o mezashite* (Basic guidelines for support measures for the foreign residents of Higashiosaka City: Developing a community friendly to people of all national origins).

Higuchi, Naoto, 2000, 'Gaikokujin no seiji sanka' (Foreigners' political participation), *Nichiō imin seisaku no sai to shūren: Nashonaru/ rōkaru reberu, kōteki/shiteki ryōiki* (Differences and convergence of Japanese and European immigration policies: National/local public/ private domains), Proceedings of the Rikkyo University International Symposium, 44–51.

Higuchi, Yūichi, 2002, *Nihon no Chōsen/Kankokujin* (North Koreans and South Koreas in Japan), Tokyo: Dōseisha.

Hokkaidō Utari Kyōkai Sapporo Shibu, Buraku Kaihō Dōmei Chūō Josei Taisakubu, Apuro Josei Jittai Chōsa Purojekuto and Hansabetsu Kokusai Undō Nihon I'inkai, eds., 2007, *Tachiagari tsunagaru mainoritī josei: Ainu josei, buraku josei, zainichi Chōsenjin josei niyoru ankēto chōsa hōkoku to teigen* (Minority women beginning to build networks: Results and proposals from a survey on Ainu women, buraku women, Korean women), Osaka: Kaihō Shuppansha.

Hondagneu-Sotelo, Pierrette, 1994, *Gendered Transitions: Mexican Experiences of Immigration*, Berkely: University of California Press.

hooks, bell, 1984, *Feminist Theory: From Margin to Center*, New York: South End Press.

————, 1994, *Teaching to Transgress: Education as the Practice of Freedom*, New York: Routledge

Hottorain Jamae (Sister's Hotline), 2004–2007, *Hottorain Jamae*, Inaugural issue, Vol. 5.

Ikuno Omoni Hakkyo 20-shūnen Jikkō I'inkai (Ikuno Mothers School 20th Anniversary Executive Committee), 1997, *Ikuno omoni hakkyo*, Vol. 4, (The 20th anniversary of the founding commemorative essays).

Inatomi, Susumu, 1988, *Mugunfa no kaori* (The fragrance of the rose of Sharon), Tokyo: Yojisha.

————, 1990, *Moji wa kūki da: Yakan chūgaku to omonitachi* (Literacy is like air: Night school and omonis), Tokyo: Yojisha.

Ito, Ruri, 1995, 'Jendā, kaikyū, minzoku no sōgo kankei: Ijū jōsei no jōkyō o tegakari toshite' (Interrelationships among gender, class and race: In the light of immigrant women's status) in Shun Inoue et al. eds., *Iwanami kōza gendai shakaigaku dai-11-kan: Jendā no shakaigaku* (Iwanami lectures on contemporary sociology vol. 11: Sociology of gender), Tokyo: Iwanami Shoten.

————, 1999, 'Furansu no imin tōgō to "chūkai suru joseitachi": Shakai-bunka chūkai ni kansuru yobiteki kōsatsu' (Integration of immigrants in France and 'mediation by women': A preliminary analysis on socio-cultural mediation), *Shakaigaku kenkyūka ronshū* (Review of of Graduate School of Sociology), 6: 7–16.

———, 2000, 'Kyūjū-nendai Furansu ni okeru imin tōgō seisaku to "josei chūkaisha": Chi'iki no nakade tamesareru Furansugata tōgō' (Integration policy of immigrants in 1990s France and 'female mediators': French integration model attempted at local level), Miyajima Takashi ed., *Yōroppa tōgōka no seiō shokoku no imin to imin seisaku no chōsa kenkyū* (Research studies on immigration and immigration policies in Western Europe under the European unification), (Report of the grant-in-aid for scientific research by Ministry of Education, Science, Sports and Culture), 143–159, Rikkyo University.

Iwai, Yoshiko, 1989, *Omoni no uta: Shijūhachisai no yakan chūgakusei* (Songs of omoni: A forty-eight-year-old night school student), Tokyo: Chikuma Bunko.

Iwakami, Mami, 2003, *Laifu kōsu to jendā de yomu kazoku* (Sociology of the family: Gender and life course perspectives), Tokyo: Yuhikaku.

Jayawardena, Kumari, 1986, *Feminism and Nationalism in the Third World*, London and New York: Verso.

Jūgun Ianfu Mondai Uriyoson Nettowāku (Military Comfort Women Issue Uri Yeoseong Network), 1991, *Gasshuku hōkokushū Katariakasō! Zainichi josei no asu ni mukatte: Yoon Jung-ok san to Chōsenjin jūgun ianfu mondai o kangaeru* (The workshop report Let's talk the night away for the tomorrow of Korean women in Japan: Thinking about the issue of military comfort women with Yoon Jung-ok).

———, 1992, *Kono 'han' o tokutame ni: 'Moto jūgun ianfu Kim Hak-sun san no hanashi o kiku tsudoi' o oete (1991-nen 12-gatsu 9-ka Tokyo ni oite)* (To untangle our sorrow: After 'the gathering to listen to the story of former comfort woman Kim Hak-sun' [in Tokyo 9 December 1991]).

———, 1992–1996, *Allim* (Announcement), (Inaugural issue–Vol. 17).

———, 1993, *Yoson Net nenji hōkoku (1992-nendo)* (Yoson Net annual report [the year 1992]).

———, 1994, *Yoson Net nenji hōkoku (1993-nendo)* (Yoson Net annual report [the year 1993]).

Jūgun Ianfu Mondai o Kangaeru Zainichi Dōhō Josei no Kai (Association of Fellow Countrywomen in Japan to Consider Military Comfort Women Issue) (tentative name), 1991, *Watashitachi wa wasurenai Chōsenjin jūgun ianfu: Zainichi dōhō josei kara mita jūgun ianfu mondai* (We will not forget Korean military comfort women: The military comfort women problem from the perspective of Korean women in Japan).

Jung, Yeong-hae, 1986, 'Ie no kaihō to hirakareru "minzoku": Han gaikokujin tōroku hō undō no tenkai kara' (Liberation of families and open "nation": From the perspective of the development of anti-alien registration act movements), *Kaihō shakaigaku kenkyū* (The liberation of humankind: A sociological review), 1: 83–96.

———, 1993, 'Zainichi to ie seido' (Koreans in Japan and the family system), *Horumon bunka 4: Zainichi Chōsenjin yureru kazoku moyō* (Hormone culture 4: Changing families of Koreans in Japan), Tokyo: Shinkansha, 41–55.

———, 1994, 'Hirakareta kazoku ni mukatte: Fukugōteki aidentitī to jiko ketteiken' (Toward open families: Compound identity and a right to self-determination), *Joseigaku nenpō* (Annual report of women's studies), 15: 8–14.

———, 2003, '"Sengo" tsukurareta shokuminchi shihai' ('Postwar' creation of colonial domination), *Tamigayo seishō* (Let's sing our national anthem, not for the Japanese Emperor but for us, the people), Tokyo: Iwanami Shoten.

Kajimura, Hideki, 1993, *Zainichi Chōsenjinron* (The discussion of the Koreans in Japan), Tokyo: Akashi Shoten. (Chapter 2 'Kaihōgo no zainichi Chōsenjin' [Koreans in Japan after liberation] first published in 1980 by Kōbe Gakusei Seinen Sentā Shuppanbu).

Kandiyoti, Denise, 1988, 'Bargaining with Patriarchy', *Gender and Society*, 2(3): 274–90.

Kang, Young-ja, 1995, 'Jimichi na gaikokujin kyōiku no torikumi o' (Calling for constant efforts in education for foreigners), *Zainichi no omoni wa ima* (Korean mothers now), Osaka: Zenchōkyō bukkuretto.

———, 2008, *Watashi niwa Asada sensei ga ita* (My teacher Asada was there for me), Tokyo: San'ichi Shobo.

Karpinski, Eva C., 1999, 'Choosing Feminism, Choosing Exile: towards the Development of a Transnational Feminist Consciousness', Alena Heitlinger ed., *Émigré Feminism: Transnational Perspectives*, Toronto, Buffalo and London: University of Toronto Press, 17–29.

Kashiwazaki, Chikako, 2000, 'The Politics of Legal Status: The equation of nationality with ethnonational identity', Sonia Ryang ed., *Koreans in Japan: Critical Voices from the Margin*, London and New York: Routledge, 13–31.

———, 2002a, 'Kokuseki no arikata: Bunkateki tayōsei no shōnin ni mukete' (How the nationality should be: Toward an approval of cultural diversity), in Kondō Atsushi ed., *Kōza gurōbaruka suru nihon to imin mondai dai-2-kan: Gaikokujin no hōteki chii to jinken yōgo* (Japan and immigration issues in globalization series vol. 2: Foreign nationals' legal status and protection of their human rights), Akashi Shoten.

———, 2002b, 'Teijū gaikokujin no zōka to jichitai no hannō: "Kokusaika" o koete' (Increasing long-term foreign residents and reaction of municipalities: Going beyond 'internationalization'), in Furukawa Shun'ichi and Menju Toshihiro eds., *Jichitai henkaku no genjitsu to seisaku* (Japan's road to pluralism: Transforming local communities in the global era), Tokyo: Chuo Hoki Shuppan.

Kawano, Yukio, 2007, 'Zainichi Korian no kōreika to esunishiti' (Aging Koreans in Japan and their ethnicity), in Kawamura Chizuko and Sun Wonsuk eds., *Ibunkakan kaigo to tabunka kyōsei: Darega kaigo o ninau noka* (Healthcare for people with different cultures and multicultural symbiosis: Who will take responsibility for healthcare?), Tokyo: Akashi Shoten, 28–47.

Kawasaki Kodomo o Mimamoru Omoni no Kai (Kawasaski Omoni Society for the Protection of Children) 1995, *Hikari ni mukatte, 20-shunen kinenshi* (Toward the light, the 20th anniversary commemorative issue).

Kawase, Shunji, 1978, *Yakan chūgakko setsuritsu undo: Nara kara no hōkoku* (Movements to establish new night schools: A report from Nara), Tokyo: Taimatsusha.

Kim, Sung-woong (director), 2004, *Hana hanme* (Flower grandmother).

Kim, Chan-jung, 1982, *Chōsenjin jokō no uta: 1930-nen Kishiwada bōseki sōgi* (Songs of female factory workers: the 1930 Kishiwada Cotton Spinning dispute), Tokyo: Iwanami Shoten.

Kim, Eun-shil, 2000, 'Minzoku gensetsu to josei: Bunka, kenryoku, shutai ni kanusuru hihanteki yomikata no tameni' (The discourse of nationalism and women: Critical readings on culture, power and subject), Nakano Noriko tr., *Shisō* (Thought), 914: 63–87.

Kim, Isaja, 1994, 'Zainichi josei to kaihō undō: Sono sōseiki ni' (Korean women in Japan and the rise of liberation movement), in Inoue Teruko ed., *Ribu to feminizumu* (Women's lib and feminism), Tokyo: Iwanami Shoten.

Kim, Jackie J., 2005, *Hidden Treasures: Lives of First-Generation Korean Women in Japan*, Lanham, MD: Rowman and Littlefield Publishers.

Kim, Mi-seon, 2008, 'Imin josei to shikiji mondai ni tsuite: Yakan chūgaku ni manabu zainichi Korian issei no shikiji senryaku' (On migrant women and the literacy problem: Literacy strategies of first-generation Koreans in Japan studying at evening schools), *Kotoba to shakai* (Language and society), 11: 69–92.

Kim, Pu-ja, 2005, *Shokuminchiki Chōsen no kyōiku to jendā: Shūgaku fushūgaku o meguru kenryoku kankei* (Education and gender in colonial Korea: Power relations surrounding schooling and non-schooling), Yokohama: Seori Shobo.

———, 2009, 'Zainichi Chōsenjin josei to Nihon gun "ianfu" mondai kaiketsu undō: 1990-nendai no Yoson Netto no undō keiken kara' (Korean women in Japan and campaign to solve the Japanese military 'comfort women' problem: From experience of Yeoseong Net campaigns in the 1990s), *Sensō to sei* (War and sex), 28: 100–111.

Kim, Si-jong, 2001, 'Sarasareru mono to sarasu mono to: Chōsengo jugyō no ichinen han' (Exposer and exposed: A year and half of Korean language classes), *'Zainichi' no hazama de* (Caught in 'being-in-Japan'), Tokyo: Heibonsha.

Kim, Tae-young, 1999, *Aidentiti poritikusu o koete: Zainichi Kankokujin no esunishiti* (Beyond identity politics: Ethnicity of Koreans in Japan), Kyoto: Sekaishisosha.

Kim, Young and Kim, Pu-ja, 1993, *Dainiji Sekai Taisen 'kaihō' chokugo no zainichi Chōsenjin undō* (Campaign by Korean women in Japan immediately after the 'liberation' from Colonialism), Tokyo Josei Zaidan research activity report on women.

Kim, Young, 2009, 'Kaihō chokugo no Josei Dōmei ga mezashita "josei kaihō"' ('Emancipation of women' sought by Josei Dōmei immediately after the liberation), *Sensō to sei* (War and sex), 28: 112–117.

Kim, Young-Soon, 1979, 'Zainichi Chōsenjin katei no onna tachi' (Women in Korean families in Japan), *Onna Erosu* (Women eros), 13: 129–132.

Kinki Yakan Chūgakkō Renraku Kyōgikai (Kinki Liaison Council of Night Junior High Schools) http://www.akebi.sakura.ne.jp/~kinyachu/index.htm

Kokusai Shikijinen Suishin Higashiosaka Renrakukai (International Literacy Year Coordinating Committee Higashiosaka Liaison Meeting), 1990, *Osaka tono taiwa: Paulo Freire shi Osaka hōmon hōkoku* (Dialogue with Osaka: A report on Paulo Freire's visit to Osaka).

Kokusai Shikijinen Suishin Osaka Renrakukai, 2001, *21-seiki ni yakan* chūgaku ga dekita: Taiheiji Yakan Chūgakkō no dokuritsu (A night school born in the 21st century: The independence of Taiheiji Night Junior High School), Filmed and edited by Yoshimura Ryūji and Enomoto Ashio.

Komatsu, Hiroshi, Kim Yong-tal and Yamawaki Keizō, 1994, *'Kankoku Heigō' mae no zainichi Chōsenjin* (Koreans in Japan before the annexation of Korea), Tokyo: Akashi Shoten.

Kurihara, Akira, Tess Morris-Suzuki and Yoshimi Shunya, 2000, 'Gurōbaruka to tasō na "kōkyōken"' (Globalization and multilayered public sphere), *Shisō* (Thought), 915: 88–112.

Landes, Joan, 1988, *Women and the Public Sphere in the Age of the French Revolution*, Ithaca: Cornell University Press.

Lee, Hyo-jae, 1997, 'Kankoku no kafuchōsei to josei' (Patriarchy and women in South Korea), Yang Jingja tr., in Ajia Joseishi Kokusai Shimpojiumu Jikkō I'inkai ed., *Ajia joseishi: Hikakushi no kokoromi* (The history of women in Asia: Explorations in comparative history), Tokyo: Akashi Shoten.

Lee, Soon-ae, 1977, '"Kinyūkai" oboegaki' (Memorandum of 'Kinyūkai'), *Zainichi Chōsenjinshi kenkyū* (Journal of history of Koreans in Japan), 1: 33–41.

——, 1978, 'Zainichi Chōsen josei undō (1915–1926): Joshi ryūgakusei o chūshin toshite' (Korean women's movement in Japan (1915–1926): Focusing upon the female foreign students), *Zainichi Chōsenjinshi kenkyū* (Historical review of Koreans in Japan), 2: 29–45.

Lim, Jie-hyun, 2000, 'Chōsen hantō no minzokushugi to kenryoku no gensetsu: Hikakushiteki mondai teiki' (Nationalism on Korean Peninsula and the power discourse: Introduction of the issue from a comparative history perspective), *Gendai shisō* (Review of contemporary thought), 27–28: 126–144.

Lister, Ruth, 1997, *Citizenship: Feminist Perspective*, New York: New York University Press.

Lowe, Lisa, 1996, *Immigrant Acts: On Asian American Cultural Politics*, Durham: Duke University Press.

Mackie, Vera, 2001, 'The Language of Globalization, Transnationality and Feminism', *International Feminist Journal of Politics*, 3(2), 180–206.

——, 2003, *Feminism in Modern Japan*, Cambridge: Cambridge University Press.

Marshall, T. H. and Tom Bottomore, 1992, *Citizenship and Social Class*, London: Pluto Press.

Matsudoshi ni Yakan Chūgakkō o Tsukuru Shimin no Kai (Citizen's Group to Create Night School in Matsudo City), 2003, *Matsudo jishu yakan chūgakkō no 20-nen* (The 20 years of voluntary night schools in Matsudo), Tokyo: Keisō Shobō.

Mearihoe, 1993–1999, *Meari* (Echo), Vol. 1–23.

Mindan Shinbun, 1999, 'Zainichi dōhō ni totteno chesa: Sosen uyamau kokoro wo gishiki ni kazoku daikaigō no ichidai ibento (What Jesa means to Koreans in Japan: A major event that unites family together for ancestor honoring ceremony)', *Mindan Shinbun*, February 10th, 1999.

Ministry of Education, Culture, Sports, Science and Technology, 2015, *Heisei 27-nendo Monbu Kagaku Haksho* (White Paper on Education, Culture, Sport, Scinece and Technology, 2015).

Minzokumei o Torimodosu Kai, 1990, *Minzokumei o torimodoshita Nihonseki Chōsenjin: Uri irumu* (Koreans with Japanese nationality who reclaimed their ethnic names: Uri ireum), Tokyo: Akashi Shoten.

Mizuuchi, Toshio, 2005a, 'Mainoritī/shūen kara mita sengo Osaka no kūkan to shakai' (Space and society in post-war Osaka from the perspective of minority/marginality), *Nihon toshi shakaigakukai nenpo* (The annals of Japan association for urban sociology), 23: 32–56.

——, 2005b, 'Sengo Osaka no toshi seiji ni okeru shakaiteki kūkanteki haijo to hōsetsu: Burakumin, zainichi Korian, hiyatoi rōdōsha tono kanren ni oite' (Exclusion and subsumption in the social space of post-war Osaka: In relation to people of discriminated communities, Koreans in Japan and day laborers), *Rekishigaku kenkyū* (Journal of historical studies), 807: 129–140.

Mohanty, Chandra Talpade, 1991, 'Cartographies of Struggle', C. T. Mohanty, A. Russo and L. Torres eds., *Third World Women and the Politics of Feminism*, Bloomington: Indiana University Press.

Molyneux, Maxine, 1998, 'Analysing Women's Movements', Cecile Jackson and Ruth Pearson eds., *Feminist Visions of Development*, London: Routledge, 65–88.

——, 2001, *Women's movement in International Perspective, Latin America and Beyond*, New York: Palgrave.

Moon, Ok-pyo, 1997, 'Gendai Kankoku josei no seikatsu ni okeru Jukyō no eikyō' (The influence of Confucianism on the lives of women in contemporary South Korea), Inoue Kazue tr., in Ajia Joseishi Kokusai Shimpojiumu Jikkō I'inkai ed., *Ajia joseishi: Hikakushi no kokoromi* (The history of women in Asia: Explorations in comparative history), Tokyo: Akashi Shoten.

Mori, Yasuyuki, (director), 2003, *Konbanwa* (Good evening).

Morita, Yoshio, 1996, *Sūji ga kataru zainichi Kankoku Chōsenjin no rekishi* (The history of resident Koreans illustrated by statistics), Tokyo: Akashi Shoten.

Motohashi, Tetsuya, 2005, *Posuto koroniarizumu* (Postcolonialism), Tokyo: Iwanami Shoten.

Munekage, Tadashi, 2005, Yakan chūgaku no zainichi gaikokujin (Foreign residents at night school), Tokyo: Kōbunken.

Nikkan Mondai o Kangaeru Higashiosaka Shimin no Kai (Higashiosaka Citizens' Group for Considering the Problems of Japanese-Korean Relations) http://www.e-sora.net/shimin/index.html

Nozawa, Kazuyuki (director), 2004, *Haruko*.

Oguma, Eiji, 1998, *'Nihonjin' no kyōkai: Okinawa, Ainu, Taiwan, Chōsen, shokuminchi shihai kara fukki undō made* (The boundaries of the 'Japanese': Okinawa, the Ainu, Taiwan and Korea. From colonial domination to the return movement), Tokyo: Shinyosha.

Okin, Suzan, 1999, 'Is Multiculturalism Bad for Women?', Joshua Cohen et.

al. eds., *Is Multiculturalism Bad for Women?* Princeton: Princeton University Press.

———, 2005, 'Multiculturalism and Feminism: No Simple Question, No Simple Answers', Avigail Eisenberg et. al. eds., *Minorities within Minorities: Equality, Rights and Diversity*, Cambridge: Cambridge University Press.

Ōnuma, Yasuaki and Suh Yong-dal, 2005, *Zainichi kankoku-chōsenjin to jinken [shinpan]* (Koreans living in Japan and human rights [new edition]), Tokyo: Yuhikaku.

Osaka Chame (Osaka Jamae), 2000, *Gambatteiru zainichi Korian josei e: Wākushoppu & kōkai kōza hōkokusho* (To striving Korean women in Japan: A report on workshops and public lectures).

Pak, Il-bun et al., 1977, 'Nisei josei ōini kataru' (Second-generation women speak out), *Tong il pyong ron* (Unification review), Vol. 147.

Pak, Il-bun, 2002, *Ikite, aishite, tatakatte: Zainichi Chōsenjin issei tachi no monogatari* (Live, love and fight: Stories of first-generation Koreans in Japan), Tokyo: Chōsen Seinensha.

Pak, Sam-sok, 1997, *Nihon no naka no chōsen gakkō* (Korean schools in Japan), Tokyo: Chōsen Seinensha.

Park, Hwa-mee, 1993, 'Kazoku no onna no jiishiki' (Women's self-awareness within families), *Horumon bunka 4: Zainichi Chōsenjin yureru kazoku moyō* (Hormone culture 4: Changing families of Koreans in Japan), Tokyo: Shinkansha, 56–66.

Park, Kyoung-Sik, 1989, *Kaihō go zainichi Chōsenjin undōshi* (Post-liberation history of movements by Koreans in Japan), Tokyo: San'ichi Shobō.

Parker, Andrew, M. Russo, D. Sommer and P. Yaeger, 1992, 'Introduction', A. Parker et al. eds., *Nationalisms and Sexualities*, New York and London: Routledge, 1–18.

Pateman, Carole, 1988, *The Sexual Contract*, Cambridge, U.K.: Polity Press.

Peterson, V. Spike, 2000, 'Sexing political identities / nationalism as heterosexism', S. Ranchod-Nisson and M. A. Tétreault eds., *Women, States, and Nationalism: At home in the nation?* London and New York: Routledge, 54–80.

Porter, John, 1967, *The Vertical Mosaic: An Analysis of Social Class and Power in Canada*, Toronto: University of Toronto Press.

Quiminal, Catherine, 2000, 'The Associative Movements of African Women and New Forms of Citizenship', J. Freedman and C. Tarr eds., *Women, Immigration and Identities in France*, Oxford and New York: Berg, 39–56.

Roth, Benita, 2004, *Separate Roads to Feminism: Black, Chicana, and White Feminist Movements in America's Second Wave*, Cambridge: Cambridge University Press.

Ryan, Mary P., 1990, *Women in Public: Between Banners and Ballots, 1825–1880*, Baltimore: Johns Hopkins University Press.

———, 1992, 'Gender and Public Access: Women's Politics in Nineteenth-Century America', in Craig Calhoun (ed.), *Habermas and the Public Sphere,* Cambridge: MIT Press, 259–88.

Ryang, Sonia, 1998, 'Nationalist Inclusion or Emancipatory Identity? North Korean Women in Japan', *Women's Studies International Forum*, 21(6), 581–97.

Sai, Takanori, 2001, 'Chesa wa danjo sabetsu?! (nandarōna)' (Is jesa gender discriminatory?! [The answer is probably yes]), *Hamkke Yokohama dayori* (Together Yokohama letter), No. 40.
Saitō, Junichi, 2000, *Kōkyōsei* (Publicness), Tokyo: Iwanami Shoten.
Sakamoto, Kazue, 2005, *Aidentitī no kenryoku: Sabetsu o kataru shutai wa seiritsu suruka* (Identity and power: Is it possible to create a speaking subject that speaks about discrimination?), Tokyo: Shinyosha.
Satomi, Minoru, 2010, *Paulo Freire 'hiyokuatsusha no kyōikugaku' o yomu* (To read Paulo Freire's *Pedagogy of the Oppressed*), Tokyo: Tarojirosha Editus.
Seishun Gakkō Jimukyoku, ed., 2004, *Tabunka kyōsei no machi zukuri: Seishun gakkō 10-nen no jissen kara* (Creating a multicultural symbiotic town: From ten years of experience of Seishun Gakkō), Tokyo: Akashi Shoten.
Seo, Akwi, 2005a, 'Zainichi Chōsenjin josei ni yoru "taikō teki na kōkyōken" no keisei to shutai kōchiku: Osaka ni okeru yakan chūgaku dokuritsu undō no jirei kara' (Creating a counterpublic and subject formation: Case studies on Korean women's night school independence movement in Osaka), *Jendā kenkyū* (Journal of gender studies), 8: 113–128.
———, 2005b, 'Zainichi Chōsenjin josei no shutai kōchiku: "Jūgun ianfu" mondai o meguru undō kara' (The emergence of a new subjectivity for Korean women in Japan: A case study of the 'comfort women' redress movement), *F-GENS jānaru* (Frontiers of gender studies), 4:93–101.
———, 2006, *Zainichi Chōsenjin josei ni yoru "kai no taikō teki na kōkyōken" no keisei: yakan chūgaku, oyobi "jūgun ianfu" o meguru undō jirei kara* (Creating a 'subaltern counterpublic': Case studies on Korean women in night school and the problem of 'military comfort women') Unpublished dissertation, Ochanomizu University Graduate School of Humanities and Sciences.
———, 2008, 'Zainichi Chōsenjin josei ni miru sedai kan no renkei to esunishiti: Higashiosaka ni okeru deihausu no jirei kara' (Intergenerational solidarity among Korean women: Case studies on day care homes in Higashiosaka), Ito Ruri and Adachi Mariko eds., *Kokusai idō to 'rensa suru jendā': Ekkyō suru shutai, henyō suru Ajia* (International migration and 'chained gender': Transgressing subjects and Asia's transformation), Tokyo: Sakuhinsha.
———, 2009a, 'Formation of ethnic identity through elder care: An analysis of Korean women's inter-generational solidarity in a day home in Osaka,' *Journal of Asian Women's Studies*, vol. 17 (Gender and Welfare), pp. 17–30.
———, forthcoming, 'Toward Postcolonial Feminist Subjectivity: Korean Women's Redress Movement for "Comfort Women",' J. C. Bullock, A. Kano and J. Welker eds., *Rethinking Japanese Feminisms*, Honolulu: University of Hawai'i Press.
Shin, Sug-ok, Cho Yeh-ho, Park Hwa-mee and Jung Yeong-hae, 2000, 'Paneru disukasshon "zainichi" onna gatari' (Panel discussion 'Koreans in Japan' talks by women), *Korian mainoritī kenkyū* (Korean minority studies), 4: 5–45.
Shirai, Zengo, 2006, *Yakan chūgaku wa ima*, No. 1–11, http://www.journalist-net.com/home/

Siim, Birte, 2000, *Gender and Citizenship: Politics and Agency in France, Britain and Denmark*, Cambridge: Cambridge University Press.
Sim, Stuart, 1999, *The Routledge Critical Dictionary of Postmodern Thought*, New York: Routledge.
Song, Youn-ok, 2002, '"Zainichi" josei no sengo shi' (Postwar history of "zainichi" women), *Kan* (Kan: History, environment, civilization), 11: 166–177.
―――――, 2005, 'Zainichi Chōsenjin josei towa dareka' (Who are the Korean women in Japan), Iwasaki Minoru ed., *Keizoku suru shokuminchi shugi: Jendā/minzoku/jinshu/kaikyū* (Continuing colonialism: Gender, nation, race and class), Tokyo: Seikyūsha.
―――――, 2009, *Datsu teikoku no feminizumu o motomete: Chōsen josei to shokuminchi shugi* (Searching for the de-imperialistic feminism: Korean women and colonialism), Tokyo: Yūshisha.
Song, Pu-ja, 2007, *Aisuru toki kiseki wa tsukurareru: Zainichi sandaishi* (When you love, that's when miracles are born: History of three generations of Koreans in Japan), Tokyo: San'ichi Shobo.
Spivak, Gayatri C., 1985, 'Subaltern Studies: Deconstructing Historiography', R. Guha and G. Spivak eds., *Subaltern Studies* Vol. IV, New Delhi: Oxford Press.
―――――, 1988 'Can the Subaltern Speak?', C. Nelson and L. Grossberg eds., *Marxism and the Interpretation of Culture*, Basingstoke: Macmillan Education, 271–313.
Stasiulis, Daiva and Abigail Bakan, 2003, *Negotiating Citizenship: Migrant Women in Canada and the Global System*, Basingstoke: Palgrave Macmillan.
Stasiulis, Daiva and Nira Yuval-Davis, 1995, *Unsettling Settler Societies: Articulation of Gender, Race, Ethnicity and Class*, London: Sage.
Statistics Bureau, Ministry of Internal Affairs and Communications, 2005, *Heisei 17-nen kokusei chōsa jinkō gaikan sirīzu 6: Rōdo jōtai, sangyō, shokugyō betsu jinkō* (2005 population census of Japan overview series 6: Population by labour force status, industry and occupation).
―――――, 2005, *Heisei 17-nen kokusei chōsa hōkoku dai-7-kan: Gaikokujin ni kansuru tokubetsu shūkei kekka* (2005 population census of Japan No. 7: Results of special tabulation on foreigners).
Stivens, Maila, 2000, 'Introduction: Gender politics and the reimagining of human rights in the Asia-Pacific', Anne-Marie Hilsdon et al. eds., *Human Rights and Gender Politics: Asia Pacific Perspectives*, London and New York: Routledge, 1–36.
Sugihara, Tōru, 1996, 'Chōsenjin o meguru taimen, gensetsu kūkan no keisei to sono isō: 1930-nendai no Osaka o chūshin ni' (Formation of interactive discourse space surrounding Koreans and its phases: Focusing upon 1930s Osaka), Iyotani Toshio and Sugihara Tōru eds., *Nihon shakai to imin: Kōza gaikokujin teijū mondai dai-1-kan* (Japanese society and immigrants: Series 1: The issue of long-term foreign residents), Tokyo: Akashi Shoten.
―――――, 1998, *Ekkyō suru tami: Kindai Osaka no Chōsenjin shi kenkyū* (People transgressing borders: Research on the history of Koreans in Osaka), Tokyo: Shinkansha.

Tachi, Kaoru, 1995, 'Josei no sanseiken to jendā' (Women's suffrage and gender), *Sōkan Shakaigaku 2: Jendā* (Interdisciplinary social sciences 2: Gender), 122–140.

Taiheiji Yakan Chūgakkō Seitokai, Chōei Yakan Chūgakkō Seitokai, Chōei Taiheiji Yakan Chūgakkō Dōsōkai (Taiheiji Night Junior High School Student Council, Chōei Night Junior High School Student Council and Chōei and Taiheiji Night Junior High School Alumni Association), 2001, *Taiheiji Yakan Chūgakkō no dokuritsu o iwau kai* (Meeting to celebrate the independence of Taiheiji Night Junior High School).

Takano, Masao, 1975, *Runpuro gannen charippu: Yakan Chūgaku Undō 10-nen no kiroku* (Independence, the first year of the lumpen proletariat era: A record of 10 years of night school movements).

——, 1993, *Yakan chūgakusei Takano Masao: Buki ni naru moji to kotoba o* (Night school student Takano Masao: Writing and speaking as weapons), Osaka: Kaihō Shuppansha.

Tanaka, Hiroshi, 1995, *Zainichi Gaikokujin (shinpan)* (Foreign residents in Japan [new edition]), Tokyo: Iwanami Shoten.

Tonomura, Masaru, 2004, *Zainichi Chōsenjin shakai no rekishigakuteki kenkyū* (Historical research of the Korean community in Japan), Tokyo: Ryokuin Shobō.

Touraine, Alain, Z. Hegedus, F. Dubet, and M. Wieviorka, 1980, *La prophétie anti-nucléaire*, Paris: Editions du Seuil.

Uri Hakkyo o Tsuzuru Kai, 2001, *Chōsen gakkō te donna toko?* (What is a Korean school like?), Tokyo: Shakai Hyōron Sha.

Uri Seodang, 2009, *'Uri Sodan' to Taiheiji Yakan Chugakkō: Sodan Taiheiji no kaikōshiki ni atatte* ('Uri Seodang' and Taiheiji Night Junior High School: At the opening ceremony of Seodang Taiheiji).

Woolf, Virginia, 1966[1938], *Three Guineas*, San Diego: Harcourt Brace & Company.

Yakan Chūgaku Sonohi Sonohi (Night school, from one day to the next) (Shirai Zengo) http://www.journalist-net.com/shirai/

Yakan Chūgaku Zōsetsu Undō Zenkoku Kōryūshūkai, 1986, *Za yakan chūgaku: Moji o kaese 170-mannin no sakebi* (The night school: Give us back the art of writing, 1.7 million people's outcry), Tokyo: Kaisōsha.

——, 1994, *Benkyō ga shitai gakkō ga hoshi* (We want to study, we want a school), Nara: Uta Shuppan Kikaku.

——, 1997, *Shinpen moji wa inochiya, gakkō wa takaraya* (Writing is life, school is treasure, new edition), Tokyo: Kaisōsha.

Yamada, Yōji (director), 1993, *Gakkō* (School).

Yamawaki, Keizō, 2001, 'Sengo Nihon no gaikokujin seisaku to zainichi Korian no shakai undō' (Policy for foreigners in post-war Japan and social movements of resident Koreans), in Kajita Takamichi ed., *Kōza shakai hendo dai-7-kan: Kokusaika to aidentitī* (Series social transition vol. 7: Internationalization and identity), Kyoto: Mineruba Shobō.

Yamawaki, Keizō, Kashiwazaki Chikako and Kondō Atsushi, 2003, 'Taminzoku kokka Nihon no kōsō' (A vision for a multiethnic Japan), in Kaneko Masaru et al. eds., *Keizai kōsō kyōsei shakai rekishi ninshiki: Higashi Ajia de ikiyō* (Economic vision, multicultural

society and understanding history: Let's live in East Asia), Tokyo: Iwanami Shoten.
Yang, Young-hoo, 1994, *Sengo Osaka no Chōsenjin undō: 1945–1965* (Korean people's movement in post-war Osaka: 1945–1965), Tokyo: Miraisha.
Yang, Young-jee, 1997, 'Kokka minzoku ni honrō sarenai hitori no ningen toshite ikitai' (I want to live as an individual human not controlled by the nation-state), *Onnatachi no 21-seiki* (Women's 21st century), Vol. 11 (Summer), Asia-Japan Women's Resource Center, 15–18.
Yoneyama, Lisa, 2003, '"Hihanteki tabunkashugi" no kangaekata' (An approach to 'critical multiculturalism'), *Bōryoku, sensō, ridoresu: Tabunkashugi no poritikusu* (Violence, war and redress: The politics of multiculturalism), Tokyo: Iwanami Shoten.
Yoon, Ga-ja, 1987, '"Zainichi" josei no hyōgensha tachi' (The 'resident Korean' female artists), *Shin Nihon bungaku* (New Japanese literature), 471 (4): 84–93.
Yuval-Davis, Nira, 1993, 'Gender and nation', *Ethnic and Racial Studies*, 16(4): 621–32.
———, 1994a, 'Identity Politics and Women's Ethnicity', V. M. Moghadam ed., *Identity Politics and Women: Cultural Reassertions and Feminisms in International Perspective*, Boulder, San Francisco, Oxford: Westview Press, 408–24.
———, 1994b, 'Women, ethnicity and empowerment', K. Bhavnani and A Phoenix eds., *Shifting Identities, Shifting Racisms, special issue of Feminism and Psychology* 4(1): 179–98.
———, 1997, *Gender and Nation*, London, Thousand Oaks, New Delhi: Sage Publications.
Yuval-Davis, Nira and Floya Anthius, 1989, *Woman-Nation-State*, London: Macmillan Press.
Zainichi Chōsenjin Sōrengokai (General Association of Korean Residents in Japan) http://www.chongryon.com/
Zainichi Daikan Kirisutokyō Fujinkai Zenkoku Rengōkai (Korean Christian Church in Japan National Christian Women's Association), 1999, *Yonjūnenshi (1948–1988)* (Forty-year history [1948–1988]).
Zainichi Daikan Kirisutokyō Zenkoku Kyōkai Josei Rengōkai (Korean Christian Church in Japan National Christian Women's Association), 1999, *Gojūnenshi (1989–1999)* (Fifty-year history [1989–1999]).
Zainichi Kankoku Gakusei Dōmei (Korean Students League in Japan) http://youth-forum.soc.or.jp/members/kangakudo.html
Zainichi Kankoku Minshu Joseikai (Korean Women's Society in Japan for Democracy) (Osaka Headquarters), 1998–2010, *Porappi* (Purple), Vol. 128–246.
Zainichi Kankoku Minshu Joseikai (Korean Women's Society in Japan for Democracy) (Tokyo Headquarters), 1987–2005, *Minjuyeoseong* (Democratic women), Vol. 1–103.
Zainichi Kankoku Minshu Joseikai (Korean Women's Society in Japan for Democracy) http://yeoseong.korea-htr.com/
Zainichi Kankoku Minshu Tōitsu Rengō (Federation of Koreans in Japan for Democracy and Unification) http://www.korea-htr.com/chuo/japanese/index-cj.htm

Zainichi Kankoku Seinen Dōmei (Korean Youth Alliance in Japan) http://www.han-chung.com/
Zainichi Kankokujin Gakusei Kyōgikai (Student Council of Koreans in Japan) http://hakseng.korea-htr.com/
Zainichi Kōreisha Chōsa I'inkai, 2004, *Zainichi Korian kōreisha seikatsu jittai chōsa hōkokusho* (Report on the survey of socio-economic conditions of elderly Koreans in Japan).
Zainichi Korian Mainoritī Jinken Kenkyū Sentā (Korean Residents Minority Human-rights Research Center of Japan), 1998, 'Fukushi genba kara mita zainichi Korian kōreisha fukushi no genjō to korekara (Current and future state of welfare for elderly Koreans in Japan as seen in welfare institutions)' in *Kikan Sai*, Vol. 29.
———, 2000, 'Kōreisha ni taisuru jinken ishiki o takamete hoshī (Calling for better awareness of human rights for elderlies)' in *Kikan Sai*, Vol. 35.
Zainihon Chōsen Minshu Josei Dōmei Chūō Jōnin I'inkai (Korean Democratic Women's League in Japan Central Standing Committee), 1998, *Nyeoseongdongmaeng jarangchan 50nyeon: 1947–1997* (Proud 50 years of Nyeoseongdongmaeng: 1947–1997).
Zainihon Chōsen Minshu Josei Dōmei (Korean Democratic Women's League in Japan), 1997–2002, *Joseonnyeoseong* (Korean women), Vol. 537–551.
Zainihon Chōsen Minshu Josei Dōmei (Korean Democratic Women's League in Japan) http://www4.ocn.ne.jp/~nyomeng/index.htm
Zainihon Chōsenjin Jinken Kyōkai (Human Rights Association for Korean Residents in Japan), 2003, *Jinken to seikatsu* (Human rights and life), Vol. 16.
Zainihon Chōsenjin Sōrengōkai (General Association of Korean Residents in Japan), 1991, *Chosun Chongryun*.
Zainihon Daikanminkoku Fujinkai (Korean Residents Union in Japan Women's Association), 1999, *Fujinkai 50-nenshi* (Buinhoe 50-year history).
Zainihon Daikanminkoku Fujinkai Osaka Honbu (Korean Residents Union in Japan Women's Association Osaka Headquarters), 1992, *Osaka Fujinkai 45-nenshi* (Osaka Buinhoe 45-year history).
Zainihon Daikanminkoku Fujinkai Tokyo Chihō Honbu (Korean Residents Union in Japan Women's Association Tokyo Regional Headquarter), 1993, *Fujinkai Tokyo hanseikishi* (Tokyo Buinhoe 50-year history).
Zainihon Daikanminkoku Fujinkai Tokyo Chihō Honbu (Korean Residents Union in Japan Women's Association Tokyo Regional Headquarter) http://mindan-tokyo.org/hujinkai.htm
Zainihon Daikanminkoku Mindan (Korean Residents Union in Japan) http://mindan.org/index.php
Zenkoku Yakan Chūgakkō Kenkyūkai (National Night Junior High School Study Group), *Zenkoku Yakan Chūgakkō Kenkyū Taikai: Taikai kiroku* (National Night Junior High School Study Conference: Proceedings), Annual issues.
Zenkoku Yakan Chūgakkō Kenkyūkai Dai-51-kai Taikai Jikkō I'inkai, 2005,

Yakan chūgakusei: 133-nin kara no messēji (Night school students: Messages from 133 people), Tokyo: Toho Shuppan.

———, *Zenkoku Yakan Chūgakkō Kenkyū Taikai: Taikai shiryō* (National Night Junior High School Study Conference: References), Annual issues.

Zenkoku Zainichi Gaikokujin Kyōiku Kenkyū Kyōgikai (National Foreign Residents Educational Research Council) http://members.at.infoseek.co.jp/zencho/

Zenkoku Zainichi Gaikokujin Kyōiku Kenkyū Kyōgikai Osaka (National Foreign Residents Educational Research Council Osaka) http://kangaerukai.net/index.htm

Name Index

Althusser, Louis, 16, 159
Anthius, Floya, 68

Bunch, Charlotte, 151–152

Coll, Kathleen M., 68
Crenshaw, Kimberley W., 15

Enloe, Cynthia, 14

Fraser, Nancy, 5, 11–12, 210, 212
Freire, Paolo, 145, 209

Habermas, Jürgen, 11–12
hooks, bell, 13, 145, 152

Ito, Ruri, 188

Jung Yeong-hae, 19, 21, 32, 34

Kandiyoti, Denise, 129–130, 217
Kashiwazaki, Chikako, xiii, 33, 75, 177, 231

Kim Pu-ja, 52, 119
Kim Young, 52

Mizuuchi, Toshio, 8, 80, 83, 223
Molyneux, Maxine, 45

Oh Ki-moon, 54. 220
Okin, Suzan, 212

Park, Hwa-mee, 217, 219

Quiminal, Catherine, 187–188

Roth, Benita, 15
Ryang, Sonia, 34, 60, 151

Song Youn-ok, 22, 26, 28–29, 32
Spivak, Gayatri C, 16, 151

Takano Masao, 90, 97

Yuval-Davis, Nira, 45

Subject Index

abolition of night school, *see* 'night school'
activism, 15, 34, 36, 44, 59, 65, 67, 71, 87, 97
African-American women, 15, 216–217
African women (in France), 187–188
agency, 5, 140
aging, 189–190
alien registration, 20–21, 54, 217
alternative public space, 202, 211 see also 'public space'
Asian Women's Association, 73, 77
assimilation as 'Japanese', 27, 198, 202 *see also* 'colony/colonial'
autonomy, 2, 53, 204
  autonomy of women's movements, 44–45
  organizational autonomy, 45

banjjokbari, 169, 198
bargaining with patriarchy, 129–130, 140, 205 *see* 'patriarchy'
board of education, 3, 67, 73, 78, 98, 101–105, 164, 166–167, 174
bourgeois public sphere, 11 *see also* 'public sphere'

Buinhoe (Korean Residents Union in Japan Women's Association), 51, 54, 56–58, 60–61
buraku (descendants of outcast communities), 4, 8, 79
buraku liberation movement, 81, 83
Buraku Liberation League, 97

charye (Confucian ceremony conducted at home for New Years), 200, 202, 211
Chōei Night Junior High School, 84
Chongdaehyup, 49, 64, 71
Chongryun (The General Association of Korean Residents in Japan) 28, 43, 51, 58, 86
Chosun, 215
citizen, 11–13, 21, 91
  maternal citizen, 68
citizenship, 68, 71, 180, 232
civic subject, 66 *see also* 'subjectivity'
civil public sphere, *see* 'public sphere'
collective identity, *see* 'identity'
colony/colonial, 6, 21
  colonial legacy, 27, 74
  colonial policy, 20

Subject Index

assimilation as 'Japanese', 27, 198, 202
colonial rule, 10, 30, 162, 182
colonialism, 27
comfort women, 64, 70
Confucian/Confucianism, 29, 120, 129, 196, 200, 211
correlation between nation and gender, 14 *see also* 'gender', 'nation'
counterpublic, 155
   subaltern counterpublic, 8, 11–13, 84, 109, 143, 156–157, 184, 200–203, 205, 216
   formation of the subaltern counterpublics, 210
cross-domain public sphere, *see* 'public sphere'

discourse of emancipation, 34
discrimination, 10, 13, 20 *see also* 'oppression'
   ethnic discrimination, 27–28, 199, 201
   gender discrimination, 28, 32
   racial discrimination, 21–22, 147
   sexual discrimination, 19
diversity of the public sphere, 84, 211 *see also* 'public sphere'
Dokushokai (Korean Women's History Reading Society), 70
domestic responsibility, 27
domestic sphere, 14, 68

education
   educational opportunity, 83
   ethnic education, 57, 87–88, 146
   literacy education, 34–35, 183 *see also* 'literacy'
   modern educations, 9
employment, 7, 21, 23–26, 31
   Hitachi Employment Discrimination Incident, 26
ethnic
   ethnic and class order, 158
   ethnic boundary, 200–201, 205
   ethnic class, 83, 88, 157 *see also* 'ethnic education'
   ethnic community, 4, 19, 28, 60, 150, 173–174, 184, 186, 190, 209
   ethnic discrimination, 27 *see also* 'discrimination'
   ethnic education, 57, 87–88, 146 *see also* 'education'
   ethnic identity, 149 *see also* 'identity'
   ethnic movement / ethnic rights movement, 2, 4, 15, 33–34, 43, 67
   Korean civil rights movement, 65
   Korean unification movement, 64
   ethnic name, 146–147, 149
   ethnic order, 201 *see also* 'discrimination'
   ethnic organization, 7, 28, 33, 43, 55–56, 58, 153
   ethnic resource, 42, 196–7
   ethnic school, 133, 142, 150, 157 *see also* 'education'

ethnic sphere, 143
ethnicity, 8, 13, 28, 39–41, 44, 51, 60, 67, 110, 130, 142, 158, 170, 190, 198, 202, 205
  intersection of ethnicity and gender, 39, 51 see also 'gender'

family, 19, 22, 29, 31
  family gender roles, 51, 61, 69, 142, 204 see also 'gender'
  family-operated businesse, 22, 197
  modern family, 24, 55
feminism, 19
first-generation women, 186, 189, 193, 197–198 see also 'generation'

gender
  gender discrimination, 28, 32 see also 'discrimination'
  gender division of labor, 2, 13–14, 43, 63
  gender order, 18, 199–202
  gender role, 4, 14–15, 28, 30, 41, 51, 57, 61, 63, 65, 73, 123, 204, 212
  gender segregation, 28 see also 'discrimination
  gender structure, 207, 212
  gendered ethnic identity, 35 see also 'identity'
  correlation between nation and gender, 14
  intersection of ethnicity and gender, 39, 51
  intersectionality of nation and gender, 41
generation, 11, 77, 203, 234

first-generation women,10, 18, 34, 38, 40, 117, 154, 176, 186, 189, 193, 197–198
second-generation, 18, 19, 25–26, 65–66, 70–71, 81, 83–84, 143, 146, 194–195, 198, 201
third-generation, 77
grassroots activism/movements, 65, 69, 80
'great *omoni*' discourse, 60 see also '*omoni*'
Gurūpu Chame (Sisters' Group),, 72

halmoni (grandmother), 10, 108, 179, 181–182, 194, 209
Hanshin Education Struggle, 82, 87, 153, 163, 164
  Second Hanshin Education Struggle, 101, 161, 208
Hantongryun (Federation of Koreans in Japan for Democracy and Unification), 61–62, 86
Hitachi Employment Discrimination Incident, 26
host society, 20, 42, 120, 158, 199, 207
  voluntary activities of female immigrants in a host society, 187

identification, 17, 34
identity, 4, 8, 13, 17, 19, 33–34, 72, 75, 79, 83, 165, 167, 209
  identity politics, 33
  collective identity, 206
  ethnic identity, 149
  gendered ethnic identity, 35

Subject Index

national identity, 52
recognition of identity, 16
Ikaino, 7, 64, 82, 85–86, 169, 194
illiteracy, 9–10, 121–122, 151, 197 *see also* 'literacy'
intergenerational solidarity, 11, 185, 187, 196–197, 199, 207 *see also* 'generation'
International Literacy Year, 97, 145
intersectionality
  intersectionality of ethnicity and gender, 39, 51 *see also* 'ethnicity', 'gender'
  intersectionality of nation and gender, 41 *see also*, 'gender', 'nation'
  intersectionality of oppressions, 15 *see also* 'oppression'

Japanese feminist, 44
Japanese teacher, 154
Jeju, 6–7, 29, 86, 166, 120, 122, 139, 148, 184
Jeju Uprising, 6
jesa (patrilineal succession ceremony), 28, 120, 198, 234

Kansai region, 8, 78–80, 84
Kawasaki Omoni no Kai (Mother Society for the Protection of Korean Children), 66, 69
Korean civil rights movement, 65 *see* 'ethnic movement'
Korean name, 66–67, 113, 148 *see* 'ethnic name'

Korean unification movement, 64 *see* 'ethnic movement'

legal status, 20
life course, 9, 11, 41, 111–113, 205
literacy, 98, 112, 117, 120, 145, 149, 152, 157, 224 *see also* 'illiteracy'
literacy class, 91, 121
literacy education, 34–35, 183
literacy education in South Korea, 183
literally 'mothers' school, 181
local multiculturalism, *see* 'multiculturalism'
local society, 186
long-distance nationalism, *see* 'nationalism'

mainstream
  mainstream public sphere, 12, 76, 212 *see also* 'public sphere'
  mainstream society, 2, 4, 13, 83, 87, 144, 152, 198, 200, 206
marriage, 32, 58, 168–169, 196
  pro-marriage ideology, 58
  public sphere after marriage, 196
maternal citizen, *see* 'citizen'
Mearihoe (Meari Association: Association for promotion of human rights and ethnic education for Korean school children in public schools), 66–69
mediation, 189
migrant women, 188

Mindan (the Korean Residents Union in Japan), 28, 43, 52, 54, 58, 86
Ministry of Education, 89, 91, 157, 162
minority movement, 80
Minsokukyo (the Association for Ethnic Education Promotion), 88, 102, 108, 174, 231
modern education, *see* 'education'
modern family, *see* 'family'
motherhood, 68
multicultural, 68–69
  multicultural symbiosis, 69–70
  multiculturalism, 48, 177, 179–180, 212
  local multiculturalism, 177
multiplicity, 12
  multiplicity of oppression, 13, 18, 74, 196 *see also* 'oppression'
  multiplicity of publics, 79, 84, 107, 109 *see also* 'public sphere'
munhae (literacy), 108, 183, 212 *see also* 'literacy education in South Korea'
mutual assistance, 188

national identity, 52 *see also* 'identity'
national pension, 26, 116, 190
nationalism movements, 14, 51
nationalist public sphere, *see* 'public sphere'
nationality, 13, 17–18, 21, 32, 34, 67, 76–77, 83

Nationality Clause, 26, 116, 158, 190, 233
nation
  correlation between nation and gender, 14
  nation-state, 8, 21, 75–76
  intersectionality of nation and gender, 41
naturalization, 1, 27
night junior high school expansion movement, 89, 156
night school, 3, 73
  abolition of night school, 89
Nikkan Shimin no Kai (Group for Considering the Problems of Japanese-Korean Relations), 107, 177
Nyeomaeng (the Korean Democratic Women's League in Japan), 51, 55–59

official public sphere, *see* 'public sphere'
Okinawans, 81
omoni (mother), 58
oppression
  dual oppression of race and gender, 72
  intersectionality of oppressions, 15
  multiplicity of oppression, 13, 18, 74, 196
  sexist oppression, 22
oppositional public sphere, 109 *see also* 'public sphere'
oppositional subject, 10, 17, 28, 160, 168, 173–174, 200, 206 *see also* 'subjectivity'

Ordinance for ethnic school closure, 162
organizational autonomy, 45 see also 'autonomy'

patriarchy, 18–19, 21, 28, 30, 34, 170, 211, 217
  bargaining with patriarchy, 129–130, 140, 205
patriotic motherhood, 34, 59–60
political subject, 155, 159
postcolonial, 19, 53, 73–74, 77, 79, 111
prejudice, 10
private sphere, 51, 76, 143, 168, 186, 188, 206
pro-marriage ideology, 58 see also 'marriage'
public authority, 10, 45, 79, 84, 87, 158, 161, 168
public education, 68, 157, 205
public space, 141, 151, 202
  alternative public space, 202, 211
public sphere, 11, 188
  public sphere after marriage, 196 see also 'marriage'
  bourgeois public sphere, 11 see also 'public sphere'
  civil public sphere, 213
  cross-domain public sphere, 212
  diversity of the public sphere, 84, 211
  France's public sphere, 188
  mainstream public sphere, 12
  multilayered public sphere, 211
  nationalist public sphere, 12
  official public sphere, 216
  oppositional public sphere, 109

racial discrimination, 21–22, 78, 147 see also 'discrimination'
racial order, 207 see also 'discrimination'
recognition of identity, 16 see also 'identity'
repatriation project, 21
returnees (from China), 97, 179

San Francisco Peace Treaty, 21, 233
Sarangbang (a service center for older Korean women), 74, 176, 185
School Education Law, 90
second-class citizen, 20
  see also 'colonial', 'discrimination'
second-generation, see 'generation'
self-directed night school, 90–91 see also 'night school'
seodang (village school, private traditional schools in Korean), 117, 120, 228
sexist oppression, 22 see also 'oppression'
sexual discrimination, 19 see also 'discrimination'
sexual violence, 62
sit-in, 102, 167
social actor, 5, 109, 143
social integration, 188
social movement sphere, 79, 203

socio-cultural mediation, 11, 186–189, 199, 206–207
student council, 153–155
spatial axes, 6, 10
subaltern counterpublic, 8, 11–13, 84, 109, 143, 156–157, 184, 200–203, 205, 216 *see* 'counterpublic'
  formation of the subaltern counterpublics, 210
  transnational subaltern counterpublic, 212
subaltern women, 16, 143, 151
subjectivity, 5, 16–17, 141–142, 189, 200, 209
subsequent-generation women, 186, 189, 196–198 *see also* 'generation'

Taiheiji Extension Class, 100, 102–103
Taiheiji Night Junior High School Independence Movement, 73, 96, 105, 108, 142, 145, 148, 153, 155, 158, 163, 165, 174, 177, 185, 205
Taiwan, 20–21
temporal axis, 9–10
third-generation, 77 *see also* 'generation'
transnational life space, 5, 203

transnational subaltern counterpublic, *see* 'subaltern counterpublic'

Uri Seodang ('our village school': a learning institution for Korean women), 74, 105, 176, 179, 181, 184, 185

'wise mother and good wife', 14, 19, 35, 51, 55, 150, 204
women's liberation, 19, 44, 55
women's liberation movement, 14–15, 33, 43, 63, 71, 207
women's liberation movement in South Korea, 62
women's organization, 52
women's solidarity, 199

Yeoseong Net (Military Comfort Women Issue *Uri Yeoseong* Network), 70–74
Yeoseonghoe (the Korean Women's Society in Japan for Democracy), 61–64, 174

Zenkokoku Yakan Chūgakkō Kenkyū Taikai (National Night Junior High School Study Conference), 92